OUT OF FOCUS

OUT OF FOCUS

Power, Pride, and Prejudice—
David Puttnam in Hollywood

Charles Kipps

CENTURY

LONDON   SYDNEY   AUCKLAND   JOHANNESBURG

FOR SUE

First Published in USA by William Morrow & Co Inc
Published in Great Britain in 1990 by Century
An imprint of Random Century Ltd
20 Vauxhall Bridge Road, London SW1V 2SA

Century Hutchinson Australia (Pty) Ltd
20 Alfred Street, Milsons Point, Sydney, NSW 2061, Australia

Century Hutchinson New Zealand Ltd
PO Box 40-086, 32-34 View Road, Glenfield, Auckland 10, New Zealand

Century Hutchinson South Africa (Pty) Ltd
PO Box 337, Bergvlei 2012, South Africa

Charles Kipps's right to be identified as the author of this work has been asserted by him in accordance with the Copyright, Designs and Patents Act, 1988.

Printed and bound in Great Britain by
Mackays of Chatham, Chatham, Kent

British Library Cataloguing in Publication data

Kipps, Charles
  Power, pride and prejudice: David Puttnam in Hollywood.
  1. British cinema films. Production. Puttnam, David, 1941-
  I. Title
  791.430232092

ISBN 0-7126-3911-X

ACKNOWLEDGMENTS

Not long ago, I completed the final chapter of *Out of Focus* and raced off to William Morrow with the manuscript. As I carried the weight of several hundred pages along Madison Avenue, I couldn't stop thinking about how insurmountable the prospect of writing a book had once seemed. Days of sheer terror flashed before my eyes. Midnight encounters with my computer. Torturous confrontations with insecurity. But even as I remembered a lone struggle, so did I recall certain people who had freely offered their support and provided indispensable assistance.

Jane Dystel, my agent, exhibited an unwavering faith in my ability throughout the development of this book. Every writer should have a dynamo like Jane on his side.

Sherry Arden, publisher of Silver Arrow Books, always endeavored to make me feel important, much more important than any first-time author has a right to feel.

Jim Donahue, my editor at Silver Arrow, consistently proffered suggestions that greatly enhanced the manuscript. So did Jennifer Williams, who also edited these pages.

Richard and Arlene Gersh, who have been friends forever, proved how valuable true friends can be, especially to a writer in the midst of a project.

Two generations of the Carney family—Paul and Debbie, and Jean and Art—provided more comfort than they realize.

Roger Watkins, editor of *Variety*, challenged me to seek an ever higher caliber of journalism, and I am grateful to him for his emphasis on excellence.

To all those who took the time to offer on-the-record comments, I owe a huge debt of gratitude. People such as Herbert A. Allen, Jarvis Astaire, Warren Beatty, Jake Eberts, Bertram Fields, Howard Franklin, Richard Gallop, Peter Guber, Tom Hansen, Norman Jewison, Victor Kaufman, David Matalon, Guy McElwaine, Dan Melnick, Frank Price, David Puttnam, Martin Ransohoff, Bob Robinson, Don Safran, Don Simpson, Ray Stark, Dawn Steel, and Brandon Tartikoff.

And, of course, long before I even started this project, my mother, Harriet Kipps, led me to believe I could accomplish anything. A writer herself, she has never run short of encouraging words. Likewise, my sister, Ginger, and my brother, Glenn, have long been sources of encouragement.

Many more people made contributions to this book, particularly Janet Garrison and Robin Green. Still others furnished invaluable background information but chose to remain anonymous. To them, a genuine thanks as well.

OUT OF FOCUS

PART I

CHAPTER ONE

The last place David Puttnam thought he would be on April 11, 1988, was Toronto, Canada. In a hotel suite. Alone.

He fully expected to be three thousand miles west, in another country, indeed another world. And certainly not alone. He had envisioned a congregation of worshipers pushing in around him, shaking his hand and kissing his cheek.

David knew this would be a day of dizzying personal glory. He had counted on it. Planned for it.

But he was wrong.

April 11 marked the date of Hollywood's most stellar annual event, the Academy Awards presentation. Major stars would gather on stage, powerful movie business moguls would fill the audience, and armies of reporters and photographers would record every glittering moment.

David Puttnam, however, would watch the Oscars on television. Alone. In Toronto, Canada.

It was quite a change from a year before, when David sat atop Columbia Pictures as its chairman and chief executive officer with a million-dollar-a-year salary and a $300,000,000 production budget at his fingertips. Now he was teaching a class on the motion picture industry to twelve residents of the Canadian Centre for Advanced Film Studies. No salary. No budget.

What could the dozen students learn from David Puttnam? How to make a movie, perhaps. David, an independent British film producer, had gained a solid reputation via a series of motion pictures which were critically acclaimed, crowned in 1981 with a Best Picture Oscar for *Chariots of Fire*.

What else could they learn? Certainly, if David chose to impart such wisdom, they could find out how *not* to run a studio.

There was one other lesson David Puttnam could teach the twelve Canadian film students: how to handle the media. Reporters around the globe had been notified of his whereabouts on an evening which promised both irony and drama. *The Last Emperor*, a film David brought to Columbia, had been nominated for nine Academy Awards while another picture he shepherded into the studio, *Hope and Glory*, had been given four Oscar nominations by the Hollywood creative community.

So it was that the focus of the entertainment world was not only centered in Los Angeles on this night, but also on the other side of the North American continent. Hollywood was set to honor its own while an exiled outsider who had once held the most powerful job in the motion picture industry sat by himself in front of a television screen.

One by one, the envelopes were opened. And the winner was . . .

Sound: *The Last Emperor*.
Costume Design: *The Last Emperor*.
Art Direction: *The Last Emperor*.
Original Score: *The Last Emperor*.
Film Editing: *The Last Emperor*.
Cinematography: *The Last Emperor*.
Screenplay Adaptation: *The Last Emperor*.
Direction: *The Last Emperor*.
Best Picture: *The Last Emperor*.

Although *Hope and Glory* had been shut out, *The Last Emperor* had swept an incredible nine out of the nine awards for which it was nominated. Equally incredible was the fact that *none* of the Oscar recipients bothered to thank former Columbia chief David Puttnam.

Three thousand miles away, the switchboard at the Four Seasons hotel hummed with activity.

"Mr. Puttnam please . . ."

"Mr. Puttnam please . . ."

"Mr. Puttnam please . . ."

"Hello." David's voice was subdued.

"Mr. Puttnam, how do you feel about not being mentioned in any of the acceptance speeches?"

What could he say? Was there an answer?

"Those who made the film," David responded, "deserve all the credit."

Jeremy Thomas, producer of *The Last Emperor*, apparently felt the same way. When he was asked after the ceremony why he didn't offer a word of appreciation for David Puttnam's role in the film, Thomas snapped, "He didn't produce the picture."

Actually, David's name had been invoked once, by Jonathan Sanger, the coproducer of a film "short" entitled *Ray's Male Heterosexual Dance Hall*. The minimovie had been sponsored—at David's insistence—by Columbia Pictures' parent corporation, The Coca-Cola Company. So at least there was a modicum of recognition for the ousted studio head.

"Mr. Puttnam . . ."

"Mr. Puttnam . . ."

"Mr. Puttnam . . ."

A seemingly endless stream of phone calls extended into the early morning hours of Eastern Standard Time.

"Nine Academy Awards," David told *Variety* reporter Todd McCarthy, "will do wonders for *The Last Emperor*, as far as extending the audience is concerned."

While the appraisal was certainly correct, the one detail David omitted was that Columbia would not participate in the financial reward reaped from that extended audience, typically represented by foreign theatrical exhibition, broadcast and pay television, and home video. Indeed, Columbia's participation in the picture was limited to theatrical release and even those rights were not worldwide, including just five territories: United States and Canada (considered one territory for distribution purposes), the United Kingdom, Australia, New Zealand, and certain sections of South America. Ticket buyers in France, Germany, and Japan would fill the coffers of some other entity, not Columbia Pictures.

Hollywood wasted little time in labeling *The Last Emperor* a "dumb deal."

"Remember that crack in the trade press the other day," David sighed during one telephone conversation, "about *The Last Emperor* being a 'dumb deal?' How many studios would like to have *The Last Emperor* right now?"

The answer, of course, was both all and none, depending on the nature of the agreement and expectation of financial return. Would any studio eschew a picture with nine Oscars? Certainly not. But, at the same time, those studios would want to benefit from the ancillary markets now greatly enhanced by the Academy Awards sweep—something Columbia Pictures would not be able to do.

Well past midnight in Toronto, late night on the West Coast, *Los Angeles Times* writer Michael Cieply elicited this response from a now-weary David Puttnam:

"I joined Columbia to get Coca-Cola a studio it could be proud of. The job is half done."

Yet, this statement, too, required qualification. While David had often spoken of the "mandate" he received from Columbia's parent corporation, Coca-Cola, the truth was that executives of the giant soft-drink manufacturer had watched the hoopla surrounding David's arrival at Columbia Pictures more as spectators than a group bent on issuing specific directives. The corporate structure just didn't work in such a way that David Puttnam, merely a division head within a sprawling hierarchy, had any direct connection to the upper echelon of The Coca-Cola Company. Indeed, there was a spider's web of diverging lines on the organizational chart separating David from Coke president Donald Keough.

A king in Hollywood, David Puttnam was at best a knight in Atlanta, Georgia, where the headquarters of Coca-Cola were located.

So, when the British producer *insisted* on visiting Atlanta to meet Don Keough and Coke chairman Roberto Goizueta before accepting the Columbia post, there was mild bewilderment from the two executives. Despite this, they agreed to a meeting with their new studio chief as a *courtesy*. David, however, placed far more significance on this courtesy than was actually warranted and misunderstood the true relationship between Coca-Cola and Columbia Pictures.

And making decisions based on a misunderstanding is—at the very least—a perilous thing to do.

The metallic black limousine seemed out of place as it swept past weeping willow trees, rolling lawns, and antebellum-style homes. It was a setting more suited for horse and carriage than internal-combustion engine. A scene from *Gone With the Wind.*

This was Atlanta, Georgia, early morning on June 24, 1986. Except for the Cadillac slicing through the tranquil illusion, it might have been a century ago.

The chauffeur's sole function that morning was the delivery of two passengers, British film producer David Puttnam and his wife Patsy, to the headquarters of The Coca-Cola Company.

David had jetted in from London to meet with Coke regarding the conditions of his proposed employment.

The terms were attractive: one million dollars a year and an iron-clad three-year contract. So was the position. Chairman and chief executive officer of Coke subsidiary Columbia Pictures.

But David Puttnam hadn't flown five thousand miles to haggle over contractual clauses. In fact, the decision to hire the British producer had already been made by Fay Vincent, chairman of Columbia Pictures Industries. Coke executives had not even asked to be a part of the process.

Yet David had wanted to confer with the Coca-Cola top brass so he could make sure his new employers understood how he intended to run their motion picture studio. And he wanted a chance to talk about his favorite subject, the philosophy of film-making.

The limo eased through the gate of Coca-Cola's office complex, four highrise structures secured by a tall steel-picket fence with both humans and electronic surveillance equipment keeping a constant vigil around the perimeter.

David and Patsy emerged from the car and walked into the main building. As the couple wended their way, those who were aware of the purpose of David's visit curiously examined their new colleague.

Many were surprised to see a man who looked more like a college professor than someone seeking to grab the reins of a $300,000,000 movie production budget. He wore a solid dark-blue suit, a plain white shirt, and a conservative tie. A salt-and-pepper beard framed his face, while tousled brown hair fell around his ears and over the back of his collar. When he smiled, he revealed rows of jagged teeth.

David seemed randomly put together, imperfect in contrast with the neatly attired and well-coiffed corporate executives who noted his progress. Observers were equally surprised to see Patsy. Wives were generally invisible in corporate America, yet David's spouse marched beside him, seeming to be very much a part of the team.

All of this—David's disheveled appearance coupled with the presence of Patsy—added up to the distinct impression that there was something very different about the new studio chief. It was as if David had planned to foster this off-center perception of himself as a precursor to the business at hand, staging a scene from a movie and providing visual clues for what he was about to say.

David and Patsy continued toward the Coke conference room, half in awe and half in satisfaction over what they had been able to achieve during their thirty-year relationship since they'd been childhood sweethearts. David was just sixteen when he'd met a thirteen year-old schoolmate named Patricia Mary Jones.

It might have been a quaint and proper love story from that point except for the fact that David, driven by ambition, dropped out of school to become a messenger for a London publishing firm. During the next four years, David strove to better his position. But just as David seemed to be gaining momentum in his professional pursuits, Patsy became pregnant. So, in 1961, Patsy, too, left school and they were married.

Suddenly David Puttnam was a twenty-year-old dropout with a teenage wife and a child on the way. Since he was earning a meager fourteen pounds a week, the outlook for the Puttnams was about as bleak as it could be in 1960s England.

Now, as their footsteps echoed in the corridors of one of America's largest corporations, they were light years away from those days. Yet, the roles were familiar. David always seemed to be one step away from something monumental. And Patsy was always there, leading a cheer.

In late 1967, for example, David left the security of a job at prestigious London advertising agency Collet, Dickinson and Pearce to set up his own photographers' agency. Patsy backed this move, which ultimately paid off when one of David's clients, Richard Avedon, landed a photo session with The Beatles and, in a flash (literally), David Puttnam Associates was off and running with the rights to a stunning set of prints of the world's most famous musical quartet.

Despite his instant success as an agent, however, David was restless. There was only one thing he *really* wanted to do.

He wanted to make movies. More to the point, he wanted to make *his* kind of movies.

In order to accomplish this, David discontinued active operational involvement in his photographers' agency and linked with two fellow Britons, Ross Cramer and Charles Saatchi, to form a film production company. But Saatchi quickly became disillusioned with David's rapid-fire burst of cinematic ideas and left to form an advertising agency with his brother Maurice—Saatchi & Saatchi—now the leading hawker of products in the world.

On his own again in 1968, David resolved to produce a motion picture. Besides the normal obstacles facing a film producer in search of cash, David bore the onus of trying to fund a *first* project.

This time David entered into a partnership with music business agent Sanford (Sandy) Lieberson, forming Visual Programmes Systems/Goodtimes Enterprises Production Company. They decided on a project entitled *Melody*, signed as screenwriter a British writer of television commercials, Alan Parker, and then set out to raise the money to produce it.

The financing came together in patchwork fashion, and *Melody* finally emerged as the coproduction of two entities: Sagittarius and Hemdale. As is the case with most money deals, the pair of companies represented myriad investors, including Seagram's chairman, Edgar Bronfman.

Since David had no track record, he had to rely on sheer persuasion to mount his initial project. First he had to convince investors that *Melody* was a worthwhile movie and then he had to further demonstrate that, though he had never done so before, he could act as producer.

To facilitate a monetary commitment, David provided potential backers with two "hooks" upon which they could hang their confidence: casting and music.

The casting was timely. David chose two young actors, Jack Wild and Mark Lester, who had just starred in the hit film *Oliver*. The presence of the child celebrities gave *Melody* a promotional edge.

The music, too, added a luster to the picture. David engaged the Bee Gees—brothers Robin, Maurice, and Barry Gibb—to perform songs for the soundtrack. The Bee Gees had made the U.S. pop charts *four* times in 1968, with "The New York Mining Disaster 1941 (Have You Seen My Wife Mr. Jones?)," "To Love Somebody," "Holiday," and "The Lights Went Out in Massachusetts."

Although David was a rookie producer, he was exhibiting a flair for packaging commercial cinematic product. Stars. Salable soundtrack. Yet, there was one aspect of *Melody* which was decidedly not commercial.

The screenplay.

The movie related the bittersweet love story of two ten-year-olds who want to get married. No car chases. No shooting. Just a simple preteen romance.

Major U.S. film distributors were not impressed, dismissing *Melody* as an odd bit of cinema. Stars and music aside, there was no room amid the hungry gears of the American movie machine for such a genteel motion picture.

The sour note *Melody* struck in Hollywood was to be expected. In 1970, while David was attempting to find an outlet for his offbeat reel of celluloid, action movies were exploding on the screen.

There was a disaster film: *Airport* (Universal), which spawned a series of successful sequels. Three military pictures: *M*A*S*H* (Twentieth Century–Fox), *Patton* (Twentieth Century–Fox), and *Catch-22* (Paramount). A James Bond entry, *On Her Majesty's Secret Service* (United Artists). And a futuristic adventure, *Beneath the Planet of the Apes* (Twentieth Century–Fox).

When American films did explore relationships, the treatment was *very* adult. Columbia Pictures' *Bob & Carol & Ted & Alice* and Twentieth Century–Fox's *Beyond the Valley of the Dolls*, for example.

Rebuffed in Hollywood, *Melody* was ultimately distributed in North America by New York-based distributor Levitt-Pickman and premiered Spring 1971.

Reviews were kind; *Variety* dubbed it " 'The Graduate' for and about 10-year-olds." But *Melody* was flat at the box office and quickly disappeared from American screens. On a worldwide basis, *Melody* did not fare any better, except in Japan. Tokyo audiences were fascinated with the confused libido of two Western children and the intake of yen covered much of the film's cost.

Before continuing with the dramatic form, David took a brief detour and fulfilled his desire to produce what he termed "socially relevant cinema" with several documentaries including *The Double-Headed Eagle*, *Swastika*, and *Brother, Can You Spare a Dime?* But, while documentaries may have provided a sense of purpose, they did not contribute much to the income statement of Goodtimes Enterprises.

Next up for David and Sandy was a version of the children's story, *The Pied Piper*, also funded by Sagittarius and Hemdale. The film was undistinguished, except for the music of pop star Donovan underlying the images. But *The Pied Piper* represented the first David Puttnam production released by a major American studio, Paramount, and for that reason it was significant.

In 1972, David coproduced, with Sandy Lieberson, a picture called *That'll Be the Day*, a saga of youthful self-discovery in the 1950s which was financed by EMI Films. Once again, David looked to the music business in an effort to enhance a film. He cast British rock star David Essex in the lead and enlisted ex-Beatle Ringo Starr to play an ensemble of supporting roles.

Upon its 1973 release, *Variety* called *That'll Be the Day* a "nice bit of nostalgia," adding that the film possessed a "literate script, appealing performances" and was a ". . . technically superior job" with ". . . superior period feel evident in details of setting, action and dialog."

But critics liked the movie better than theatergoers and *That'll Be the Day* remained an obscure, though well done, motion picture.

By this time, the dossier on David Puttnam was definitive. He could raise money. And he could make quality films. But he chose esoteric scripts with limited box-office potential.

In the fall of 1974, *Stardust*—the sequel to *That'll Be the Day*—twinkled onto movie screens via EMI. The film found David Essex reprising his role as a strung-out musician in search of himself. Ringo Starr, however, was otherwise engaged and did not appear in the picture.

Stardust explored the dark side of the rock music world, depicting guitarist Jim Maclaine (Essex) in a nightmarish life crisis.

From *Variety:* "The harrowing finale finds hero a drained, confused recluse in his Spanish castle, his inspiration (and courage) lost, unable any longer to come to grips with life, much less a career. It is a sobering, often shattering picture . . ."

The film drew avid David Puttnam fans but few others. However, with a production cost of just a million dollars, *Stardust* performed well enough at the box office to eke out a profit.

In late 1974, David took one step back from production and acted as executive producer on a movie entitled *Mahler*, a biographical look at the life of turn-of-the-century composer Gustav Mahler. It was released in the United States by Columbia Pictures.

An executive producer credit usually carries little weight in the motion picture industry and generally is considered to be an ambiguous description. In this case, however, *Mahler*—a slick period piece—was so much like previous David Puttnam pictures that it became associated with him rather than with its actual producer, Roy Baird, or its well-known director, Ken Russell.

Mahler was not a film for everyone. The script contained numerous references which were designed specifically for those "in the know" and played its intellectual theme to the point of snobbery.

"Pic [*Variety* abbreviation for motion picture] also has 'in' jokes for the cognoscenti," *Variety* said in its April 1974 review, "such as a visual reference to Visconti's Mahler-influenced 'Death in Venice.' "

The cognoscenti flocked to see *Mahler*. Unfortunately, there are not that many cognoscenti.

Cranking up the camera in 1976, David co-produced (with Allan Marshall) a movie entitled *Bugsy Malone*, once again teaming up with *Melody* screenwriter Alan Parker. The Rank Organization issued the picture outside North America while Paramount handled the U.S. and Canada.

Bugsy Malone was a most unusual film. In fact, the advertising slogan stated: "There's never been a movie like it!" With a cast made up entirely of children—Scott Baio, who went on to network television, and Jodie Foster, who later grew into more serious screen roles, were two of the child stars—*Bugsy Malone* was set in the 1940s. *Variety* sized up the picture by bold-facing the following sentence: "Gangster spoof musical entirely played by (very able) juveniles. Captivating and winning, but a hard sell nonetheless."

The appraisal proved to be accurate. Paramount reported just $1,756,146 in film rentals. (Rentals represent the portion of box office which is income to the studio; about 45 percent. Thus, *Bugsy Malone* grossed about $3,800,000 at the theaters, with $1,756,146 returning to the studio and the balance being retained by exhibitors.) But, with its cost of $2,000,000, *Bugsy Malone* wound up being marginally profitable after exhibition in foreign territories and income from ancillary sales.

By contrast, the year's top picture, *Star Wars*, did $193,500,000 in U.S. film rentals during the same period, while movies like

Saturday Night Fever and *Smokey and the Bandit* generated $74,100,000 and $58,949,900 respectively.

Following his now familiar pattern, David next produced yet another period picture, *The Duellists*, set during the time of Napoleon. As the title suggested, it was the saga of two Napoleonic lieutenants who fought a series of duels.

Another aspect of *The Duellists* was to become a David Puttnam trademark: the presence of a first-time feature director. In this case it was Briton Ridley Scott.

Developed under the Enigma Productions banner—David's own company—and released by CIC, *The Duellists* starred Keith Carradine and Harvey Keitel.

Variety dubbed the film "an item of festival and archive interest but more difficult for commercial chances."

Predictably, *The Duellists* was shot down at the box office.

So, by 1976—after a decade in the film industry—David Puttnam had managed to gain a reputation as a producer of quality, if rather esoteric, pictures. He had also managed to do something else. Lose money. In fact, he was deep in debt following the financial failure of *The Duellists*.

But that was ten years ago. Now David stood at the threshold of motion picture power, knocking on the door of The Coca-Cola Company and seeking to run Columbia Pictures. It would have been a truly exhilarating feeling except for one thing.

David was unable to shake the memory of the last time he took a job in Hollywood.

And vowed he would *never* come back.

CHAPTER

TWO

In 1976, the prospect of leaving England was most appealing to David Puttnam. The British film industry was in decline and the outlook was anything but promising. In fact, a survey being conducted at the time by the Department of Trade and Industry would provide a damning statistical confirmation of what filmmakers already knew.

During the previous decade, there had been a downward trend in which the number of theaters dropped from 1,871 to 1,583. Admissions took an even steeper dive. Although 291,000,000 people a year were purchasing tickets ten years earlier, only 107,000,000 had filed into British cinemas during the most recent twelve-month period.

While inflation raged throughout the United Kingdom, box office had risen modestly since 1967 to seventy-five million pounds from sixty million, indicating that even a sharp rise in ticket prices could not keep pace with the rapidly shrinking attendance.

As bleak as the government report was, it was only half of the bad news for British filmmakers. At the same time the *market* for their pictures was dwindling, their *market share*, too, was contracting. Increasingly, American movies dominated England. Hollywood sent 127 motion pictures into the United Kingdom in 1977, versus 42 local efforts. As a result of all the imports, the number of Britons employed by the English film industry plummeted to 18,443 from 34,766, a 47 percent decrease.

It was no wonder David Puttnam wished to cross the Atlantic.

Besides his desire to flee the constraints of the British Isles, David wanted to come to America and be part of the Hollywood mechanism that dazzled the world with its cinematic magic. Casablanca Filmworks offered him that opportunity. Small by Hollywood standards, Casablanca was a partnership between film producer Peter Guber and music business maven Neil Bogart.

Peter Guber had just produced *The Deep* for Columbia Pictures, an adaptation of a book by the same title from Peter Benchley, the author of *Jaws*. It boasted a stellar cast—Robert Shaw, Jacqueline Bisset, and Nick Nolte—and turned in $31,266,000 in domestic rentals.

Neil Bogart—dubbed the "king of bubblegum" during the sixties ("bubblegum" was a term used for a teen-oriented pop music style)—founded New York–based Buddah Records before moving to Los Angeles to establish Casablanca Records. At Casablanca he broke through with rock-group Kiss and disco-queen Donna Summer. By the time he linked up with Peter Guber to form Casablanca Filmworks, Neil Bogart had been responsible for sixty gold records (a million dollars each in sales) and twenty-four platinum records (two million dollars each).

Neither Peter nor Neil had aspirations to run Casablanca on a day-to-day operational basis. So they sought out someone who would serve as president of the company.

They chose David Puttnam.

Many in Hollywood were surprised by the choice. There were scores of qualified candidates for the job living right in Beverly Hills. And none of David's movies was the kind of box-office hit which would warrant bringing in an *outsider* to run an American film company.

But Peter and Neil were impressed with the quality of production inherent in David's previous pictures and opted to take a chance that the British producer could bring those skills to bear on the process of commercial filmmaking. Based on this extrapolation, Casablanca chairman/CEO Peter Guber signed David Puttnam to a three-year pact as president of Casablanca Filmworks.

Immediately after arriving in Burbank, however, David's first official act as a studio chief was to leave for Malta where the Casablanca film *Midnight Express* was about to get under way. He didn't go to Malta for a visit, however. He went there for an extended stay as coproducer of the picture.

It was highly unusual that a corporate officer would prefer

standing behind a camera to sitting behind a desk. After all, the position of president carried with it certain duties which would remain unfulfilled during the shooting of the picture.

There was an explanation for David's expedition to Malta. Alan Parker, who had directed *Bugsy Malone*, and Alan Marshall, who had coproduced *Bugsy Malone*, were at the helm on *Midnight Express*. David wanted to be reteamed with the men who had generated his most successful film to date. The difference between then and now, however, was that *then* David was an independent producer and *now* he was president of a company.

Midnight Express proved to be a rude awakening for a young British filmmaker who had become accustomed to complete autonomy. Until then, all the pictures David produced had been done on his own terms, in his own country. He had always chosen scripts which suited his own personal tastes. Even though his movies generally were relegated to what he himself referred to as the "art ghetto"—a group of small theaters in major urban areas—at least David had never had to accommodate the wishes of superiors.

Midnight Express required learning a fundamentally different set of rules.

David did not choose the script, nor had he developed the story. Instead, he was handed a final draft and instructed to get it shot. He was not given the luxury of time to dally over aesthetics. There was a strict production schedule and a theatrical release date already on the calendar.

Clearly, *Midnight Express* was intended to be a *commercial* endeavor. Based on the true-life experience of American Billy Hayes when he was arrested in Turkey for smuggling hash, the film was peppered with violence and action. The gut-level screenplay with its graphic torture scenes was about as far away from David's filmmaking sensibilities as a motion picture could get. Yet he shot the script with few revisions, choosing not to impose his will in making any significant modifications.

Even the box-office expectation for *Midnight Express* was alien to David's previous experiences. In fact, the business Casablanca *expected* from *Midnight Express* represented a number which exceeded the combined gross revenue of every film David had done in the past.

Although *Midnight Express* did not reach the box-office heights of *The Deep*, the wrenching drama was a major financial success and ultimately generated $15,065,000 in U.S. film rentals.

David Puttnam might have been happy—he now had a production credit on a certified hit—but he was not. Instead of taking bows for the financial success of the film, David became obsessed with the reviews. Many critics had found *Midnight Express* offensive. A good example was *Time* magazine's appraisal:

"One of the ugliest sado-masochistic trips, with heavy homosexual overtones, that our thoroughly nasty movie age has yet produced."

For most producers, the big box-office receipts which followed the critical assaults would have provided a modicum of solace. David, however, had spent ten years cultivating an image of himself, both in the media and via the content of his films, as a champion of cinematic purity. He was having difficulty explaining his philosophy on the one hand, and *Midnight Express* on the other.

While shooting *Midnight Express* David actively sought to put together another film: *Agatha*. Dustin Hoffman was cast in the lead male role of the mystery, which was to be shot in England with David producing.

Agatha was promoted as "an imaginary solution to an authentic mystery," purporting to explain the disappearance of writer Agatha Christie in 1926. Vanessa Redgrave was Agatha and Dustin Hoffman played the American journalist who was investigating the story. No *Midnight Express* this time, *Agatha* was pure Puttnam. A period piece with an intellectual slant.

One of the people David had enlisted as a financial backer was London businessman Jarvis Astaire. Jarvis had meticulously set up a budget for *Agatha* under a provision called EADY, a British film-subsidy program. All calculations were based on EADY and, in order to qualify for certain government concessions, the cast and crew had to be largely British.

The linchpin of the deal was British producer David Puttnam. It was David's involvement which had attracted Vanessa Redgrave and Dustin Hoffman to the project. And, of more consequence, the idea to turn the Kathleen Tynan story of the celebrated mystery writer Agatha Christie into a film entitled *Agatha* was all David Puttnam's idea.

Two weeks before the cameras were set to roll, Jarvis Astaire received a letter from David Puttnam. The letter stated that, for tax reasons, David could only come into England a maximum of twenty days for the remainder of the year. David indicated that, despite his limited presence, he would still produce *Agatha*.

Jarvis was infuriated, finding David's suggestion that he could produce *Agatha* part-time an unacceptable compromise. So, in order to salvage the EADY subsidy, Jarvis—himself a Briton—co-produced the movie with partner Gavrik Losey.

Had there been sufficient time, Jarvis might have been able to find a substitute for David. But, with production fourteen days away, and no way to postpone the start without severe financial penalties, he had no alternative other than proceeding with *Agatha* himself.

"The last thing in the world I want to do," Jarvis grumbled as shooting began, "is produce a picture."

So *Agatha* completed principal photography with Jarvis Astaire in charge and the film's originator, David Puttnam, having never set foot on the set.

For his initial efforts, David did get a production credit in a roundabout way. The opening title sequence read: "A Warner Brothers–First Artists release of a Sweetwal production in association with Casablanca Filmworks." The Casablanca reference, however, had little to do with production input, rather it was an obligatory mention because of a minor financial stake Casablanca had in the film.

At the time, David explained his absence from *Agatha* by blaming actor Dustin Hoffman. In the *Los Angeles Times* Calendar section, David was quoted as saying:

"Dustin is a gifted actor on the screen, but my experience with him was an unhappy one. There seemed to be a malevolence in him, a determination to make other human beings unhappy. . . . He gave me such a hard time on *Agatha*, I became totally neurotic."

When Dustin Hoffman saw the article, he was shocked. And angered. So he sought out the *Los Angeles Times* a month later and countered David's allegations:

"What is extraordinary is that I've never worked with this man. As far as I know, I've only met him three times. And yet he goes around saying these terrible things about me."

Jarvis Astaire, upon reading the *Los Angeles Times* point-counterpoint, told anyone who would listen: "David Puttnam was getting a tax breather. That's why he didn't produce *Agatha*. He created this *myth* that he couldn't get along with Dustin Hoffman."

The *Agatha* episode would not have been an issue had the British producer so crucial to the project not been David Puttnam. Such financial maneuvering is especially common among those whose income soars into lofty tax brackets. But the difference between most citizens and David Puttnam was his frequent rhetoric about social responsibility in which he cast himself as the conscience of the film industry.

Dustin Hoffman, at least, saw the sudden disruption in the production flow of *Agatha* as not only an inconvenience, but as a contradiction in David Puttnam.

With a minimum of effort, David suddenly found himself with something very difficult to shake: a Hollywood enemy.

In 1979, David was reunited with *Bugsy Malone* star, Jodie Foster, for *Foxes*, a film which depicted the trials of four teenage girls as they learned about sex, drugs, parents, etc.

But somewhere in the translation, *Foxes*, instead of being *about* teenagers, turned out being a teenage movie. The difference was in the telling. Slapstick versus dialogue.

Neither critics nor audiences embraced the uneven motion picture. It marked the first time a David Puttnam production (actually a coproduction with Gerald Ayers) had *entirely* missed the mark. The British producer who had traveled to America with such high hopes was inconsolable.

David abruptly ended his relationship with Casablanca Filmworks in 1979 and limped back to London. He felt he had lost creative control in America and proceeded to distance himself from Hollywood via a series of interviews with the press.

In a piece which appeared in *Variety* June 11, 1980, reporter Simon Perry observed of David's time at Casablanca Filmworks:

"While in Hollywood, he admits, he discovered he was not equipped to make 'a North American film,' because he couldn't apply his own instincts in the way he could to British settings and characters that are 'the fabric of my upbringing.' "

David cited the difficulty he encountered even in something as basic as choosing jewelry for a female star.

"In order to know, for example, whether Sally Kellerman was good casting for *Foxes*, he had to rely on the best expertise he could hire, not his own gut feeling. It unnerved him to be at one remove from the subject.

" 'If I was casting a similar part in England,' he explains, 'I'd know instinctively if someone was physically right for it, whether the associations were right, and exactly how she'd look—all the way down to what earrings she'd wear. I'd have a basis of knowledge to draw on going back to when I was born."

In fact, David found the Casablanca Filmworks experience so distasteful, it prompted him to conclude: "I absolutely now know that I want to live in Britain."

Yet here he was five years later, asking to return to the glitter of Hollywood in a most exalted and visible position.

Chairman of Columbia Pictures.

"David, Patsy. Good to see you again."

The voice belonged to Francis T. (Fay) Vincent, Jr., chairman of Columbia Pictures Industries and president of the Coca-Cola Entertainment Business Sector. As far as he was concerned, David Puttnam already was the new chairman/CEO of Columbia Pictures. Fay had come to terms with David a few days earlier in New York and hired him. It was Fay's decision to make, and he had made it.

Although Coke had never second-guessed his authority, it appeared David was doing just that. The meeting in Atlanta was not necessary within the normal corporate protocol. Was Fay's position not high enough to satisfy David Puttnam?

Fay wondered why his new employee was so adamant about meeting the upper echelon of Coca-Cola. David had been vague and somewhat mysterious regarding the purpose of his visit to Coke headquarters. What was he planning to say?

Fay hated surprises. Especially when it threatened to challenge his scope of power.

A forty-eight-year-old attorney, Fay Vincent had served for a time in the Division of Corporate Finance at the Securities and Exchange Commission before joining Columbia Pictures Industries in 1978. Balding and bespectacled, he was the antithesis of the top man at a major entertainment entity.

Fond of saying he knew nothing about movies, Fay wore his ignorance of the motion picture industry as a kind of badge, a reminder that there were *two* words in the phrase "entertainment business"—entertainment and business. In fact, there was a sharp delineation between the two concepts within the structure of Columbia Pictures.

Coca-Cola was the parent corporation. The division of Coke that owned Columbia—as well as an interest in Tri-Star Pictures, Merv Griffin Productions, and other entertainment entities—was dubbed the Entertainment Business Sector.

Then there were the two Columbias. Columbia Pictures Industries was a subsidiary of Coca-Cola, while Columbia Pictures existed as a division of Columbia Pictures Industries.

Although the uninitiated often became confused when discussing Columbia Pictures Industries and Columbia Pictures, the two similar names represented entirely different functions. Columbia Pictures (without Industries tacked on) embodied the creative and distribution mechanism. This was the company that David Puttnam would head as chairman/CEO.

Columbia Pictures Industries—the administrative overseer—was the company of which Fay Vincent was chairman.

Fay had always created the impression that he had the *business* in hand. Now, with the addition of David Puttnam as creative chief, he had told Coca-Cola he would have the entertainment aspect under control too. But how much did Fay really know about the British filmmaker? Every time someone asked him about David, his reply was always the same.

"You know. David Puttnam. The film producer. The guy who won an Oscar for *Chariots of Fire.*"

David's triumph at the 1982 Academy Awards had obscured all other details of his cinematic background. That one brief instant in time became the essence of David Puttnam's entire past. Certainly it was an event which swayed Fay Vincent, and landed David Puttnam in Atlanta that June morning.

Early in 1980, David had focused on the concept of a film about two runners in the 1924 Olympics. He would use running as a metaphor in order to explore the internal conflict of two real-life characters, Eric Liddell and Harold Abrahams. Liddell, a Scottish Christian, was running to serve the Lord, while Abrahams, a British Jew, was running for recognition in an effort to overcome his feeling of persecution.

Once again, the Puttnam fingerprint was on a film project. Period piece. Intellectual slant.

Even though he had spent three years at Casablanca Filmworks, David found his ability to raise money as sharp as ever. He approached film-financier Jake Eberts, a Canadian residing in

London, and asked for $50,000 as seed money for the movie. Jake obliged.

Next David brought in Dodi Fayed as coproducer. Notwithstanding any production talent Dodi may have had, his father was Mohammed El Fayed, owner of such establishments as the Ritz Hotel in Paris and Harrods in London. Dodi brought a requisite bankroll with him when he came on board.

Billionaire Mohammed was not prepared, however, to fund an open-ended budget. So David was obligated to proceed carefully with *Chariots of Fire*, staying within a well-defined cost structure.

As he had done in the past, David exhibited a sensitivity toward the music, opting to employ contemporary instrumental artist Vangelis to do the score instead of filling the soundtrack with 1920s period tunes. The *Chariots of Fire* theme became a giant hit, spurring admissions for the movie. As the movie drew huge numbers at the box office, it fueled album sales, which in turn attracted listeners to the theater, which led to still more record sales.

The result was $30,600,000 in U.S. film rentals, a record, at the time, for a foreign motion picture. And an Academy Award nomination to boot.

The year 1981 had been particularly fertile for Hollywood stalwarts involved with exceptional films, as the Best Picture nominations demonstrated. *Reds* from Warren Beatty; *On Golden Pond*, boasting the seemingly unbeatable trio of Henry Fonda, Jane Fonda, and Katharine Hepburn; the George Lucas–backed, Steven Spielberg–directed *Raiders of the Lost Ark* with Harrison Ford in the starring role; and *Atlantic City*, sporting a strong performance by Burt Lancaster, all vied for top prize. Perhaps the only nominated picture not given any chance at all was the British import *Chariots of Fire*. It was a *small* picture. A foreign entry. And it had no stars.

If there was a favorite among the four Hollywood-grown movies, it was *Reds*. Besides Best Picture consideration, *Reds* received eleven other nominations and the general opinion in Hollywood was that Warren Beatty's epic would cut a wide swath through the awards on its way to claiming top honors.

The press loved the contrast and much of the pre-Oscar buildup centered around the perceived David and Goliath contest between heavy favorite *Reds* and dark horse *Chariots of Fire*. When the envelope was opened, however, it was David Puttnam, not

Warren Beatty, who stepped to center stage to accept the Best Picture Oscar, pulling off a stunning upset.

But as spectacular as the *Chariots of Fire* victory was, there existed an underlying explanation for its unexpected triumph. With *Reds, On Golden Pond, Radiers of the Lost Ark*, and *Atlantic City* going head-to-head, a split in the votes developed, working to the advantage of *Chariots of Fire*.

Although *Chariots of Fire* won Best Picture, its director, Hugh Hudson, was snubbed in favor of Warren Beatty for the Best Direction Oscar. Most observers saw this as not only a showing of support for Beatty, but also as a definitive affirmation that David Puttnam's association with a film severely limited the amount of credit which would be bestowed on the balance of the production crew.

David did attempt to ease the tension between him and Hugh Hudson by telling reporters at the post-Oscar press conference that Hudson was a much better director than Warren Beatty, but all the British producer succeeded in doing was further alienating the *Reds* star/director/producer.

Prior to Oscar night, David had spoken freely with members of the British press regarding Warren Beatty and *Reds*.

"I have a lot of problems with *Reds*," he offered. "Not with the film, but with the affluent manner in which it was produced. It upset me immensely to be forced to spend a year getting a director I was working with to conform to a set of rigid disciplines to avoid going over budget while someone else was being given a carte blanche to exceed his budget."

Although David was always accessible to the press, Warren Beatty was not. Consequently, David's statements went unanswered.

But David Puttnam now had *two* enemies in Hollywood: Dustin Hoffman *and* Warren Beatty. He must have known he had miffed two major stars, but what David did not realize was that by doing so, he had gained a third and perhaps more formidable foe, attorney Bertram Fields.

Both Dustin and Warren happened to be represented by Bertram Fields, considered one of the most influential lawyers in the movie business.

Bertram was mystified. First the *Agatha* run-in. Then *Reds*. "Who the hell does David Puttnam think he is?" Bertram asked himself.

***

When *Chariots of Fire* was released, David and his film were the constant subject of newspaper and magazine articles. While David willingly obliged armies of reporters and related anecdotes about the production, he used the press opportunity for quite another purpose: a continuation of his attack on Hollywood.

On May 13, 1981, *Variety* carried a story headlined: HOPE OF A DISPIRITED BRITAIN.

"The concept of no compromise," wrote Roger Watkins, *Variety*'s London bureau head at the time, now the paper's editor-in-chief, ". . . is based on Puttnam's belief that audiences react favorably to cinematic honesty, respond well to emotional accuracy . . . no matter where the film comes from.

"The universality of a picture comes not from the fact that the cast is littered with internationally known names, or locales in a half dozen different countries. International accessibility of basic themes such as love, pain, achievement, loneliness and so on, are recognized by producer Puttnam."

The article laid out David's views and gave fair warning that he stood a world apart—literally and figuratively—from the Hollywood establishment.

"It's Puttnam's view," Watkins continued, paraphrasing the content and spirit of David's remarks, "that one of the reasons that U.S. majors make so many bad pictures is because film production is forced to fit a studio's distribution commitment. Ready or not, a pic [motion picture] often has to go into production on a given date to fulfill a major's distribution schedule, hence many roll imperfectly cast, without satisfactory script and other supposed prerequisites. 'They become,' says Puttnam, 'product.'

"The argument for a picture to be true to itself is overwhelming, according to Puttnam, and for him to 'get it right' he feels he has to be on his own turf, making pictures in which, instinctively, he knows if nuances are right or wrong.

"Two years in America where, as a producer for Casablanca Filmworks, he had to rely on the interpretation of others for his 'feel,' was enlightening. It persuaded him that England was where he wanted to work."

Before Fay Vincent, David, and Patsy reached the door to the conference room, Richard Gallop emerged. Dick was president of Columbia Pictures Industries and executive vice president of the

Coca-Cola Entertainment Business Sector. Although Fay had made the final determination on David's employment, Dick had been the negotiator.

"They're all waiting," Dick said.

Coca-Cola chairman Roberto Goizueta, president Donald R. Keough, and executive vice president Ira Herbert rose as Patsy walked in ahead of David.

After exchanging pleasantries, Patsy spoke first.

"David asked me to come here with him so I could see that he hadn't sold out."

The Coke executives were surprised at her choice of words and challenging demeanor.

Patsy continued: "David's ideals are important. Coke must understand that."

Was she putting Coca-Cola on trial? Did she expect those present to *defend* the company? As far as Roberto, Don, and Ira were concerned, the *only* purpose of the meeting was to accommodate the request of a new employee who had asked to meet the people he would be working for. It wasn't supposed to be the British inquisition.

"It's vital for us to know," Patsy went on, "that you understand David's deep commitment to making quality movies. And that you will back him a hundred percent on that."

Dick Gallop was beginning to lose patience.

"I understand your commitment to quality," Dick said, directing his comment at David rather than Patsy, "but, by the same token, I know you are aware that Columbia Pictures is a profit-oriented company. We certainly want films the studio can be proud of, but we want them to do well at the box office too."

Dick felt uneasy with David's constant references to *quality* pictures. It seemed to him the word was being used as a *substitute* for profitable, rather than as a measure of worth.

"Making a quality film," Dick added, "does not preclude making a commercial film."

The observation was intended as a peace offering, requiring only a nod of agreement.

"That's true," David acknowledged, "but it is not true in reverse. I would never make a picture purely for commercial reasons. Take *Rambo*, for example."

The mention of *Rambo* riveted the attention of everyone in the room. *Rambo: First Blood Part II* had been the most successful movie ever for Coke's other motion picture subsidiary, Tri-Star Pictures, generating $78,919,250 in domestic film rentals. The figure placed the action/adventure sequel at number twenty-one on *Variety*'s all-time rental champions. In other words, of all the movies *ever* made, *Rambo* had been bested at the box office by just twenty other pictures.

"Even if I knew *Rambo* was going to be as big as it was," David offered, "I would never have made it. It's just not a film I would be interested in."

"We're not asking you to make *Rambo* specifically," Dick Gallop shot back, "but we do expect you to make commercial films generally."

David seemed to be mulling over Dick Gallop's statement, yet he did not respond. It was suddenly clear to both men that communication had all but broken down.

CHAPTER THREE

Several hundred miles north of Atlanta, Herbert A. Allen worked in his New York office. While he was aware of David Puttnam's visit to Coca-Cola, he had little interest in the outcome of the meeting. Notwithstanding his hands-off policy in this case, it occurred to him that all the controversy in the movie business during the last decade seemed to center around Columbia Pictures. Certainly this was true since July 1973, when Herbert had become a major stockholder in the studio.

It wasn't that controversy bothered the forty-six-year-old Wall Street investment banker. It didn't. It was just that Columbia Pictures had generated more than its share of aggravation considering its relative size among his varied holdings and he certainly had more to worry about than the ongoing turmoil of Hollywood.

For the past nineteen years Herbert had expended a great deal of energy building Allen & Company, Inc. into a respected financial firm, having stepped in as chief executive at the age of twenty-seven.

"I was a shell of a president," Herbert says of his professional origins, "heading a shell of a company."

Most people are surprised by this assessment, confusing Allen & Company, Inc. with Allen & Company (without the Inc.), a firm formed by Herbert's Uncle Charlie in 1922 and joined by Herbert's father, Herbert, Sr., a few years later. Despite almost identical corporate names, the two companies are entirely separate entities.

In nephew/son Herbert, the senior Allens saw a willing and capable executive, so they placed him in charge of the newly formed corporation, Allen & Company, Inc., giving him a chance to either prove himself or fail. Whatever happened, it was entirely up to young Herbert A. Allen and no one else. It would be sink or swim, profit or loss.

Herbert didn't disappoint them. From the moment he slid behind his highly polished rosewood desk in 1966, it became clear that he possessed the same curious mix of outward panache and inner caution as his ancestors. He was an Allen all right. Every pound as tough as Uncle Charlie. Every ounce as thoughtful as father Herbert.

Yet Herbert Allen proved to be independent of the past. He did not exhibit the blind arrogance usually born of highbrow genealogy. Nor did he hide behind a veil of tradition. Before long, it was clear that Herbert intended to be a progenitor of the family business rather than a caretaker of the family tree.

Herbert's independence was never more apparent than it was the summer of 1973 when he decided to buy a huge block of shares in Columbia Pictures even though the studio was one reel away from bankruptcy.

However, a factor that had nothing to do with the balance sheet ultimately convinced Herbert Allen to invest in the film industry: a strong vote of confidence regarding Columbia Pictures from producer Ray Stark, a long-time Allen family friend and a man Herbert considered an expert regarding motion pictures.

Ray, fifty-seven at the time, had produced, directly or indirectly, over one hundred movies. His credits read like a history of motion pictures. *Night of the Iguana. Reflections in a Golden Eye. Funny Girl. The Electric Horseman. The Goodbye Girl. The Way We Were.*

So, along with Ray Stark, Herbert opted to buy stock in Columbia Pictures.

The first action Herbert took as controlling stockholder of Columbia was to elevate President Leo Jaffe, who had been with the studio since 1930, to the position of chairman. Next, he moved Alan Hirschfield, an investment banker at Allen & Company since 1959, into the president's office.

Alan Hirschfield's association with Allen & Company, though it spanned more than a decade, was preceded by an even longer relationship. Alan's father, Norman, had begun doing business with Herbert's uncle Charlie in the 1920s. So the Allens and the Hirschfields had something very important, especially when hundreds of millions of dollars were at stake. The two families had a history.

Herbert and Alan chose super-agent David Begelman to oversee the studio's creative endeavors. By 1973, David Begelman had become one of Hollywood's most influential representatives of major talent, listing Paul Newman, Robert Redford, and Cliff Robertson among his clients.

But a few months after buying the studio, Herbert's move into the motion picture industry appeared to have been sheer folly as Columbia reported a loss for fiscal 1973 of nearly $50,000,000.

Yet Herbert was not ruffled. He had expected a gush of red ink—maybe not quite the flood which occurred—but red ink nonetheless.

Almost immediately after the shedding of the $50,000,000, however, the purchase of the troubled movie studio began to shape up as a stroke of pure genius. Within two years, Columbia was rolling the cameras and rolling in box-office receipts from pictures like *Funny Lady*, *Tommy*, and *Shampoo*. More success ensued and, by 1977, *Close Encounters of the Third Kind*, with Steven Spielberg in the director's chair, was in the works.

The turnaround at Columbia had been phenomenal.

Then, without warning, Herbert Allen's carefully constructed company disintegrated in a most unexpected manner. No financial debacle. At least that could be measured in dollars and analyzed by accountants. What actually happened defied explanation.

David Begelman, the white knight who guided Columbia Pictures along a dazzling comeback trail, embezzled $10,000 from the studio by forging and cashing a check made payable to actor and former client Cliff Robertson.

Herbert was stunned. David Begelman was *very* highly paid. Why would he steal $10,000?

As the affair progressed, it became uglier every day and eventually spawned a best-selling book entitled *Indecent Exposure* (William Morrow, 1982) by David McClintick.

The story presented in *Indecent Exposure* has been a source of controversy ever since its publication. Although David McClintick offered fascinating details regarding the Begelman scandal, the recollections which provided the foundation of *Indecent Exposure* apparently were those of Alan Hirschfield.

According to Hirschfield, upon learning about the forgery, he called for Begelman's immediate dismissal over the objections of the Columbia board of directors.

But Herbert Allen remembers a much different scenario.

Hirschfield *did not* immediately suggest that Begelman be fired. And the Columbia board was not opposed to taking action against the beleaguered studio chief. On the contrary, the board of directors reacted swiftly and properly.

First of all, the board directed management to speak with Los Angeles district attorney John Van de Kamp and the Securities and Exchange Commission on *day one* of the board's discovery of the forgery. And the board of directors, too, took several *instantaneous* steps in the Begelman case. By the end of the first week, the board stripped Begelman of all corporate titles, took away his board seat, and relieved him of his in-the-money stock options worth $1,300,000, representing the largest cash penalty ever imposed on an executive of a public company.

"If these facts were made public at the time," Herbert Allen states now, "there would not have been any basis for a book."

Ray Stark also figured prominently in *Indecent Exposure*, but the producer states: "I talked to McClintick once for an hour during lunch at Kosherama and I had a public relations representative with me. Yet he quoted me inaccurately three hundred times."

Following an investigation, and subsequent to Begelman's acquiescence to a demand by the board that he seek psychiatric help, the deposed studio chief was reinstated, although it was without his previous corporate title and stock options.

But two months later, after a bitter and prolonged struggle between Alan Hirschfield and Herbert Allen—one that undid generations of good will—David Begelman was forced to resign.

Suddenly, Herbert Allen not only found himself in an unwanted media spotlight but with a company in disarray as well. To Herbert, ownership was desirable, but having to divert time and energy to day-to-day operations was quite another matter.

When David Begelman exited Columbia, Alan Hirschfield encouraged Columbia president of production Dan Melnick to act as interim studio head. Dan, who was forty-three years old, was reluctant. He had spent ten years within the web of network television, eight with David Susskind's production entity, Talent Associates, and four at MGM as head of production. Now, after seven months at Columbia, Dan was thinking more in terms of independent production than reorganizing a major studio.

But, because of his relationship with Alan Hirschfield, he relented, on the condition that his role clearly be interim in nature. Alan agreed, and set out to find a permanent studio head.

Alan Hirschfield's executive search came up empty, so he went back to Dan Melnick and offered him the permanent president's post. Dan agreed, but once again placed a condition on his acceptance: a number-two man who could ultimately assume Dan's responsibilities would be hired as well.

At the strong suggestion of mutual friends, Alan met with Frank Price, the president of MCA/Universal Television. Frank was riding high at MCA, and many were certain he would someday assume control of the entire company.

Frank had joined MCA Television nineteen years before as a writer, graduated to an associate producer, then became a producer, next a vice president, and finally the president. But all his corporate ladder-climbing was within the television department, and Frank dreamed of seeing his projects on the great expanse of the silver screen. MCA did not extend him the opportunity, but Alan Hirschfield did, offering him the position of president of production at Columbia Pictures.

At the age of forty-seven, Frank very much wanted the job but he responded to the overture with caution.

"I keep reading that you're not going to be with Columbia for very long," he bluntly told Alan Hirschfield. "I don't want to become a political appointment. I think I should talk to Herbert Allen."

It was a savvy move on Frank's part. Alan Hirschfield was an *employee* of Columbia. Herbert Allen was an *owner*. Frank knew that Herbert's approval was vital if he was to have any longevity at the studio.

A meeting between Herbert Allen and Frank Price was arranged. It was brief. But by the time it was over, Frank was on his way to Columbia Pictures.

When MCA chairman Lew Wasserman heard that Frank was leaving, he was not amused.

"Frank, you're making a mistake," Wasserman warned. "Why are you doing this?"

"Because," Frank replied, "I don't want to look in the mirror twenty years from now and realize I never made a motion picture."

Lew Wasserman knew there was only one thing that would convince Frank to stay: a job in the movie division. But Lew was happy with the current motion picture executives—they were doing their jobs very well—and he really viewed Frank as a *television* man, so he didn't make the offer.

Frank Price left Lew Wasserman's office and began extricating himself from a twenty-year relationship to become Columbia's president of production.

On July 5, 1978, Alan Hirschfield resigned as president of Columbia Pictures Industries and Herbert Allen moved to fill the administrative void by bringing in Fay Vincent.

The selection of Fay Vincent was undoubtedly a reaction to the David Begelman experience. Herbert hoped a conservative lawyer, a graduate of Yale Law School, would provide a steadying influence in his attempt to bring the shaky management situation under control.

Both Fay and Herbert had gone to Williams College. Although they were not really classmates—Fay had graduated two years ahead of Herbert—the alumnus factor weighed heavily in Fay's favor.

Following Fay Vincent's arrival, studio chief Dan Melnick resigned and Frank Price assumed his post. To fill the production president job, Frank Price chose Guy McElwaine, a former professional baseball player, agent, and studio production chief.

Guy's rise within the motion picture business was textbook in nature, but his entry into films was not. While playing pro baseball in the Pacific Coast League, he'd sustained an injury that ended a promising athletic career. Guy was then recruited by MGM for its industrial softball team and given a job in the publicity department.

He left MGM and became an agent at ICM before accepting a position as head of production at Warner Brothers. Then it was back to ICM as head of the motion picture department.

But Guy was hired away from ICM, this time landing at Ray Stark's Rastar Productions as president. Finally, Guy McElwaine left Rastar to become president of production at Columbia, reporting to Ray Stark's friend, Frank Price.

During Frank Price's term as president, Columbia distributed the biggest money-maker in the studio's history, *Ghostbusters*, which scared up $128,264,005 in domestic film rentals. In addition, Frank fostered films like *Kramer vs. Kramer*, starring Dustin Hoffman and Meryl Streep, and brought in the highly acclaimed *Gandhi*, which won nine Academy Awards.

Another picture released during the Frank Price administration was *Annie*, a $40,000,000 film version of the Broadway play. Originally, David Begelman was to produce the picture as part of the severance package provided him by Columbia Pictures. However, Begelman accepted a position at MGM as president of production shortly after leaving Columbia, and Frank Price was forced to find another producer for the project.

Reasoning that Ray Stark was the only filmmaker at Columbia who had any real experience with movie musicals, Frank persuaded Ray to step in as producer. Ray chose John Huston as director, and assembled a well-known cast including Carol Burnett, Bernadette Peters, Tim Curry, Albert Finney, and Ann Reinking.

"I tried to make the film more acceptable to a broader spectrum of the audience," Ray says now, looking back at the production of *Annie*.

Even though the movie returned $75,000,000 to the studio in film rentals and ancillary income, there is a general perception in the entertainment industry that *Annie* was not profitable.

"As it turned out," Ray observes, refuting this notion, "the film did well for the studio, despite the critics who reviewed the budget rather than the film. While the budget was forty million dollars, we inherited twelve million of that expense for stage rights and screenplay. The actual production cost was approximately twenty-eight million, which is not so much for a period musical on location in New York."

While Frank Price was exerting his authority, Herbert Allen once again tried to focus his attention on Allen & Company, Inc. And, once again, Columbia Pictures diverted him.

This time it was corporate raider Kirk Kerkorian who provided the fireworks. Kerkorian made a run at the studio in 1979, attempting a hostile takeover. Herbert fought back, successfully thwarting the effort.

Although Herbert was the *effective* power at Columbia he was not the top man by title. In April 1981, when Leo Jaffe resigned as chairman, Herbert assumed *both* the title and the power.

One year later, chairman/CEO Herbert Allen put together a deal with Coca-Cola, selling Columbia Pictures Industries for $750,000,000. His own 495,800 shares, at $72.835 per share, were valued at $36,111,593 on June 21, 1982 when the sale was finalized—a particularly worthwhile investment when measured against Herbert's initial cash outlay of about $1,500,000.

The Coke deal concluded, Herbert felt that Columbia Pictures Industries was at last in good shape, with a solidifying management team and a blue-chip corporate parent.

Confident that the team he put together could carry on without his direct, day-to-day, involvement, Herbert—though he remained on the board of directors and wielded an identical measure of power—stepped down as chairman of Columbia Pictures Industries and elevated Fay Vincent to that post. Fay then moved Richard Gallop into the president's office.

Dick Gallop had begun working with Columbia as outside counsel in 1978. As it turned out, he was at the right place at the right time.

After a few months of handling routine legal paperwork, the forty-year-old attorney found himself in the hot seat, squaring off against billionaire Kirk Kerkorian. He worked closely with Herbert Allen and Fay Vincent to repel Kerkorian's attack on Columbia stock, thus earning two powerful allies. As a reward for his efforts, Dick Gallop was made senior vice president and general counsel of Columbia Pictures Industries in 1981.

But, as Dick Gallop's authority redoubled, Frank Price realized his own authority was shrinking and he was being increasingly distanced from the power core in New York, specifically Herbert Allen. The chain of command—originally consisting of direct contact between Frank and Herbert—now went from Frank to Dick Gallop to Fay Vincent and *then* to Herbert Allen. Frank told friends he was beginning to feel like a "plant manager" instead of a president.

In fact, Frank Price reached a point in the summer of 1983 where he could no longer tolerate what he perceived to be an encroachment on his territory as studio chief. So he left Columbia and returned to Universal.

Frank's job passed, by default, to Guy McElwaine.

Many of those who knew Guy McElwaine well thought he was in over his head. The consensus was that Guy was "terrific in talent relations and exhibited all the attributes of a good agent," but his real skill was bringing in people rather than projects.

One of the first pictures Guy McElwaine green-lighted was *Sheena, Queen of the Jungle.*

Sheena, which cost $26,000,000 to make on location in Africa, returned a mere $2,690,000 in domestic film rentals in 1984. The safari had cost Columbia a lot of money and, although it didn't happen instantaneously, it eventually cost Guy McElwaine his job.

Other than *Sheena,* the film most associated with the Guy McElwaine tenure at Columbia Pictures was *The Karate Kid* (although it actually had been developed by Frank Price), also a 1984 release. Produced by Jerry Weintraub, the movie was in the *Rocky* vein: little guy beats all the odds and turns up a winner. Audiences love that sentiment and proved it by generating $42,835,838 in rentals.

While *The Karate Kid* atoned for the financial sins of *Sheena,* it could not erase the image that was burned into the memory of Columbia management: elephants stampeding away with $26,000,000 clutched in their trunks.

Even when *The Karate Kid Part II* outdid the original with a domestic rental figure of $57,700,000, the thunder of millions charging off into the jungle still drowned out the jingle of the cash register.

Sensing he was in trouble, Guy began renewing or initiating deals with several of Hollywood's most politically connected players. Screenwriter/director Lawrence Kasdan. Director Norman Jewison. Former-Columbia-president-turned-producer Dan Melnick. Producer/director Taylor Hackford. And, of course, producer Ray Stark. Guy signed deals with major stars for upcoming pictures, *Ishtar,* with Warren Beatty and Dustin Hoffman, for example. In other words, he positioned himself so that seeking strong box-office performance for Columbia through big names might provide a measure of safety for himself as well.

But even surrounding himself with such solid citizens did not save Guy McElwaine. In April 1986, before the deals could generate much product, Guy resigned, and Columbia Pictures was once again without a studio chief.

Herbert Allen thought about all the times he had been forced into the role of personnel director during the last decade and longed for a lasting solution to the Columbia Pictures employment sweepstakes.

Meanwhile, two East Coast attorneys, three executives from a southern-based soft drink manufacturer, one British producer, and one British producer's wife convened in Atlanta, Georgia to talk about a job in the most insular town in the world.

Hollywood.

CHAPTER

FOUR

"I've prepared a statement," David Puttnam said as he pulled a sheet of paper from his pocket, "which explains how I feel about movies."

Fay Vincent raised his eyebrows. What now?

David handed out several copies of the document. It said:

"I was brought up on and by the movies. They formed, far and away, the most powerful cultural, social and ethical impact on my formative years. They were the movies of the fifties and, for the most part, they were American movies.

"Many of them were made by Columbia Pictures. I was one among millions of young people around the world who basked in the benign, positive and powerful aura of post–Marshall Plan, concerned and responsible America.

"The first day that I came to this country in 1963 was, in many ways, the most exciting of my life. Part of me was coming home. That's how powerful the effect of the American cinema had been on me.

"Far more than any other influence, more than school, more even than home—my attitudes, dreams, preconceptions, and pre-conditions for life had been irreversibly shaped five and a half thousand miles away in a place called Hollywood. I labour over all of this in order to explain exactly where my passion for cinema stems from—exactly why it hurts me that the movies so frequently sell themselves short; unable or unwilling to step up to the creative or ethical standards the audience is entitled to expect of them.

"The medium is too powerful and too important an influence on the way we live, the way we see ourselves, to be left solely to the tyranny of the box-office or reduced to the sum of the lowest common denominator of public taste; this public taste or appetite being conditioned by a diet capable only of producing mental and emotional malnutrition.

"Movies are powerful. Good or bad, they tinker around inside your brain. They steal up on you in the darkness of the cinema to form or confirm social attitudes. They can help to create a healthy, informed, concerned, and inquisitive society or, in the alternative, a negative, apathetic, ignorant one—merely a short step away from nihilism. In short, cinema is propaganda. Benign or malign, social or anti-social, the factual nature of its responsibility cannot be avoided.

"To an almost alarming degree, our political and emotional responses rest, for their health, in the quality and integrity of the present and future generation of film and television creators. Accepting this fact, there are only two personal madnesses that film-makers must guard against. One is the belief that they can do everything and the other is the belief that they can do nothing.

"The former is arrogant in the extreme. But the latter is plainly irresponsible and unacceptable.

"Without doubt, film-makers will continue to stagger from real to imagined crises and back again for years to come. The film industry is no place for faint-hearted time-servers. It needs thorough-going professionals with a love for cinema and respect for its audience.

"There can be no place for heroic posturing or overnight reputations. We have a business to nurture and build and that will require patience and a form of application which allows reputations the opportunity to develop and mature. Only those with a long-term interest in the film industry can expect to be rewarded. Speaking from experience, the rewards for that patience and faith are enormous."

When everyone finished reading, there was a stunned silence. Then a few obligatory comments. Then silence again.

Roberto Goizueta and Don Keough hadn't expected such a detailed statement of purpose. Nor did they wish to engage in a discussion of the pros and cons of the motion picture industry.

"I'm sure Fay told you," David interjected, "that I will only be signing on for three years."

"Three years with one six-month option," Fay corrected.

"The point is, whenever my contract is up, I will leave. I will not reenlist."

It was a startling declaration which led to a befuddling question: Why would David announce his retirement before he had even begun the job?

The answer could be found in David's notion that it was *imperative* he limit his term. He knew he had often blasted Hollywood, frequently telling reporters he would never return. By placing parameters on the deal, David somehow was able to convince himself he had not sold out.

David raised other contractual points.

"Did Fay mention that we worked it out so all overseas operations will report to me?"

"I'm happy about that," Don Keough responded, "after all, that is your bailiwick. Besides, I'm certain that you will get along with Pat Williamson, who I feel is a very able executive."

Originally, Fay Vincent had offered David control of Columbia's *domestic* operations, but not the foreign. It was a bizarre exclusion, considering David's nationality.

The sticking point was Columbia's foreign distribution chief, Pat Williamson. Williamson had been with Columbia for over forty years and he reported directly to Fay Vincent. David wanted control of overseas operations with Williamson reporting to him. Neither Fay nor David would budge from their position on the issue.

David knew there was only one man who could break the impasse.

Ray Stark.

Although Ray was not an officer of Columbia, the veteran producer had maintained a close relationship with the studio and had acted as a consultant for years. He had produced thirty-four films there since 1969 and Ray was consistent. His pictures almost always made money.

Besides his track record, there was his friendship with Herbert Allen. Obviously, that relationship was strengthened when Herbert and Ray bought Columbia and the outcome was millions of dollars in profit for both of them.

It was therefore a natural and sensible move on David Puttnam's part to seek the help of a man considered to be one of the most powerful figures, not just at Columbia, but in all of Hollywood.

Despite this perception of power, Ray Stark has always objected to the use of the word. In fact, Ray maintains that he doesn't believe in the concept of power at all, and any power he may be perceived to have is merely a result of his tenacious persistence in pursuing film projects.

It is a matter of semantics. Generally, power evokes an image of dominance as in military power, or control as in corporate power. But in Hollywood, power has a much more subtle basis. It is not seized by force nor can it be obtained by right of transfer. It must be *cultivated* over a long period of time.

True power in the motion picture business is never exercised, only alluded to, and imposing one's will does not reflect power, it reveals weakness.

A powerful man in Hollywood is one who merely makes a suggestion and things happen. A man like Ray Stark.

Ray did not come by his extraordinary position in the Hollywood hierarchy overnight. He had invested decades in the movie business, developing relationships and accumulating allegiances. Many of the people Ray helped along the way were now major stars or studio heads or successful directors, writers, and producers. Those people, in turn, often came to Ray's aid on a project. Thus, a mutual exchange of favors and ideas propelled Ray and his acquaintances forward.

Ray Stark got his start in show business as a publicist at Warner Brothers·Pictures in the 1930s before moving on to Fawcett Publications as West Coast entertainment editor. At Fawcett, he made contact with a great many writers. These contacts provided all the impetus Ray needed to leave Fawcett and become a literary agent. Soon he was representing authors like Raymond Chandler, J. P. Marquand, James Gould Cozzens, and Ben Hecht.

Although he was successful in the literary arena, Ray craved a different kind of action. Building on his network of associates, he became a partner with Charlie Feldman at Famous Artists Agency and quickly rose to prominence as an agent, with Lana Turner, Ava Gardner, William Holden, Kirk Douglas, and Richard Burton among his clients.

But, by the mid-1950s, acting as an advocate for major stars had lost its luster for Ray Stark. He no longer wanted to take their part in a negotiation, he wanted to *give* them a part in a motion picture.

Thus, Seven Arts Productions—a partnership between Ray and producer Eliot Hyman—was formed in 1957.

Anyone observing Ray Stark's modus operandi then would have seen the cornerstone of the methods he applied throughout his career. He relied on his access to story material and his many relationships when mounting movies at Seven Arts.

Working with friends he'd made while a literary agent, Ray acquired for Seven Arts the rights to an array of books and Broadway plays including *West Side Story, The Nun's Story, Anatomy of a Murder, By Love Possessed,* and *The World of Suzie Wong.*

In 1961, Ray deliberated over a move into independent production and began appraising the various projects on hand to find one that could be his signature film. Since *West Side Story* would always be associated with Jerome Robbins, its creator on Broadway, and *Anatomy of a Murder* was developing at the time as an Otto Preminger film, Ray felt that *The World of Suzie Wong* was the perfect property, a film with which he could create his own personal imprint. Consequently, he allowed *West Side Story* and the other films that he had acquired for Seven Arts to remain with that studio, and *The World of Suzie Wong* became Ray Stark's first movie as an independent producer. Remembering his former clients, Ray cast William Holden, whom he had represented at Famous Artists, in the male lead.

Although *The World of Suzie Wong* proved to be a success, Ray returned to Seven Arts after the film's release. In 1964, however, he left Seven Arts again, this time to produce the Broadway musical version of *Funny Girl*, the story of legendary singer-performer Fanny Brice. Besides her attributes as a vocalist and comedienne, Fanny was Ray's mother-in-law by virtue of Ray's marriage to Fanny's daughter Fran.

That same year, Ray launched his second independent project, *The Night of the Iguana*. He cast two more former clients—Richard Burton and Ava Gardner—in the film, an MGM release directed by John Huston. And in 1966, still another former client—Kirk Douglas—appeared in Ray's next production, *Is Paris Burning?*, released by Paramount Pictures.

Heartened by the box-office success of his independently produced pictures, Ray Stark founded his own production company, Rastar, in 1968. Rastar was formed for the purpose of producing a screen version of the hit Broadway musical *Funny Girl* for Columbia Pictures.

Starring Barbra Streisand, Omar Sharif, and Walter Pidgeon, *Funny Girl* paid off in 1969 with $26,325,000 in domestic film rentals and proved to Hollywood that Ray Stark could deliver the megahit motion picture. (Adjusted for current ticket prices, *Funny Girl* represented the kind of phenomenon twenty years ago that a $100,000,000 picture does today.)

Ray spent the next decade chalking up more than a billion dollars in box office and, in the process, definitively launched a number of careers. For example, Rastar produced four additional Streisand films for Columbia Pictures: *The Owl and the Pussycat* (1970), *The Way We Were* (1973), *For Pete's Sake* (1974), and *Funny Lady* (1975.)

During the filming of *Funny Girl*, Ray enjoyed his collaboration with Herbert Ross, the director of musical sequences. Over the next eight years, Ross directed several more Rastar pictures: *The Owl and the Pussycat* (Columbia) in 1970, *The Sunshine Boys* (MGM) and *Funny Lady* (Columbia) in 1975, *The Goodbye Girl* (MGM/Warner) in 1977, and *California Suite* (Columbia) in 1978. (Ross went on to direct two more Rastar-produced films: Universal's *The Secret of My Success* in 1987 and *Steel Magnolias* for Tri-Star in 1989.)

Ray did four films with legendary filmmaker John Huston: *The Night of the Iguana* (MGM/Seven Arts) in 1964, *Reflections in a Golden Eye* (Warner/Seven Arts) in 1967, *Fat City* (Columbia) in 1972, and *Annie* (Columbia) in 1982.

And he worked with director Sydney Pollack on three films: *This Property Is Condemned* (Paramount/Seven Arts) in 1966, *The Way We Were* (Columbia) in 1973, and *The Electric Horseman* (Columbia/Universal) in 1979.

Ray produced and Neil Simon wrote *nine* Rastar pictures between the years 1975 and 1986: *The Sunshine Boys* (MGM), *Murder by Death* (Columbia), *The Goodbye Girl* (MGM/Warner), *The Cheap Detective* (Columbia), *California Suite* (Columbia), *Chapter Two* (Columbia), *Seems Like Old Times* (Columbia), *The Slugger's Wife* (Columbia), and *Brighton Beach Memoirs* (Universal). (Simon would later add *Biloxi Blues* [Universal, 1988] to his ongoing list of collaborations with Ray Stark.)

Besides people, the other common thread in Ray Stark films was their profitability. Ray chose accessible themes to go with all-star casts, a combination that filled theaters. Consequently, he enjoyed a reputation for being bankable at the box office.

Ray Stark became one of an elite group of producers who—as Twentieth Century–Fox chairman Barry Diller put it—"can get films made anywhere."

It was not just two men who met, but two diametrically opposed philosophies, when David Puttnam sat down with Ray Stark at his Holmby Hills home.

David faced Ray across a table which overlooked a perfectly landscaped backyard. He noted the extraordinary number of statues by Henry Moore and other well-known sculptors, and then got down to the business at hand.

"Ray, there's a problem with Fay Vincent. I'd like Pat Williamson to report to me but Fay tells me that is not possible."

"Anything is possible," Ray replied. "If it's logical."

Ever the agent, Ray figured there had to be a way to bring David, whom he considered to be a bright young producer, and Pat Williamson, whom he thought was one of the keenest international marketing executives, into alignment.

Yet Ray must have wondered why David wanted the job in the first place. Except for the short period as an officer of Seven Arts Productions, Ray had avoided any executive position which would tie him down and encroach on his status as a true independent producer. He had no desire to answer to stockholders or deal with potential conflicts of interest. And he certainly never succumbed to the lure of power inherent in the job of studio chief, a lure which David apparently was unable to resist.

"I'll try to help," Ray offered.

In fact, Ray did help. After David left, Ray called Don Keough in Atlanta and offered his appraisal of the Pat Williamson–David Puttnam impasse. Ray suggested that an amicable solution might be worked out which took advantage of "David's European background and Pat's experience and business acumen."

Ray added that he felt Fay Vincent was being unnecessarily stubborn about the European problem and seemed to be trying to protect his authority as chairman of Columbia Pictures Industries.

A few days later, the matter was settled. David Puttnam would be in charge of European operations.

But the significance of the resolution of the European problem did not lie with the resolution itself, but rather in the *manner* in which it was resolved.

David Puttnam, of his own volition, had sought out Ray Stark's help.

And then accepted it.

No matter what David Puttnam said, the Coca-Cola contingent did not react. Although it sometimes seemed that David was deliberately trying to provoke a debate, Roberto Goizueta, Don Keough, and Ira Herbert chose not to oblige. The meeting was merely an opportunity for them to confirm Fay Vincent's decision, an opportunity they had not even asked for.

The meeting in Atlanta was a fitting finale to the Columbia/Puttnam negotiation. Both had been a study in nonsequiturs and neither was exactly what it was intended to be.

Except for the initial phone call to Fay Vincent from David's New York attorney, Tom Lewyn—in which Lewyn had pitched his client for the job—the Columbia/Puttnam encounter appeared to be one of Columbia Pictures chasing a reticent David Puttnam and *forcing* him to become chairman/CEO.

Yet the situation was not that at all. David wanted the job, and wanted it very badly. The perception that indicated otherwise had nothing to do with David, but rather with Fay Vincent.

A high-level job opening like that of studio chief draws countless inquiries from an aggressive mob of young hopefuls and an army of out-of-work war-horses. Since Guy McElwaine's sudden departure from the studio a few weeks before, Fay's existence had become mired in the fielding of an endless stream of phone calls. For Fay Vincent, the only way to return to a normal life was to fill the position. Fast.

No one in Hollywood quite met all of Fay's requirements, however. In fact, he was facing a real dilemma in that most of the applicants broke down into two professions: lawyers and agents.

Fay may have been reluctant to hire an attorney because he himself was an attorney, reasoning that, since he knew nothing about the creative workings of a studio, most lawyers didn't either. Although the logic was flawed, it was an understandable conclusion.

Agents, on the other hand, conjured up the likeness of David

Begelman. Arriving at Columbia in the wake of the Begelman scandal, Fay was wary of a sequel.

Notwithstanding Fay's stack of messages from the outside world, there were two likely candidates currently employed by Columbia: Steve Sohmer and Peter Sealy. But each had a handicap which disqualified them in Fay's eyes.

Steve Sohmer, president of the studio, was filling in for his ex-boss, Guy McElwaine. But Fay remembered that Guy had assumed control by virtue of his proximity to Frank Price. Fay, a bit wiser, was not about to repeat his previous mistake of automatic promotion from within. Ironically, Steve Sohmer, in perfect political position, was passed over as a result of the same proximity which installed his predecessor at the pinnacle of Columbia Pictures.

Peter Sealy, a marketing and distributing executive at Coca-Cola for eighteen years, possessed the management ability but not the motion picture experience. Fay did not want to find himself in a situation of the blind leading the blind.

So when Tom Lewyn phoned, it was as if he had tossed Fay Vincent a lifeline.

David Puttnam was a filmmaker. Thus, Fay wouldn't have to concern himself with the mechanics of motion picture production, something he knew nothing about.

And David Puttnam was an outsider. Since Fay found the Hollywood film community alien in the first place, he didn't relish the prospect of striking a deal with one of its members.

Fay Vincent decided he liked the idea of David Puttnam as chairman/CEO of Columbia Pictures very much. But he latched onto the notion so completely, he became obsessed.

After talking with Fay, Tom Lewyn realized that the odds against David Puttnam winding up at Columbia were very long. *Never* had a major studio employed a non-U.S. citizen. Consequently, Tom readied himself for what he thought would be an intensive sales job.

A tentative date was set for an initial Vincent/Puttnam confab, but David—who was completing a new film for Warner Brothers called *The Mission*—was detained in London doing postproduction. Tom Lewyn informed Fay the meeting would have to wait a week or two.

"I'll fly to England," Fay obliged.

When word of the upcoming trip reached Herbert Allen, he voiced his strong opposition. Herbert felt the trip to England would create the impression that Columbia was in pursuit of David Puttnam and put the studio at a disadvantage in any negotiations which might follow.

"Get him a Concorde ticket," Herbert advised. "He's going to be working for you, so bring him over here."

But Fay was determined and flew off to London with Dick Gallop at his side.

It turned out that Herbert was right. Within hours after Fay and Dick entered the United Kingdom, the Hollywood rumor mill churned with the news that Columbia was "going after" David Puttnam. And by the time Fay Vincent and Dick Gallop arrived back in New York, Tom Lewyn's attitude toward the negotiation had undergone a dramatic change.

Another factor which aided in the perception that Columbia was the aggressor in the negotiation concerned David's production pact with Warner Bros. After *Chariots of Fire*, which was distributed by Warners via the Ladd Company, David committed himself to a multifilm deal at the studio. David was happy, Warner Bros. was happy, and the agreement still had a year and a half to run.

David's first production for Warner Bros. following *Chariots of Fire* was the story of a Houston oil company executive who travels to Scotland to buy up an entire town in order to build an oil refinery. The executive is surprised to find that, instead of resisting, the villagers become elated with the idea of profiting from the sale of their land.

The comedy/drama explored the importance of ecology and the consequences of greed. Starring Peter Riegert as oil company emissary Mac MacIntyre and Burt Lancaster as his boss, the movie was released in 1983. It was called *Local Hero*.

Once again, critics embraced the cinematic work of David Puttnam. But, as often happened in the past, the public did not.

The following year David coproduced *Cal*, the story of a nineteen-year-old Catholic youth caught up in the conflict of Northern Ireland.

Variety's review stated: "Initiated by co-producer David Puttnam and financed with British coin, pic represents a discreet, personal look at a potentially explosive subject, and limited b.o. [box-office] prospects in arthouse venues loom for U.S. play-off. . . . Pic's basic intelligence and earnestness will inspire respect in some quarters . . . but it's difficult to imagine audiences, particularly outside the British Isles, becoming too excited by this mute tale."

As predicted, the film did not perform well in American exhibition. Although it did considerably better in England and Ireland, the fact that it was done under the auspices of a major American motion picture studio did not bode well for David's future at Warner Brothers.

Redemption, however, was swift. *The Killing Fields*, David Puttnam's third film for Warners, was not only a critical success but generated a significant box office as well. The story of the friendship between an American journalist and his Cambodian guide garnered $14,300,000 in U.S. film rentals and then received seven Oscar nominations: Best Picture, Best Director, Best Actor, Best Supporting Actor, Best Screenplay Adaptation, Best Cinematography, and Best Film Editing. The film won three: Supporting Actor, Cinematography, and Film Editing.

Besides the normal fanfare surrounding a hit movie, there was a moment of unexpected poignancy.

Haing S. Ngor, an actual Cambodian refugee, had played the part of Cambodian Dith Pran in *The Killing Fields*. In his *first* role ever, Ngor won a Supporting Actor Oscar, and the scene on national television played out as one of the most dramatic in Academy Award history. The small and slightly built Haing Ngor, who had been so mired in desperation just a year before, looked overwhelmed as he hugged the golden statuette. Managing a broad smile, he stared out at the audience, now on its feet and engaged in a vigorous standing ovation.

As was the case at the 1982 Academy Award ceremony when *Chariots of Fire* beat the odds to win Best Picture, Haing Ngor's victory captivated America. For the second time in three years, the sentiment imparted to millions of viewers was one of hope. The underdog—courtesy of the American dream—could indeed come up a winner.

Haing Ngor, however, was not the true beneficiary of his own triumph. The real benefit accrued to David Puttnam as the already lustrous reputation of the British producer gained an even higher sheen following the stirring events on Oscar night 1984.

CHAPTER
FIVE

Few producers enjoyed the kind of notoriety David Puttnam did in 1984. If David had *anything* at all to do with a movie, it was referred to as a "David Puttnam film." Usually it was the *director* who was identified with a movie, based on the concept that the director was the "author" of the film.

The "auteur (author) theory" was born in France when famed French director François Truffaut, then a journalist and critic for *Cahiers du Cinéma*, wrote a commentary in the January 1954 issue of the publication regarding the "politique des auteurs." Ten years later, American film critic Andrew Sarris translated Truffaut's idea for the English-speaking world, coining the half-Anglicized phrase "auteur theory."

Essentially, the "auteur theory" is rooted in the belief that the *director* is the person whose contribution to a motion picture is most important, rather than the screenwriter or producer. Naturally, American directors readily embraced this sentiment, growing quite possessive of the title "author" during the last three decades.

But David's presence *anywhere* in the credits tended to overshadow all other names. *Chariots of Fire* director Hugh Hudson, for example, never received the recognition that many felt he deserved, as is evidenced by the ongoing classification of *Chariots of Fire* as "a David Puttnam film." Nor were the efforts of director Roland Joffe widely recognized. Even the extraordinary event of his first ever feature film, *The Killing Fields*, gaining an Oscar nomination, did not prevent the media from dubbing the movie "a David Puttnam film."

Producers, too, have fallen victim to the David Puttnam phenomenon. A case in point: Does anyone remember that the coproducer of *Chariots of Fire*, Dodi Fayed, had anything to do with the film?

David's penchant for turning to the past for motion picture subject matter manifested itself again in his next film, *The Mission*. This time he traversed backwards in time 234 years to find a story line.

In *The Mission*, Portugal is locked in a bitter dispute with Spain over territorial boundaries in South America. Besides the border battle, Spain is hindered in carrying on its illegal slave trade because of the influence of Jesuit priests who inhabit a mission deep in the jungle. Since Spain is capturing native Indians for sale as slaves, and since the Indians are the objects of the Jesuits' protection, Spain would like Portugal to take over the mission so it can free itself of the pressure from the Jesuits.

Like previous Puttnam plots, *The Mission* sounded like an interesting, but limited-appeal period film. And, with its historic relevance, it promised to do something which had become *expected* when David Puttnam produced a movie: win awards.

It is interesting to note that *The Mission* actually was a coproduction. The credit read: "Produced by Fernando Ghia and David Puttnam." But even placing Ghia first in the credits failed to negate the obscuring effect of David Puttnam's considerable shadow.

Despite its familiar Puttnam pedigree, however, *The Mission* departed from the British producer's norm in two ways: casting and budget.

David's position on "stars" was very clear. He didn't like casting them. Yet Robert De Niro and Jeremy Irons were announced as the headliners in *The Mission*.

David's position on budgets was also very clear. He often had spoken out against the excesses of Hollywood and had typically produced low-cost films. But *The Mission*—after several budget revisions—finally weighed in at $25,000,000.

Only two of David's earlier efforts—*Chariots of Fire* and *The Killing Fields*—had even earned that much at the box office. And only *Chariots of Fire* grossed enough to warrant that kind of production cost.

The Mission was David Puttnam's biggest gamble ever.

Completed in 1986, *The Mission* was entered in the Cannes Film festival in May and walked off with the Palme d'Or award. Tested for its quality, the film had performed well, but the acid test at the box office was yet to come.

Before the picture opened, however, Tom Lewyn called Fay Vincent about the Columbia job. So while Warner Bros. was preparing to launch a megabuck movie, the film's producer was off huddling with another studio.

Warner chairman Bob Daly was not particularly thrilled with the Columbia Pictures negotiation, but he opted not to stand in David's way by holding him to his contract. Daly knew that the chance to assume control of a major studio was a rare opportunity. So the Warner chairman wished David well in his pursuit of the most coveted position in Hollywood. And gave him a bit of advice as well.

"Make sure," Daly emphasized, "that Coca-Cola is aware of the kind of pictures you want to make. Be certain there is no misunderstanding. Otherwise, you will have a very tough time later on."

David Puttnam looked at Roberto Goizueta. Fay Vincent. Dick Gallop. Ira Herbert. Don Keough. Then he smiled at his wife, Patsy, and she smiled back. The smile meant a lot to David, for he felt he had done one of the things he set out to do. He had proven to his wife that he hadn't "sold out."

Finally, Don Keough spoke.

"Good luck, David," the president of Coca-Cola said. And with those words, the Puttnam era at Columbia Pictures began.

In the ensuing exodus from Coke headquarters, Fay Vincent and Dick Gallop headed north to New York while David and Patsy Puttnam boarded a plane for California.

After landing in Los Angeles, David and Patsy went straight from the airport to the home of Warner president Terry Semel.

"Congratulations," Terry said.

Warner chairman Bob Daly was there too, and offered his compliments as well.

The two Warner executives had conferred earlier in the week and outlined several scenarios which could be implemented in the event David was hired by Columbia. The Warner/Puttnam production deal would be suspended, freeing the British producer to start his new assignment.

As Terry Semel outlined the mechanics of the suspension, Bob Daly noted a certain melancholy in David's mood. Since he considered David more than a producer—a friend, in fact—he pried.

"Do you *really* want to be an executive?" Bob Daly asked.

"No, not really," David responded without hesitation.

Although Bob suspected as much, David's answer was shocking nevertheless.

"Then why are you taking the job?"

"I want a lot of the freedoms the job can give me. If being an executive comes with the job, then so be it."

"What freedoms are you talking about?" Bob laughed. "I wouldn't exactly call running a studio a freedom."

"The freedom to work at what I do. Making films. Overseeing production. The freedom of consistent income. The freedom of knowing exactly what I'm going to do each day, where I'm going to be."

Bob watched David's facial expression closely. What he saw, he didn't like.

"David, I'm concerned. Maybe you shouldn't take the job. If you want, I'll be the villain. I'll tell them you're under contract to us and we won't release you."

"No, you can't do that."

"Why not? It *is* an option for me to exercise. After all, David, we *do* have an existing agreement."

"Yes, I know. But you've been kept abreast of everything that's been happening. You just can't do that."

"You *are* valuable to Warner Brothers and I have every right to hold you to your contract."

"No," David said, "it's too late for that. I've shaken hands."

"You've done what?"

"I've shaken hands. With Fay Vincent. As far as I'm concerned, I'm already at Columbia."

There are three publications in Hollywood which are required reading every morning. *Daily Variety, The Hollywood Reporter*, and the Calendar section of the *Los Angeles Times*. Motion picture executives—no matter how busy they happen to be—take time to peruse the headlines and scan the pages.

Since the West Coast creative community is comprised of about twenty-five thousand citizens, the movie business is in many ways more characteristic of a small town than a global industry. Most people eat at the same restaurants. Everyone knows what everyone else is doing. And the favorite pastime of the locals is engaging in gossip.

As in all small boroughs, the hometown newspaper enjoys an exaggerated importance. The extraordinary thing about Hollywood, however, is that it supports not one, but *three* such journals, an indication of the insatiable desire movie moguls have for reading about the goings-on in the business. Yet these executives are not necessarily looking for *news*—they already have all the factual information they need. What really titillates a Hollywood type is *rumor*.

So, as Dick Gallop and Fay Vincent carried on their talks with David Puttnam, it became a guessing game as to which Hollywood purveyor of the printed word would "break" the story. Care had been taken to avoid leaks, and it was resolved that there would be no comment emanating from the key participants, but none of the three men actually believed they could conduct such a major negotiation in the absence of media attention.

They were right. On June 18, *all three* dailies speculated on David Puttnam's status at Columbia Pictures.

A page-one headline in *Daily Variety* stated: COL NOT RUSHING TO QUELL RUMORS RE DAVID PUTTNAM. The *Los Angeles Times* Calendar section led with the story: COLUMBIA REPORTEDLY SEEKING PUTTNAM FOR POST. And *The Hollywood Reporter* played it bigger than either *Variety* or the *Times* with a front-page banner head which blared: PUTTNAM REPORTEDLY HEADED FOR COLUMBIA FEATURES POST.

All three stories had a lot to say about David Puttnam.

"With a terse refusal to confirm or deny," *Variety* reported, "Columbia Pictures yesterday kept alive reports that British producer David Puttnam, a man not known to have aspirations of running a studio—major or otherwise—is being wooed to succeed Guy McElwaine as chairman of the company. . . . Despite the fact that many at Columbia consider Puttnam a highly improbable choice, the unlikely has become increasingly commonplace as Hollywood resonates to the noises from the constant scraping of executive musical chairs. . . . If he took the Columbia job, Puttnam would be obliged to go back on . . . [an] object of expressed distaste—living full time in the U.S., let alone Hollywood."

The *Los Angeles Times* saw it this way:

"British-based producer David Puttnam . . . has apparently been offered the top creative post at Columbia Pictures Industries, industry sources said Tuesday. . . . Puttnam, who has openly criticized the studio system in the past, is reportedly in Los Angeles . . . as is Columbia Pictures Industries president Richard Gallop. . . . The 45-year-old Puttnam is considered an unusual choice for Columbia because he has always been considered something of a renegade who doesn't fit the corporate mold, sources said.

"Puttnam, who lives in London and has made a majority of his films there, has commented openly on his disdain on the way Hollywood works. 'This is very much a fear-based community, and I can't believe that encourages real creativity,' Puttnam told *The Times* in a 1984 interview. 'That's why the creative work here is really not good enough.' "

And *The Hollywood Reporter* added its analysis:

"Industry speculation was intense yesterday that British film producer David Puttnam had been offered and accepted the key Columbia Pictures post as head of the features sector. At press time yesterday, Columbia executives were remaining mum on the widespread rumor. Puttnam, however, had reportedly been in meetings Monday in New York with Columbia Pictures Industries executives including CPI president Richard Gallop.

"Industry players who know Puttnam are questioning, in light of the rumor, why the award-winning producer would accept the L.A.-based post. Sources report that he has little interest in living full time in California. As spearhead of the current resurgence in the British film industry, Puttnam has a powerful and far-reaching power base in Europe; his network of creative contacts and ties in Los Angeles is significantly smaller, and deemed somewhat of a handicap. Also, say observers, Puttnam's orientation is less a mainstream American-style studio film than a more European-flavor cerebral style of cinema."

The Hollywood grapevine had been presented with an embarrassment of riches. From Burbank to Beverly Hills, in such famous watering-holes as Spago and the Polo Lounge, indeed, in every corner of the motion picture universe, tongues wagged incessantly about David Puttnam. And the Columbia/Puttnam rumor was especially tantalizing since it involved a confusing array of contradictions which provided an endless supply of grist for the gossip mill.

The press had dubbed Puttnam's selection "improbable" and

"unusual." Certainly—if it came to fruition—it would be.

Besides David's anti-Hollywood philosophical stance, the media noted that the British producer was under contract to Warner Brothers and about to launch his new film, *The Mission.* Given this fact, most in Hollywood considered the appointment of David Puttnam as chairman/CEO of Columbia Pictures to be inconceivable.

While David Puttnam's Warner deal and dislike for Hollywood were well known, his plan to join the faculty of Harvard University was not. So when *Variety* tagged its "appointment rumor" story with word that David Puttnam intended to join the ranks of academia, even Hollywood, a community charged with concocting unexpected plot twists, was shocked. Nothing could be more alien to the rigors of being studio chief than the civilized contemplation of an Ivy League professor. Could one man have such a flexible temperament that he could seriously consider *both* stations within his realm of ability?

Obviously, David Puttnam felt he did. Just prior to meeting with Fay Vincent in London, David sought a place on the Harvard faculty, exhibiting, and acting upon, a growing discontent with the movie business. In fact, he was all set to move to Boston and begin teaching a course on ethics when his attorney, Tom Lewyn, informed him of the interest in his talents at Columbia Pictures.

As unsettling to Hollywood as the Harvard exposition was, there existed another even more incongruous chapter in David Puttnam's life. Although it didn't make the newspapers—a rare occurrence amid an avid news-gathering movie business media—David harbored an aversion to Hollywood which was so violent, he had once turned to a Jesuit priest in an effort to cleanse himself of its influence.

After leaving Casablanca Filmworks in 1980, David returned to England feeling he had blood on his hands as a result of his role in coproducing *Midnight Express.* One of his first stops upon arriving back home was London University, where he approached Professor of Theology Jack Marney.

"I can't seem to reconcile the confusion within myself," David told Father Marney. "I think the motion picture industry is misusing its power because of its greed. And I am ashamed that I was drawn into the realm of its dark side with *Midnight Express.* I strongly feel that movies should teach. Enlighten. That's what cinema represents to me, an opportunity to give the audience something to *feel*. Something positive and uplifting."

"It's very much in your hands," Marney replied. "If you believe your medium has these qualities and these opportunities, then it's your job to steer your career in that direction."

Various versions of David's encounter with Jack Marney circulated around Hollywood, usually stemming from secondhand accounts of the meeting as related by David's friends in London. But no one actually believed it. Perhaps it was the implausibility of such a story which rendered it an unfounded "rumor," a fabrication. Even the press, in the absence of confirmation from David, discounted the anecdote as fantasy and exhibited an uncharacteristic restraint. To everyone in Hollywood, the Jesuit priest tale just seemed *too* bizarre to be true.

But the fact remained, David Puttnam, a one-time student of a Jesuit priest and a would-be Harvard professor, was in the running for a job which rested on the opposite end of the spectrum from either of those pursuits.

Coincidentally—on the day the media speculated on David Puttman's immediate plans—Dick Gallop was scheduled to address a luncheon forum of the Academy of Television Arts and Sciences at the Sheraton Premiere Hotel in Los Angeles. The morning newspapers had fostered much more anticipation of Dick's speech than its original purpose, an overall view of the entertainment industry, had warranted.

Next to Dick Gallop on the dais were acting Columbia studio chief Steve Sohmer and marketing and distributing group president Peter Sealy. The presence of the two Columbia executives fueled conjecture that Dick might use the event to make an announcement about the vacant chairman/CEO post and that either Sohmer or Sealy would be named.

During his address, however, Dick limited his remarks specifically to the television industry and gave the Columbia motion picture situation a wide berth. Attendees who had hoped to hear a declaration regarding Columbia's movie division were disappointed.

But then, in a surprise move, Dick Gallop opened the floor to questions.

"Some time has passed," a journalist noted, "since Guy Mc-

Elwaine resigned. Does this mean you are considering not replacing McElwaine per se? Do you intend to maintain the executive status quo currently in place at Columbia without actually filling McElwaine's post?"

The reference to status quo meant Sohmer and Sealy, so Dick responded to the inquiry by stating:

"Steve Sohmer and Peter Sealy have been doing a fine job during a very difficult transitional period. But we will name a new chief executive officer of the motion picture division. We fully intend to fill the post vacated by Guy McElwaine."

"When will that be?"

"I can't say at this point."

"What about David Puttnam?"

"I have no comment regarding David Puttnam."

"Can you elaborate at all on the rumors that he is headed to Columbia? Do they have *any* basis?"

"We haven't had any official statement," Dick countered sharply, "and we don't speak around our official statements."

His tone was effective in steering questions away from the subject of David Puttnam.

"What about Brandon Tartikoff? Is he in the running?"

"I have never confirmed that," Dick tersely replied.

But Brandon Tartikoff, president of NBC Entertainment, had been approached a few weeks earlier by Fay Vincent. So had ABC Entertainment president Brandon Stoddard.

Since *both* candidates were named Brandon—certainly an unlikely occurrence—Fay always experienced an initial moment of confusion whenever he answered the phone and heard:

"Hello, Fay. This is Brandon."

The Brandon-Brandon tandem overtures were a function of Fay Vincent's approach to qualifying candidates for the Columbia post, an approach that often seemed primal. To Fay, agents meant David Begelman and embezzlement; lawyers made him think of himself and his lack of movie business knowledge; while television executives brought to mind Frank Price.

Though it was true that he and Frank Price did not see eye to eye on an administrative level and there existed a personality clash between the two men, Fay could not deny the financial success of Frank's tenure at the studio. Perhaps there was an alchemy at work in which only television executives could turn film stock into gold at Columbia Pictures.

Of the two Brandons, it was Brandon Tartikoff who came closest to seizing the reins of Columbia Pictures. Even though Brandon had been at NBC for six years when Dick Gallop approached him, a recent change in ownership of the network, as well as a pending shift in management, made Gallop's offer all the more appealing.

"I absolutely seriously considered it," Brandon Tartikoff states now, recalling his brief encounter with Columbia Pictures. "Technically, I was under contract. But I felt I should take a look around and evaluate new challenges. From my perspective, it was really a critical juncture in my career. Grant Tinker was leaving and there was a new owner in G.E."

General Electric had purchased NBC in December 1985, and a short time later NBC chairman Grant Tinker announced that he would vacate his post. Fate, it seemed, had given Columbia Pictures a running start in its efforts to lure Brandon Tartikoff into the movie business. In fact, it might have been a fait accompli had it not been for one small request by Brandon Tartikoff and one big mistake by Fay Vincent.

"I knew they were under pressure to fill the position," Brandon remembers, "but I was knee deep in the middle of pilots and I didn't want to be distracted during the most critical time of the year. I told them I could not make a decision before the affiliates' meeting in June."

Affiliates are the local stations around the country that carry network programming. Each year, all three networks gather their affiliates in order to present new shows, known as pilots, which are candidates for the upcoming fall schedule. It is imperative that the man who nurtured the pilots, in this case Brandon Tartikoff, be present at the annual get-together. NBC would host the 1986 meeting in Hawaii and all Brandon was asking was that he be given an opportunity to hand-deliver his package of sitcoms and dramas across the Pacific and perhaps have a day or two to overcome jet lag when he returned.

Fay Vincent, however, paid little heed to Brandon Tartikoff's request.

"They kept the courtship going hot and heavy during that period," Brandon recounts.

But it was not Fay Vincent's ardent pursuit that was the undoing of the deal; rather it was Fay's idea of fair play that cost Columbia the services of Brandon Tartikoff. Here again, Fay's background betrayed him. After all, there is a different set of rules in the entertainment business than at the Securities and Exchange Commission.

As it happened, Fay Vincent was a good friend of G.E. chairman/CEO Jack Welch. Fay felt that the "gentlemanly" thing to do was to inform Welch of his talks with Brandon Tartikoff.

"Ultimately Jack Welch got into the middle of things," Brandon remarks. "He's a very dynamic and persuasive person. He said, 'No way!' It was resolved in three days after he got involved."

What was resolved was this: NBC immediately signed Brandon Tartikoff to a brand-new long-term contract.

The incident became another example of Fay Vincent's well-meaning, honorable, but certainly naive approach to the entertainment industry.

Dick Gallop, annoyed at the assault by the media concerning various unattributed reports as to who would be taking over the studio, chastised the entertainment business press.

"There have been many instances where the leaks were actually untrue. And—though there have been some cases when they were true—I'm not sure the public gained by knowing these things two days early."

Ending on a confrontational tone, the meeting between Dick Gallop and the media had done nothing to clarify the most burning question in Hollywood:

Was David Puttnam *really* about to become chairman/CEO of Columbia Pictures?

Copies of *Daily Variety*, *The Hollywood Reporter*, and the *Los Angeles Times* were fanned out on Bertram Fields's desk like a hand of three-card poker. As Bertram studied the three newspapers, he had the look of a man with a huge stake in the kitty but no aces among his cards.

Certainly his stake *was* sizable. Two of his clients, Warren Beatty and Dustin Hoffman, were immersed in making a new movie for Columbia Pictures. The film, *Ishtar*, was a big-budget project and would require a matching monetary marketing thrust. (Actually, *three* of Bertram's clients were involved in *Ishtar*. Elaine May, director of the picture, also was his client.)

Considering the fact that David Puttnam seemed to relish launching media attacks on Warren Beatty and Dustin Hoffman, Bertram was truly perplexed by the rumor of David's appointment. Dustin had played a major role in two of Columbia's biggest films, *Kramer vs. Kramer* and *Tootsie,* and Bertram found it incomprehensible that Fay Vincent would entertain the idea of hiring someone who had made it a point to denigrate one of Columbia's most stellar performers.

What would happen to Warren Beatty and Dustin Hoffman and *Ishtar* if David Puttnam became head of the studio?

Bertram Fields shuddered at the thought.

CHAPTER
SIX

The official announcement that David Puttnam would become chairman/CEO of Columbia Pictures and senior executive vice president and director of Columbia Pictures Industries came at a press conference on Thursday, June 26, 1986. The venue was the Beverly Hills Hotel and the men at the dais were Fay Vincent, Dick Gallop, and David Puttnam.

There had not been a press conference with this much energy in recent memory as those in attendance prepared to witness a unique event: the installation, for the first time ever, of a non-U.S. citizen at the helm of a major Hollywood studio. And, put another way—which made the occasion loom even more remarkable—the ascension of Hollywood's most outspoken critic to a position of power atop the object of his criticism.

David Puttnam, who once called Hollywood a "godless place," was becoming a member of the congregation.

"I think it says a lot for Columbia," the new chairman observed, "and I think it says a lot for European cinema that a European has been invited to come to Los Angeles and have a crack at influencing the ideas, dreams, and aspirations of people all around the world."

When the applause finally faded, David launched into an articulate message-laden speech in which he demonstrated that he had not altered his attitudes even though his status of employment had changed dramatically.

"We all believe that budgets can and should be brought down," David said as he alluded to the excesses of the studio system.

"Maybe I'm being naive," the British producer offered regarding the question of art versus commerce, "maybe I'm going to get the most terrible shock in the coming years, but I do trust the audience. I think if you give them good films, they'll respond."

The appeal in David Puttnam's remarks lay in the unassailable nature of the content. Who wasn't in favor of lower budgets? Who could deny that quality was a good thing?

David gained considerable momentum when he explored the ramifications of the international marketplace, citing Coca-Cola as a model for what he intended to accomplish as studio chief.

"I find it incredibly refreshing to work with a company whose outlook is by definition international, sixty-five percent of whose income is derived from what you term 'abroad.' I should try very hard to see if Columbia Pictures couldn't do likewise."

At that point, Fay Vincent interjected with a concurrence and an endorsement.

"We have agreed on the outlines of strategy and on the opportunities. And we stress that there are magnificent opportunities in the worldwide entertainment business. Since Coca-Cola is essentially an international company where over 60 percent of our business is done outside the U.S., the appointment of David to run our film business is consistent with our belief that this is an international market, and the opportunities internationally are significant."

Indeed, the *reality* for American product overseas was already significant. As Fay and David spoke, the rest of the world was importing Hollywood output with a gusto.

In London, for example, *Variety* reported that eight of the top ten movies at the time were from major U.S. studios including Columbia's own *Jagged Edge*. Nine of ten in Australia. Five of the eight films listed for France were Hollywood-grown, a reissue of Columbia's *Tootsie* among them. Six of eight in Sweden. Four of eight in Denmark. Four of five in Finland.

Regardless of the territory, the dominance of Hollywood was evident, and big, star-laden extravaganzas from America were obviously the choice of the global audience. With worldwide market share knocking around 80 percent for U.S. films, the export outlook could hardly have been better. Yet David dwelled on the fact that Columbia would become an "international" studio under his direction. The thrust of what he was saying, however, had little to do with another marketing approach, rather it outlined another filmmaking approach.

"The films I will make will be humanist without being sentimental, and commercial without being condescending. I will strive for *both* virtue and profit. Cinema has a massive responsibility, and I question whether all the responsibility has been addressed in the last decade. I'll do my best. I'll live by my likes. I'll make the films I believe in and hope to God there's an audience out there that will want to see what I'm making."

After elaborating on his philosophy of filmmaking, David alluded to the meeting he had had with Coca-Cola executives in Atlanta. His appraisal of the talks contained a fine point, one most in attendance probably missed.

"I went to Atlanta early in the week and was a skeptic," David announced, "although they had made it perfectly clear it was a journey I didn't have to make. I came away a convert. I met three utterly remarkable men. Roberto Goizueta, Donald Keough, and Ira Herbert. They made me feel that what I could bring to the studio was valuable to them. The problems I would bring with me, and the attitudes I would bring with me, and the experience I would bring with me, were things they were prepared to live with."

As the applause swelled, many thought they had just heard broad praise of the Coca-Cola management trio, but there was a subtle countertheme in David's words. The new chairman/CEO was placing a very important fact on the record: Coca-Cola's approval of the David Puttnam doctrine of filmmaking.

But *was* it a fact? Since Roberto Goizueta or Don Keough had not met with David Puttnam until *after* he was hired by Fay Vincent and since the two Coke executives were merely being accommodating to David, much of the nodding and smiling that took place in Atlanta stemmed more from polite demeanor than agreement with what was being said.

The scene at the Beverly Hills Hotel was a repeat of Atlanta. It didn't matter what David said, it was *how* he said it. The frequent bursts of applause were born of reaction, not understanding. David was making it clear that he intended to *change* the way Hollywood operated and the response seemed to indicate that Hollywood welcomed that change.

According to the newly installed chairman/CEO, Coca-Cola condoned his concept of filmmaking. It was as if David was saying: "I am going to shake up this town. And, if you don't like it, keep in mind that I have the enforcement power of a six-billion-dollar soft drink manufacturer in my back pocket." This was not only an erroneous conclusion on David's part, it was a dangerous supposition regarding the support he could expect from Atlanta if his actions ran contrary to the purpose of his employment: earning money.

As David entered his wrap-up, the tone of his voice changed almost imperceptibly and edged toward the ominous: "Maybe people will find me—and my style and what I want to do—uncomfortable. So I think there will be a lot of conversations."

The next morning *Variety* carried the banner headline: COL REFOCUSSING UNDER PUTTNAM. The subhead declared: NEW CHAIRMAN-CHIEF EXEC ZEROES IN ON INTERNATIONAL PIC MARKET AS TOP PRIORITY. And the opening paragraph sized up the press conference like this:

"Nurturing of the international film market has been targeted as first priority by the top command of Coca-Cola and David Puttnam, who becomes the new chairman and chief executive officer of Columbia Pictures September 1."

Obviously, the Coca-Cola reference had been heard loud and clear. The coupling in print of ". . . the top command of Coca-Cola and David Puttnam . . ." would advance the notion that each move David made was the manifestation of a mandate from Atlanta.

Virtually every publication with anything close to an entertainment section led with David Puttnam's appointment. But the most astonishing chronicle of the announcement appeared in the *Los Angeles Times*, penned by journalist Jack Mathews.

"Hollywood, like the Spanish Inquisition, has a tendency to wear the good people down. It changes their attitudes, rearranges their priorities, gets them believing that pandering to the tastes of teenagers is no vice and that art for art's sake is no virtue.

"British film producer David Puttnam, a man of immaculately mature tastes, recognized all that years ago and has never hesitated to give his opinion. Hollywood, he said, was a place he could neither live with or in.

"Thursday, after being formally named the new chairman and chief executive officer of Columbia Pictures, Puttnam smiled at a question about his past exhortations on the System and its locale and said: 'I'll have to take back a lot of what I said.'

"But the bearded 45-year-old Puttnam wasn't taking everything back . . ."

The article went on to emphasize the many passages in David's remarks which were consistent with his "past exhortations" before detailing the specifics of the Columbia appointment.

Mathews's column was extraordinary in its clear expression of adoration. It isn't often one sees that kind of tone in a major newspaper.

It did, however, convey the spirit of the media in general. Dating to 1968—and to a greater degree, following *Chariots of Fire*— David Puttnam had created many allies among the entertainment beat press corps. They responded favorably to his accessibility— anyone with press credentials knew his home telephone number by heart—and built their own reputations incorporating his brand of from-the-hip dialogue into the stories they filed.

So, on June 26, David Puttnam arrived at the Beverly Hills Hotel a conquering hero in the eyes of the media. And, since it is the media which molds the image of Hollywood that the rest of the world perceives, this fact was not insignificant.

David Puttnam was the new chairman/CEO of Columbia Pictures, despite a track record which listed low-budget, modest-box-office pictures and despite his nationality and his repeated attacks on the American motion picture industry. Indeed, the enigmatic British producer had managed an exceptional coup.

On the Saturday following the announcement of his appointment, at eight o'clock in the morning, David Puttnam met with Steve Sohmer, the studio president he inherited.

The Columbia Pictures parking lot is usually empty at that hour on a Saturday. This particular morning, however, there had been one car sitting in front of the Columbia office building since 7:30 A.M., Steve Sohmer's new Rolls-Royce.

At $160,000, a Rolls is an expensive mode of transportation. Yet it is the automobile of choice for many Beverly Hills residents, particularly the legion of aging actors and actresses who populate the city. Once it was the official car of studio executives as well, although those in the "new" Hollywood prefer to be seen in a far less ostentatious and expensive vehicle, a Jaguar or

Mercedes for example. Consequently, a traffic jam on Coldwater Canyon Drive, the snaking route that links Beverly Hills to Burbank, often looks like a parade celebrating conspicuous consumption as Rolls-Royces, Mercedes-Benzes, and Jaguars jostle for right-of-way.

While it was not unusual within the context of the movie business that Steve Sohmer should opt to buy a Rolls-Royce with his six-figure salary, David Puttnam's selection of vehicle, in that same context, was peculiar.

At 7:55 A.M. David steered a $15,000 Audi into the spot next to Steve Sohmer's Rolls-Royce.

It was as if the prince was brought to the palace in a gilded carriage while the king was deposited in an ox cart.

In most cities, this would hardly be a weighty issue, except perhaps to note the apparently unpretentious nature of David Puttnam and the expensive tastes of Steve Sohmer. Other than that observation, the Rolls-Royce and Audi resting side by side in the parking lot normally would hold no further significance.

But this was Hollywood. And in Hollywood, *everything* has significance. Especially cars.

In buying an Audi, David had broken ranks with most of his peers. Although it was merely a difference of opinion concerning a material possession, it symbolized much more, serving as an analogy of the Puttnam/Hollywood matchup. It was tangible evidence of the attitudinal chasm between the British producer and his West Coast colleagues and, to the astute observer, it hinted at a dichotomy on a much larger scale.

David climbed from his Audi and paused to examine the Rolls. It annoyed him to distraction that one of his employees was driving what he considered to be the manifestation of greed and misplaced values.

Steve Sohmer had been considered to be the likely heir to the top job at Columbia, but David Puttnam's appointment meant that he had been passed over. Worse yet, a new regime usually dispenses with the lieutenants of a previous administration.

A year earlier, Steve had left the post of executive vice president of NBC Entertainment in order to join Columbia Pictures. At the time, the step promised to be an upward career move. But now it appeared entirely likely that Steve Sohmer was headed for a dead end.

"Sorry to get you out of bed so early on a weekend," David began, "but we've got a lot of ground to cover before I go back to England next week."

For several hours, Columbia's chairman and president mapped strategy and examined particulars.

As the meeting was winding down, David became intently preoccupied, fixing his gaze out the window.

"You're being paid a great deal of money," David said as he strolled out of the building and into his Audi.

The Rolls-Royce had cost Steve Sohmer a bundle. Now, as absurd as it seemed, it looked as if it was going to cost him his job as well.

David and Patsy Puttnam were having a problem finding the perfect house, perhaps because of the unreasonable (by Hollywood standards) criteria they had placed on the selection. The British couple had specified that they be near the studio, but not be in any of the "affluent" neighborhoods. They insisted that the house *not* have a swimming pool, and that it not have a screening room.

There were, of course, many houses near Burbank without a swimming pool or screening room, but few of the size the Puttnams required. While neither David nor Patsy particularly wanted a large house, they recognized that they would often be entertaining at home and could hardly receive movie stars in the cottage both of them would have preferred.

Finally, the Puttnams opted for a modest dwelling near the intersection of Coldwater Canyon and Mulholland Drive.

The area was not one of the well-known enclaves of power and wealth like Beverly Hills, but it had become a favorite locale for many in the Hollywood creative community.

One of David's neighbors, for example, was Warren Beatty.

The following week, Columbia Pictures announced a major motion picture project: *Leonard Part 6*. The movie had been conceived by comedian Bill Cosby, who would produce it and star in it.

The deal, which had been brought to the studio by Steve Sohmer, was considered somewhat of a coup in light of the superstar status Cosby had achieved via his top-rated television situation comedy, *The Cosby Show*.

There wasn't a studio in Hollywood that hadn't attempted to sign Bill Cosby for a feature film. Yet Steve Sohmer, having worked with Cosby while at NBC, had pulled it off.

Another factor in the Cosby decision to make *Leonard Part 6* at Columbia was his million-dollar-a-year contract as a Coca-Cola spokesman. Furthermore, the actor's relationship with Coke president Don Keough was a good one and Cosby found the idea of working for a studio owned by Coke and controlled by Don Keough particularly appealing.

Although Steve Sohmer had concluded the pact with Cosby a month earlier, the signing was delayed until the resolution of the Puttnam/Columbia talks. In fact, even before officially becoming chairman/CEO, David was asked to give the green light to *Leonard Part 6*.

Leonard Part 6 was not even remotely similar to David's past cinematic efforts. It would have a budget of about $25,000,000, boast a major American television star, and was designed to be pure entertainment rather than cinema of social relevance. In short, *Leonard Part 6* was *not* a David Puttnam film.

Despite this, David may have felt he really had no viable option other than approving the project.

There was no script at that point, just an idea: a detective comedy. But even if he didn't like the concept or harbored a natural aversion to putting a Steve Sohmer project into motion, David felt compelled to approve the film for two reasons:

Number one, there was the friendship between Bill Cosby and Don Keough. And number two, there was Tri-Star Pictures, Coca-Cola's other motion picture subsidiary, waiting in the wings.

Tri-Star chairman Victor Kaufman and president David Matalon had both expressed their possible interest in *Leonard Part 6*.

David Puttnam reasoned that he could ill afford alienating Don Keough and at the same time take a chance that the movie would wind up as a giant box-office hit at Tri-Star.

Although he did not consider himself a political animal, David's first executive decision was *purely* political. It had nothing at all to do with his creative judgment, rather it was dictated by his realization that there were certain things in Hollywood that simply *must* be done.

So David expressed enthusiasm for *Leonard Part 6*, readily offering his blessing.

At least for the moment, it appeared the newcomer from Britain was willing to play the Hollywood game, despite his numerous statements to the contrary.

David Puttnam's Columbia Pictures agenda for July was full, though his duties, all administrative, were not what he had envisioned. He pulled the rip cord on Guy McElwaine's golden parachute and dealt with a number of films logjammed within the Columbia Pictures development reservoir, endeavoring to sort out which motion pictures had been irrevocably set for production by Guy and which projects could still be canceled without prohibitive financial penalty.

Topping the committed slate was *Ishtar*, already in front of the cameras and boasting a budget of $32,000,000. But David spent little time laboring over the future of the picture because he did not intend to be involved at all with the Warren Beatty/Dustin Hoffman vehicle. In fact, David had insisted that a clause be written into his agreement which specified that he not have any responsibility whatsoever for *Ishtar*.

Another picture the new chairman/CEO inherited was *The Big Town*, a $9,000,000 effort from producer Martin Ransohoff. Set in 1950 Chicago, the movie starred Matt Dillon.

The Big Town appealed to David in that it was a period piece which attempted to accurately depict an era in America's recent history. It also was attractive to the new studio chief because of the financial risk, which was zero, since the picture had been entirely financed via ancillary presales to cable, home video, and foreign markets. Although Columbia Pictures would have less upside potential due to these presold rights, David deemed the limited downside a fair exchange.

In addition to *The Big Town*, there were two more Ransohoff pictures on the "proposed" Columbia slate: *Switching Channels* and *Jagged Edge II*. David did not intend to approve either project despite the fact that Marty Ransohoff—a robust man of sixty and veteran of more than twenty years in the movie business—was a favored son in the Columbia/Tri-Star/Coca-Cola family.

Most executives at the studio felt that a sequel to *Jagged Edge* made sense. The original had brought the studio $16,464,961 in domestic rentals in 1985 and its subsequent success on home video indicated there was a large audience for the follow-up film.

However, David had said many times, "I don't like sequels," so

Jagged Edge II was stricken from consideration at Columbia Pictures.

Switching Channels, set within the world of cable network television, had a great deal of support at Columbia. David's filmmaking philosophy, however, was once again at odds with the product. While David had always said, "I don't like remakes," *Switching Channels* was to be a reworking of *The Front Page*, which originated as a Broadway play in the 1920s, was turned into a film by billionaire Howard Hughes in 1931, was reshot in 1940 as *His Girl Friday* starring Cary Grant and Rosalind Russell, and emerged again in 1974 with its original title as a Jack Lemmon/Walter Matthau/Carol Burnett comedy directed by Billy Wilder. Notwithstanding the previous versions, Marty envisioned *Switching Channels* as a star vehicle (Burt Reynolds and Kathleen Turner were later cast in leading roles), so the double-barreled violation of two very specific David Puttnam rules of filmmaking rendered the movie an untenable proposition at Columbia.

More troublesome to David than the Ransohoff pictures was one from Ray Stark called *Revenge*. The movie had been developed by Rastar Productions and was all set to roll when David was named chairman/CEO. Considering Ray's long and profitable history with Columbia Pictures, no one thought anything but a fast approval would be forthcoming.

It was not.

David wanted *Revenge* at Columbia, having read the screenplay by John Huston, but did not want Ray Stark producing it. David thought Ray's estimated budget of $16,000,000 was too "rich."

Yet Hollywood does not consider the budget to be the sole determining factor in mounting a film, rather it is the cost coupled with the expectation of profit which drives the decision-making process. Studios look to long-term players like Ray Stark to provide those profits while delivering movies within certain financial parameters.

Ironically, there was a perception in the media regarding David's philosophy on budgets which was not always the case. While he often admonished Hollywood for its conspicuous consumption on the set, his two most recent films had generous budgets. *The Mission* cost $25,000,000 and *The Killing Fields* weighed in at $15,000,000.

Were either of those pictures a better box-office gamble than

Revenge? David apparently thought so and decided to turn down the project.

Yet, by rejecting Ray Stark, David would be treading on very thin political ice. David had experienced the value of Ray Stark's relationship to Columbia when he met with Ray regarding the foreign issue.

If David approved *one* picture, reason dictated that it be *Revenge* with Ray Stark at the helm.

After all, if it was that easy for Ray to help clear the path, one might guess it could be just as easy for him to block the door.

During the machinations which had placed David Puttnam in Hollywood, a fascinating cast of characters had amassed, including Wall Street's Herbert A. Allen, Hollywood's Ray Stark, and Great Britain's David Puttnam. There were international locations: London. New York. Los Angeles. Atlanta. There were staggering amounts at stake: a $1,000,000-a-year salary, a $300,000,000 production budget. And beneath it all, there were two diverse philosophies on a collision course.

Hollywood, a town which thrives on drama, was about to get all it could handle.

Only this time, it wouldn't be on the screen.

CHAPTER

SEVEN

On one of his trips back to London in late July, David received a call from his old friend, Jake Eberts, the financier who had provided $50,000 in seed money for the development of *Chariots of Fire*. Since *Chariots of Fire* catapulted David into the forefront of the motion picture business, Jake Eberts was certainly responsible in some measure for David's success.

"David, I've got a problem," Jake said.

The "problem" involved a picture by British director John Boorman entitled *Hope and Glory* which had been caught in the financial maneuvers taking place with the sale by Coca-Cola of the Embassy film and video operations. Jake, via his company, Allied Film, had invested in the picture with the expectation it would be released through Embassy. As a result of a series of complex agreements, however, Coke wound up with a commitment to finance *Hope and Glory* and Embassy Video was set to issue the picture on video cassette, but the film had no distributor for North American theatrical release.

"Can you do anything?" Jake asked.

David was enamored with the film—the saga of World War II as seen through the eyes of children—and was happy to have a chance to help someone who had come to his aid six years before and had been a continuing source of support ever since. David's act of reciprocity would be in the form of $11,000,000 for the

North American and British theatrical distribution rights to *Hope and Glory*.

So it was that the first project David Puttnam brought to Columbia Pictures was a film with David's former London-based associate Jake Eberts serving as executive producer, and fellow Briton John Boorman in both the producer's and director's chair.

In other words, *Hope and Glory* was a modest-priced *British* motion picture.

During the next two weeks, David continued to read scripts and found three others which appealed to him. Two were by British directors. Bill Forsyth would direct the $6,500,000 *Housekeeping* and Ridley Scott would direct *Someone to Watch Over Me*, a $16,800,000 effort. The third, *A Time of Destiny* by American director Gregory Nava, would cost Columbia Pictures $9,500,000.

Ridley Scott had directed *The Duellists* for David Puttnam in 1976 and was perceived as a close associate of the new Columbia chairman/CEO. Inasmuch as David had found many occasions to chastise the American motion picture industry for "cronyism," the green light David gave to *Someone to Watch Over Me* created that very same impression. Add to the past history between David and Ridley Scott the fact that they shared the same nationality, and it is easy to see why alarms immediately began going off in Hollywood.

Ironically, it was David's earlier criticism of the Hollywood system that gave essence to what quickly became a budding controversy. It wasn't that David was practicing anything alien to the movie business or acting any differently from his American counterparts, it was just that he was doing something he had professed to despise: He had made a multimillion-dollar decision involving an old friend. Just as he had done with Jake Eberts and *Hope and Glory*, and, for that matter, Bill Forsyth and *Housekeeping*. Forsyth had directed the Puttnam-produced *Local Hero* three years before.

So, as September 1 neared, it certainly appeared that David Puttnam was as adept as anyone in providing a home at Columbia Pictures for his former associates, even though he had promised a much different scenario.

While most members of the Los Angeles filmmaking community greeted the developments as a serious threat to their well-being, Ray Stark, at least, managed a little humor.

Upon hearing of the preponderance of Britons among the initial Puttnam pictures, Ray laughed:

"Well, I guess we're going to have to call the studio *British Columbia* from now on."

David Puttnam had always made it a point to emphasize the importance of the screenwriter. As David saw it, the Hollywood studio system fostered the idea that writers were subhuman life forms at best and nonentities at worst. Stars, directors, and producers were given respect in Hollywood, but not the poor writer. Alas, the screenwriter was just a tiny sprocket in a giant wheel.

Writers, of course, quickly rallied around the crusading British producer. While David might not have been the only filmmaker who felt this way about writers, he was the only filmmaker who publicly championed the cause. So, in addition to the media, screenwriters became another subset of the Hollywood population which swarmed into David's camp.

Consequently, screenwriter Howard Franklin was excited when he was summoned to Columbia Plaza East to meet with chairman/CEO David Puttnam. Certainly Howard was filled with the enthusiasm one would expect, but that enthusiasm was spurred more by David's reputation as being empathetic to writers than it was by David's position at the studio. This, Howard felt, was his chance to correct a gross injustice which had been perpetrated on him four years before.

The injustice Howard had lived with all these years involved *Someone to Watch Over Me*. Howard had written the screenplay, working under the auspices of director Ridley Scott. Following the completion of the script in October 1982, Ridley struck a deal with MGM and the movie seemed to be on its way into production. For unknown writer Howard Franklin, it was a great beginning.

However, there was a previous obligation Ridley needed to clear up before he could start *Someone to Watch Over Me*, and that was his commitment to Universal Pictures for a movie entitled *Legend*.

Howard had worried about *Legend* when Ridley encouraged him to sign the deal with MGM for *Someone to Watch Over Me*. His concern was this: If Ridley did direct *Legend*, he would be immersed in the film for almost two years and, since it was Ridley who had brought *Someone to Watch Over Me* to MGM, it was highly unlikely the studio's interest would transcend Ridley's involvement. Howard was acutely aware of what happens to projects in limbo. They die.

"What about *Legend*?" Howard quizzed Ridley at the time.

"I'll pull out of it," Ridley assured him.

"Yes, Ridley, but you've already taken money from Universal. How are you going to do that?"

"Don't worry," Ridley insisted. "I'll get out of it."

Immediately after signing with MGM to develop *Someone to Watch Over Me*, Ridley Scott headed off to direct *Legend*.

That was Howard Franklin's first lesson about the movie business: Don't be naive. His second—never fight with a director—proved to be a more costly rule to break.

Ridley reacted to Howard's vehement protestations over *Legend* by firing him and bringing in two other screenwriters to rewrite *Someone to Watch Over Me*.

Following the rewrites, Howard obtained a copy of the new version of the screenplay. It was *nothing* like what he had written. In fact, it was a *completely different* film. While Howard had conceived a character-driven drama, the script was now laden with overt sex and peppered with violence. However, even though this was not the screenplay Howard had submitted, he would be given *sole* credit under the terms of his contract with MGM. (It is a common practice in Hollywood to bring in writers to do rewrites without on-screen credit.)

As Howard had suspected, MGM grew tired of waiting for Ridley Scott and placed *Someone to Watch Over Me* into turnaround. ("Turnaround" is a term describing the process by which a studio offers a project for sale to other studios, hoping to recoup its development costs.)

Now, after four years of anxiety, Howard Franklin was on his way to see the one man in the world who might offer a solution: David Puttnam. But David hadn't called Howard because he was a writer who needed help. On the contrary, David had sought out Howard because it was Ridley who needed help. From Howard.

Ridley Scott had contacted David about *Someone to Watch Over Me*, sent him the script, and David had agreed to bring the picture to Columbia. There was, however, one small problem. The original MGM agreement specified that if *Someone to Watch Over Me* was not in front of the cameras within four years, the rights to the movie would revert to Howard Franklin. The four years were three weeks from expiring. Since it was impossible to get the film into production before the expiration of the deal, it was up to David Puttnam to convince Howard to waive his rights.

David greeted Howard with warmth and then addressed the issue in question.

"Howard, it is absolutely regrettable that another writer was brought into your project."

"Two writers," Howard countered.

"Well, two writers then. Regrettable. Absolutely regrettable. You know, Howard, I have *never* fired a writer. Never. Never even used another writer to do a rewrite."

David paused and rubbed his beard.

"Actually, there was one time. When Robert Bolt was ill, I did have to bring in a writer for a polish, just a polish. That was the only time. By the way, I wouldn't want this to get out. No one knows about it."

Howard was flabbergasted. David continued.

"I think what we have in *Someone* is a 'thinking man's' *Lethal Weapon*. I want to do it. With your help, of course."

Now Howard was beside himself. *Someone to Watch Over Me*, as Howard saw it, was *not* an action/adventure film by *any* stretch of the imagination, but that was the least of his bewilderment. Howard wondered how David Puttnam, the man who preached social relevance in cinema, could even mouth the words *Lethal Weapon*.

"But we do have this situation here," David added. "So what do you think we should do? Really, I'd like your opinion."

"This is not the movie it should be," Howard responded tentatively. "The last third of the movie, just when the characters are supposed to take over, becomes a psycho-killer movie. I'd like to put it back the way it was."

David shook his head.

"Now, Howard, you know I can't do that. You and Ridley just don't get along anymore. And after all, this is Ridley's film."

Ridley's film? Howard was speechless. Wasn't David supposed to be sensitive to the writer?

"I'll tell you what I will do," David said. "I'll give you script approval. Unofficially, that is. Of course, I can't put it in writing, but I'll bring in another writer to restore your original idea and,

as it progresses, get your input. So Howard, do we get an extension on the turnaround or not?"

Howard mulled over his options. He could say no, but that might
mean the picture would never get made. Yet, if he said yes, a
movie which bore his name but little resemblance to his screenplay might be produced. Truly a dilemma, Howard's only hope
was that David meant what he said about returning *Someone to
Watch Over Me* to its original form. Before he could answer, David
pressed.

"Look, Howard, I want to make sure we're both on the same
team here. I'd be horrified if you called the *L.A. Times* and told
them this horrible story. Give me your solemn word of honor that
you won't ruin the picture's release by going to the press and I'll
guarantee that you will have a chance to review future versions
of the script."

"Okay, David," Howard relented.

"Great!" David exclaimed, jumping up and shaking Howard's
hand. "You've made the right decision."

"I will have the opportunity to see rewrites," Howard reiterated. "Right?"

"Absolutely!" David replied. "As soon as I have a script, you'll
have a script."

Unfortunately for Howard Franklin he had, for the second time,
violated an important Hollywood tenet: Don't be naive.

The total cost of the first four pictures brought to the studio by
David Puttnam was $43,800,000, an average of just $10,950,000 a
film. This figure was well below the $16,000,000 figure prevailing
at Columbia during the McElwaine era.

As word of the deals circulated around Hollywood, there was
mild consternation. Although no one was against keeping budgets
down, *everyone* was against limiting their payday. And it was obvious that the only way David could have cut the average budget
by 50 percent was by slashing the *above-the-line* costs.

There are two distinct categories of expense in every motion
picture budget: above-the-line and below-the-line. Below-the-line
includes the salaries of the crew, set construction, music, location
expense (Winnebagos, messengers, transportation, etc.), makeup,
sound, camera, and the like. In other words, all the nuts and bolts
of a film. Above-the-line represents the producer's fee, director,

writer, and cast. Simply put, the *glamour* of a film. The up-front creators.

When David spoke out in the past about "waste" in film production, he conjured an image among the uninitiated of a wild gluttony of excess taking place on the set. Admittedly, Hollywood is not known for moderation. But the reality of the costs involved are much different from what one might expect.

Take away a few Winnebagos, for example, and the studio could save maybe $50,000. Drop a dozen redundant members of the entourage from the payroll and shave another $100,000 from the budget. Have nonvintage California champagne brought in rather than vintage French and the bill goes down a bit more.

Try *very* hard, and the costs can be reduced a half a million. Below-the-line. Five hundred thousand dollars is a great deal of money. In the context of a $16,000,000 movie, however, it represents a reduction of 3 percent.

In order to shave $5,000,000 from a $16,000,000 film, the producer, director, writer, and cast would have to take a significant cut in salary. This raised a basic question: Were the millions being paid above-the-line worth the expenditure?

David liked to attack the amount of money received by major stars. He often assailed "rich" production deals. And he challenged the fees being paid to Hollywood directors. Behind closed doors, he would frequently bolster his argument with the following statement: "If Istvan Szabo will direct a film for $350,000, why should anyone get $3,000,000?"

Szabo—a Hungarian director whom David considered the "best pound-for-pound in the world"—had won an Oscar for *Mephisto*. Yet it was not likely he would ever direct a purely commercial film and less likely he would even want to. Szabo was content to make relevant motion pictures within the confines of what is referred to as the "Hungarian New Cinema."

The Istvan Szabo remark illustrated just how far removed David Puttnam was from the Hollywood reality. Istvan Szabo was hardly a "name" in the land of Beverly Hills. And, rather than condemning hefty fees, Hollywood defended them.

For example, former Columbia president Frank Price usually put it this way when asked about his philosophy of finance: "A twenty-million-dollar picture with stars has less risk than a ten-million-dollar picture without stars."

Given the premise that audiences are drawn into the theater by familiar names, Price reasoned that the additional amount needed to pay them fostered a measurable value at the box office. And since big-name stars are attracted to a project by a big-name director, Price considered the requisite director's fee to be a wise investment.

There was one Hollywood director David seemed to hold in high regard.

"The only American director who is any good," David would say when his Istvan Szabo reference was not convincing, "is Martin Scorsese."

Notwithstanding David's praise of Scorsese's prowess as a filmmaker, the remark was clearly intended to dismiss summarily all other American directors. The inference was this: If they weren't any good, they most certainly were overpriced no matter what they were paid.

Even as Hollywood grumbled, the media were heralding David Puttnam's appointment as nothing less than the second coming. Dozens of articles were spread out from London to Los Angeles like palm fronds, as typically hard-nosed reporters departed from a policy of uncompromising journalism and engaged in flowery editorial.

Clearly the most representative example of this media worship was written by *Los Angeles Times* columnist Jack Mathews, headlined: TO COLUMBIA'S NEW CHIEF CHARIOTEER, FROM A FAN. Presented as an open letter to David Puttnam, it was Mathews's *second* expression of adulation in four months.

"Dear Mr. Puttnam," Mathews began, "Welcome to L.A."

While expressing an allegiance to David Puttnam, Mathews interjected a few barbs for the Hollywood establishment.

"As you probably know, your decision to take this job was one of the biggest surprises in Hollywood. . . . A quality movie-maker and a major studio? What could you possibly have in common? Whatever your reasons, those of us who enjoy films more than filmed deals welcomed the news.

"At the very least, we figured the Coke folks would put either a TV or ad man in charge, someone with the proven ability to organize and reduce complex populations of people into simple slices of demographic pies. But no, they go out and hire a genuine film-maker, one with taste and dignity, and get us all excited, like maybe a major studio will again think of movies as a way to both entertain and, to use an archaic word, enlighten."

Then Mathews commented on David's past movies.

"What people may forget is that every movie you have made in the last ten years, including Oscar-winning 'Chariots of Fire,' needed patient, special handling to catch on in the American market."

The comment was revealing. If, as Mathews's observation indicated, the media were aware that David Puttnam's cinematic tastes were not an easy sell in the United States, where were the acerbic investigative pieces questioning the wisdom of placing a British producer at the top of a major *American* studio? And if a Los Angeles newspaper columnist could readily recognize David Puttnam's affinity for inaccessible motion pictures, why couldn't Coca-Cola?

Of course, the tone of Mathews's words did not warrant the adjective "inaccessible" as a description of those films. To Mathews, they were like valuable gems which only needed to be carefully mined. Unfortunately, studios have less in common with miners than they do jewelry stores.

After praising David Puttnam for several paragraphs, Mathews expressed some disappointment.

"There are some easy traps for a studio head to fall into here, and frankly, I was surprised to see you disappear into one so soon after taking this job."

The "trap" was Bill Cosby's *Leonard Part 6*. Mathews chided the new studio chief for doing exactly what he had vigorously spoken out against in the media.

"When you announced a few weeks ago that Columbia had signed Bill Cosby to produce and star in a comedy based on an idea by Cosby for Christmas '87 release, you said it signifies 'exactly what Columbia will be all about, entertainment with a heart and a mind.' When all you have is a star and idea, you don't have entertainment with a heart or a mind . . . you have a *deal*."

The article concluded with a warning.

"I hope you don't spend a lot of time trying to justify strictly commercial decisions with cliches. In the long haul, your tenure at Columbia will be measured by the mix that you create, by the number and quality of those films that will be attempted because they really do have a heart and a mind."

Perhaps Mathews should have pointed out that the measurement of David Puttnam's tenure would depend on who was doing the measuring.

The media.

Or the stockholders.

In most industries, the telephone represents a method of communication. In Hollywood, it is a device which constantly gives producers and directors an update on their relative status in the filmmaking community. Who you *can* or *can not* get on the phone is the benchmark of your entire career.

Since the *deal* is the thing, the most vital phone conversation for a filmmaker is with a studio chief. If a studio chief *originates* the call, he can celebrate. If a studio chief takes his call, he's part of the action. If a studio chief doesn't take his call but returns it within twenty-four hours, he's still okay. But, if a studio chief doesn't bother to call him back, he's history. Over. A nobody.

Such was the dilemma facing David Puttnam when he settled into his corner office at Columbia Plaza East the first week of September. As a producer, David was well aware of the significance placed on the simple act of communication. He could remember the days when even a one-minute phone conversation with a studio executive gave him great hope. And the absence of a return call sent him into despair.

David received hundreds of calls that first week, and each message was marked *urgent*. By Friday—based on whom he dialed—David had reshuffled the royal court of Columbia Pictures.

Although David answered and placed dozens of calls every hour for five days, there was one call he did not make. A call that was vital to his power base at the studio.

David did not contact Ray Stark.

The following week, his second at the helm of Columbia, David trekked from Burbank to Century City, where rows of high-rise buildings line a wide avenue named, appropriately, Century Boulevard. These monolithic structures provide office space for two of the most powerful professions in Hollywood: lawyers and agents.

Both represent talent, deriving their importance from the importance of their clients. While an individual director or actor may have great influence, a lawyer or agent who represents several directors or actors benefits from that influence to the nth power.

The purpose of David's trip to Century City was a meeting with the staff of Creative Artists Agency. Since its inception eleven years before, in 1975, CAA had become the most influential entity in the motion picture industry. Indeed, the fact that Columbia chairman/CEO David Puttnam was headed to CAA offered sufficient evidence of the scope of the agency's sovereignty in Hollywood. Clearly, the journey to Century City was one David was compelled to make.

There were five founding members of CAA, all agents at the William Morris Agency at the time. Michael Ovitz, Michael Rosenfeld, Rowland Perkins, Bill Haber, and Ron Meyer broke away from the tradition that was William Morris and set out to create their own domain of artist representation. Eighteen months later, CAA added another partner: Martin Baum. At the time, Martin was head of his own agency.

Although all five current CAA partners (Michael Rosenfeld left to become a producer) have a stake in the company, one is the undisputed leader, President Mike Ovitz. Ovitz is known for his smooth patter, excruciatingly polite behavior, and thoroughly ruthless negotiating skills. He is also known as the leading proponent of the "package."

Here again, the jargon is misleading in that the word "package" connotes something rather benign in the rest of the world but in Hollywood it is one of the more explosive words one can utter.

The "package" has been responsible for causing a major shift in the balance of power in the movie business. It has doubled and redoubled stars' salaries. And it has made Mike Ovitz and his four partners very wealthy men.

In the early days of Hollywood, motion picture studios controlled the industry because they controlled the talent. Writers, directors, and stars were signed to *exclusive* studio agreements which prevented them from working anywhere else. As a result, studios were able to pay talent whatever they chose, garnering all the monetary benefits of a hit film for themselves.

If an actor balked at his fate or otherwise became a problem, the studio would merely place him or her on "suspension." In

Hollywood, not working spells disaster. If you aren't in a movie, you are "out of the business."

The "package" turned the tables. Agents soon realized that the studios were right about one thing: control the talent and you control the industry. They also discerned something else out of the equation of control: the propensity for bigger commissions.

Thus, the "package" was born, and agencies began offering the talent on its roster in unbreakable groupings. Hence, when an agent met with a studio, he might say: "We've got the screenplay, the director, the cast. If you want one, you have to take them all."

Although the package was more expensive, the concept worked. Studios snatched up packages in order to maintain the flow of product in the distribution pipeline, just as anyone might stop by a convenience store instead of a supermarket when time is more important than money. Soon, however, studios began to rely more and more on packages instead of in-house development. Like a muscle that stops being used, the development power of the Hollywood studio quickly atrophied. And agents assumed control of the business.

It was therefore imperative, *if* he expected to survive in Hollywood, that David Puttnam come to terms with the most powerful agency of them all, CAA, and the most powerful agent of them all, Mike Ovitz.

A supercharged atmosphere of anticipation mingled with an air of apprehension when David, who had openly criticized agency packages in the past, strode into the conference room at CAA.

Most in attendance were greatly heartened by the announcement of *Leonard Part 6*. That David Puttnam gave his blessing to a twenty-odd-million-dollar pact with Bill Cosby suggested a softening of the British producer's oft-stated stance on megadeals. And David's eagerness to address the gathered staff of CAA portended good relations between the agency and Columbia Pictures.

Many—including Mike Ovitz and Martin Baum—felt David had come to his senses. They thought the reality of the job of studio chief had caused David to make adjustments in his thinking. They were certain David's visit would be a glorious afternoon of mutual respect and statement of common purpose.

They were wrong.

"I plan to be a hands-on executive," David began, "and I expect to be involved in every aspect of production, from script approval to final cut. Final cut, by the way, is something I *will not* be giving to anyone. It will reside with me."

The term "final cut" is just what it sounds like. The authority to create the *final* version of a motion picture. The right to edit the *final* print, the one which is ultimately seen in theaters. Most major directors would not work without it.

As David continued, however, it became apparent that he had no intention of working with name directors in the first place.

"I don't believe the salaries directors are being paid are worth it. If directors really think they are worth these enormous fees, then why are they so unwilling to take less on the front end and collect the rest *after* the movie has earned money at the box office?"

Mike Ovitz bristled. David's statement stabbed at the very core of the packaging concept: front-loading income to talent and the agency while placing the burden of risk on the studio.

David then elaborated on the subject of directors.

"Most directors in Hollywood are over forty-five years old and any director over forty-five is in decline. Only in Hollywood is forty-five considered young. The other day someone called Rob Reiner a 'young' director. At forty-five, I certainly wouldn't call Rob Reiner young."

A new point of contention was brought to bear on David Puttnam's relationship with the Hollywood establishment. David's appetite for low-cal budgets and his allegiance to British directors were already cause for concern. Now he was placing another parameter on his tastes, age. Considering the fact that the average age of Hollywood's power elite was probably fifty or older, the statement was potentially the *most* damaging—in terms of David's ability to operate within the Hollywood filmmaking community—that he could have made.

While his audience sat in awkward silence, David delivered the coup de grace.

"I will only be interested in pictures with a meritorious social content. I will not be shooting 'deals.' And I definitely will not consider expensive packages. So don't bother sending them to Columbia Pictures. I intend to turn Columbia into a studio again. And I will be concentrating on in-house development."

Those who wondered what the consequences of placing a filmmaker at the helm of a Hollywood studio might be no longer had to wonder. A filmmaker, especially if he happened to be David Puttnam, would do what a filmmaker does. Develop his own projects.

Yet David had been incredibly insensitive in expressing his opinion, demonstrating that he possessed very little political savvy. It might have been more prudent to refrain from offering his view in such precise terms. And the forum—CAA's conference room— was obviously inappropriate for such a controversial disclosure.

After finishing his speech, David briefly circulated around the room. When he approached Mike Ovitz, Mike was exceedingly polite. After all, civility is a well-known Mike Ovitz characteristic.

But Mike was livid and couldn't wait for David to leave. So, when David finally waltzed out the front door, Mike immediately shed his smile, his face becoming red with anger.

Martin Baum spoke first.

"We just heard something very startling," Martin noted. "How long do you think he's going to last in Hollywood?"

The look on Mike Ovitz's face answered the question better than anything he could have said.

CHAPTER EIGHT

In the few days David had spent as chairman/CEO, he learned that the gap in philosophy between him and current studio president Steve Sohmer was as wide as the price differential between Steve's Rolls-Royce and his Audi. Consequently, David would replace Steve Sohmer, and the leading candidate for the job was David Picker.

The negotiations with David Picker were laborious. Picker wanted to join Columbia, but he had various prior commitments. In fact, Picker was in Georgia at the time, where he was scouting locations for *Leader of the Band*, a film being directed by his wife Nessa Hyams for which he would act as executive producer.

Picker, an independent producer, had been in charge of a studio three times in the past. From 1969 until 1972 he was president of United Artists where his uncle Arnold was one of the controlling partners of the studio with Arthur Krim and Bob Benjamin. He served as president of Paramount from 1976 to 1978 and president of Lorimar's feature film division from 1979 to 1981.

It was a well-known fact that David Puttnam and David Picker had a long-standing relationship. Picker provided the last bit of financing for Puttnam's *Bugsy Malone* and initiated the deal which brought *The Duellists* to Paramount for U.S. distribution.

So when rumors of Picker's talks with Columbia surfaced in the trade papers, that fact was duly noted.

"David Puttnam confirmed," *The Hollywood Reporter* said on

page one, "that long-time friend and colleague Picker and the studio are negotiating the feature division presidency, though he emphasized that he expected the discussions to be protracted."

The two Davids spoke often via phone as Picker kept Puttnam informed regarding the progress of *Leader of the Band*, scheduled for completion by November. So that became the target date for Steve Sohmer's departure.

Ray Stark arrived at David Puttnam's office, exuberant as usual. He wore his normal attire—jeans and a sports shirt—while David was dressed in his "uniform," a dark suit and conservative tie. They were certainly an odd couple.

This was the first encounter between David and Ray since David arrived at the studio.

The main purpose for Ray's visit was to find out the status of *Revenge*, a film Ray had brought to Columbia earlier in 1986.

"I have been going over the book and the screenplay," David said. "Give me a few more days."

Patience is not a Ray Stark virtue.

"Fine, David, I'd like to know as soon as possible if *Revenge* will be done at Columbia," Ray pressed. "If you don't like the project, no problem, I'll take it somewhere else."

"Really, Ray," David countered, "I need more time. I've been overwhelmed here. There's a lot to do."

The first major production crisis that David had to face began to unfold on the set of *The Big Town* from the moment the picture started shooting on September 7. The initial dailies (footage viewed each day from the previous day's work) were not what producer Marty Ransohoff had expected. Nor was the film's director, Harold Becker, happy with the progress of *The Big Town*.

By September 10—just three days into the project—Marty Ransohoff was contacted by Harold Becker's agent, CAA partner Martin Baum. Both Martys—Baum and Ransohoff—agreed that the best course of action would be a "mutual parting of ways." Consequently, Marty Ransohoff found himself without a director for *The Big Town*.

The next day, Marty Ransohoff made his way to Columbia Plaza East to meet with David Puttnam.

This was the second time David and Marty had met since David had arrived in Burbank two weeks earlier. The first encounter occurred at the Bel Air Hotel, a meeting in which Marty had asked David for an answer on *Switching Channels*.

"I need a little more time," David had said. It was a sentence he would repeat over and over to anxious members of the Hollywood establishment.

Now, however, Marty's main concern was finding a replacement for Harold Becker, a difficult task in that most established directors would never step into the middle of a troubled picture. With myriad new projects being pitched their way, the filmmaking elite had no desire to engage in first aid. This left two categories of directors: old warhorses on their way down, and ambitious yearlings on their way up.

"Would you take a gamble on a young director?" David asked Marty.

"I frequently have," Marty responded. "Who do you have in mind?"

"His name is Ben Bolt."

"Ben Bolt?"

"He's Robert Bolt's son."

Robert Bolt had been the screenwriter on *The Mission*.

"Has he ever done a movie?" Marty wanted to know.

"No, he hasn't, but he's a very fine director, Marty. I've seen his work. He's done a lot of television in England. And he's done several episodes for *Hill Street Blues*, which I can have sent over to you tonight. Take a look at them."

Television was a medium Marty knew well, having spent the first twenty years of his career as head of Filmways, a company that produced such small-screen classics as *The Beverly Hillbillies*, *Mr. Ed*, *Petticoat Junction*, *Green Acres*, and *The Addams Family*. Now, after twenty years in the movie business, Marty was acutely aware of the differences between the two dramatic forms.

Could a young Briton named Ben Bolt go from directing a couple of television shows to assuming the creative responsibility for a major motion picture?

"Has Ben Bolt spent much time in this country?" Marty inquired.

"Actually, no."

"David, why would you choose a fledgling British director with no real experience in America to deal with a picture set in nineteen-fifties Chicago? This picture is a slice of Americana. And that concerns me more than the fact that he has never directed a movie."

"That may be true," David answered, "but he's brilliant and talented."

Brilliant? Talented? Marty didn't have anyone brilliant and talented ready to take over *The Big Town*.

Marty looked at David for a long time. Here was the chairman/ CEO of Columbia Pictures offering a personal endorsement of an unknown and untried director. And besides David's position at the studio, he was an independent producer who had launched the careers of many first-time filmmakers, including Hugh Hudson, Alan Parker, and Ridley Scott.

"Okay, David," Marty consented, "if he's brilliant *and* talented, we'll give it a go. Send me the *Hill Street Blues* tapes."

Although David Puttnam had stated publicly that he wanted nothing to do with *Ishtar*, his conduct behind studio walls was quite the opposite.

"I have an idea I'd like to pursue," David told the Columbia legal department. "Could we take the position that Warren Beatty would be in breach as producer of *Ishtar* if costs on the film go over a certain amount?"

David suggested that Warren Beatty immediately be put on notice regarding a proposed budget limitation. Then, David speculated, if *Ishtar* exceeded that limit, the studio would be justified in terminating Warren's agreement.

At the time, *Ishtar* was already on the books for $47,000,000. The studio expected the completion of postproduction would add at least another $2,000,000, yielding an estimated final cost of $49,000,000.

The Columbia legal department, taking a dispassionate view of the theoretical problem, returned a verdict of "possible." The consensus was that David's proposal did appear to have some merit and it was recommended that the sum that would trigger the contractual breach be $50,000,000.

Although this would give Warren Beatty a $1,000,000, or 2 percent, margin of error, it seemed certain—given the escalation from the original $32,000,000 budget—that Warren would lose his status as producer if David succeeded in carrying out his plan.

There were two major flaws in David's scenario, however. First of all, Warren Beatty had been *employed* by Columbia Pictures as producer of *Ishtar* and the terms of his agreement with the studio did not specify any responsibility for budget overruns. Besides that, Warren was a main character in the film. This fact necessitated Warren's presence during postproduction and rendered his participation in a subsequent publicity campaign highly desirable. How could the studio expect cooperation from Warren Beatty the actor when Warren Beatty the producer had just been fired?

Buoyed by a favorable response from the battery of lawyers in Burbank, David informed Columbia's senior management in New York of his intentions.

The reaction was swift and concise: "Do not proceed under any circumstances."

When David had last criticized Warren Beatty for the size of a budget, David had been an independent producer and had no power to do anything about it. In fact, it had really been none of David's business what Warren spent on *Reds* in 1981. Now, five years later, David Puttnam found himself Warren Beatty's *employer*, and it clearly was David's business what Warren spent on *Ishtar*. Yet David was strictly prohibited from exerting any authority over the man he perceived to be his nemesis.

There isn't a better definition of frustration than that.

If David Puttnam thought he was doing Ray Stark a favor by responding quickly to the *Revenge* project, he was wrong on two counts. First of all, David's method of communication, a letter, was far from being a personal touch. And second, he didn't pass on the *Revenge* project itself, he passed on Ray Stark.

The following note was hand delivered across the parking lot at the Burbank studios the day David left for England:

Ray Stark   September 16, 1986
Columbia Plaza West

Dear Ray

REVENGE

I'm just off to Europe for a couple of weeks and I thought I should set down my thoughts regarding the above property.

During the past ten days I have painstakingly picked my way through the novella, the Walter Hill and the John Huston screenplays. I came to the conclusion last night that this wasn't a property that we'll be in a position to move on in the coming months. With this in mind I suggest the following.

We arrange either formally or informally for you to have a 90 day period in which to set the film up at another studio. Failing this, it will return to Columbia without any further lien and we'll be free to offer it elsewhere.

I say this because in reviewing the film it transpired that the material had been of interest some while ago to a team of filmmakers whom I rate highly. There is always a chance that I can interest them in picking up the pieces and turn out a good film at a price that makes it attractive. I'm eager not to close us out of the possibility of being able to reinterest them on terms that we could live with.

The reason for all the neuroses regarding this property is that we have over $600,000 tied up in it and most of all I'd like the use of the money!

See you when I get back.

Warmest regards,

Yours sincerely,

DAVID PUTTNAM

Ray immediately took the letter to Bill Nestel. After reading the text, Nestel discovered an error in David's appraisal of the *Revenge* situation and his response clearly made that point.

September 25, 1986

Mr. David Puttnam
Chairman and Chief Executive Officer
Columbia Pictures
Columbia Plaza East
Burbank, CA 91505

Re: "Revenge"/RAY STARK PRODUCTIONS ("RSP")

Dear David:

I have just received a copy of your September 16, 1986 letter to my client, Ray Stark, in connection with the above-captioned project.

Inasmuch as "REVENGE" was jointly developed by RSP and Columbia Pictures, RSP is entitled to a one-year turnaround from the date of abandonment.

While we are sensitive to the fact that Columbia has incurred a significant investment in the project, Ray does not feel it is appropriate that the time within which he has the right to acquire Columbia's interest in the property be diminished.

Very Truly Yours,

WILLIAM C. NESTEL

In other words, if David wanted *Revenge* without Ray Stark, he might have a long wait.

The next member of the Hollywood establishment to fall out of favor with David Puttnam was Oscar-winning (*In the Heat of the Night*) director Norman Jewison. David had just read a screenplay sent to him by Norman entitled *The Man Who Could Work Miracles*. Unfortunately, he hated it.

Sixty-year-old Norman Jewison was one of several filmmakers with output deals at Columbia Pictures. The career of the respected director spanned three decades and included films such as *Fiddler on the Roof, Jesus Christ Superstar, The Cincinnati Kid,* and *A Soldier's Story.*

Yet David was about to turn down his latest project.

"David," Norman fumed during a phone call in which David told Norman that he didn't believe in *Miracles*, "you've just got to the studio, how can you make these decisions?"

"You asked for a quick decision," David countered. "I read it and I was bitterly disappointed. Now I'm getting right back to you. What do you want me to do?"

"Any chance of reconsidering?"

"No. If I start rethinking every decision, I'll go mad."

"Under those circumstances, I don't think there's any point in my staying at the studio."

"Norman, that's absolutely your call."

Although Herbert Allen would have preferred to keep his distance from the operations in Burbank, he felt compelled to call David regarding his remarks at CAA.

"I strongly recommend," Herbert said, "that you make an attempt to maintain a reasonable relationship with Mike Ovitz."

He did not suggest that David make any decisions which ran contrary to his philosophy, nor did Herbert purport to be intruding into David's creative territory.

As Herbert envisioned it, the position of chairman/CEO not only involved making movies, but carried mandatory political duties as well. He expected David to be tactful, especially in view of his self-imposed three-year time limit.

Ironically, Herbert was not opposed to more in-house development activity. In-house projects were certainly desirable because they cost less and were done under the studio's direct control.

But the events that weighted the balance of power away from studio production and toward agency packages had taken place over decades. Reversing that momentum would take decades as well. The term of David's contract was not of sufficient duration to effect such a drastic modification in the basic operation of the motion picture industry.

Even if Herbert wanted to pursue an in-house development course for Columbia Pictures, he knew there was more to it than just a declaration of independence from packages.

To begin with, the current employee configuration at Columbia was the exact opposite of the configuration such a change would require. Without the agencies, an immediate shortage of product would occur within the distribution system. In order to meet the distribution needs, Columbia would need more production executives.

In other words—if Columbia were to suddenly break from outside development—the studio would find itself overstaffed in its distribution arm and understaffed on the creative side.

So doing what David clearly had in mind meant a massive shift in personnel, a great deal of money and a long-term commitment.

None of the above appealed to Herbert Allen.

"I'll try to be more friendly," David promised.

It was not quite the answer Herbert would have liked, but at least it was a start.

Looking forward to a respite from the rigors of his job as studio chief, David flew to London for the world premiere of his production of Warner Brothers' *The Mission.*

The event marked the first time ever that a chairman/CEO of one studio had flown to another country to promote the film of another studio.

Even though the respective studios had amicably come to grips with the obvious conflict of interest aspect of *The Mission*, Hollywood filmmakers had not.

Many producers felt in *competition* with David Puttnam, instead of in business with him.

This feeling, of course, was more imaginary than real.

Unfortunately, there is no sharp delineation between fantasy and reality in Hollywood.

On October 9, Dick Gallop left his dual posts as president and chief operating officer of Columbia Pictures Industries and executive vice president of the Coca-Cola Entertainment Business Sector to become a senior member of Allen & Company.

The move caught the trade papers off guard, a fact which *Variety* noted the next day:

"Gallop chortled over the fact that the Allen & Company announcement did not follow a succession of rumors and speculation in the media."

When David returned from London following the premiere of *The Mission*, there was a letter which was almost burning a hole in his desk: Bill Nestel's response regarding *Revenge*. So David fired off the following counterresponse:

Dear Mr. Nestel, October 13, 1986

REVENGE/RAY STARK PRODUCTIONS

I'm sorry to have taken so long to respond to your letter of the 25th of September, but I'm afraid I have been away in Europe.

It seems that my understanding of the background to REVENGE coming to the Studio is rather more complex than your note implies. However, that's not an issue that involves any form of contention. More importantly, as I said in my original note to Ray, I am eager to increase the amount in our current development account by the $600,000 which at present is represented by our investment in REVENGE. Needless to say I'll be relieved and delighted at any word from you or Ray that a deal has been struck elsewhere.

I accept the reasons behind your insistence on one year turnaround and I assume that the clock should be deemed to have started ticking on the date of my note to Ray of 16th September.

Looking forward to hearing from you.

Yours sincerely,

DAVID PUTTNAM

c.c. Ray Stark

Ray wasted no time in replying.

October 16, 1986

Dear David:

I am in receipt of the copy of your letter to Bill Nestel of October 13, 1986. I think perhaps it would be more advantageous if, when your schedule permits, we have a meeting which would clarify some of the misunderstandings that exist between Columbia and Ray Stark Productions.

To clue you in, many years ago when Guy McElwaine was President of Ray Stark Productions, we were trying to get Richard Pryor to make a deal within Ray Stark Productions and Columbia. At that time, a writer, Joel Oliansky, told me of a project called "CHARLIE PARKER" which I thought might be wonderful bait to lure Mr. Pryor into our fold. I spent several nights with Pryor and Oliansky on "CHARLIE PARKER" and on another project, "MEN OF BRONZE," which I still am trying to package. The result of these meetings eased the way for Guy to have Pryor switch the concert film, "RICHARD PRYOR LIVE ON THE SUNSET STRIP" from Universal to Rastar. This also set the pattern for Pryor doing other pictures with us, including "THE TOY," and the eventual deal made between Columbia and Pryor directly. My main interest in "CHARLIE PARKER" was to secure Pryor's services.

For five years, I have been trying to acquire the rights to "REVENGE," which were owned by Warner Bros. I had also been trying to acquire "FIRST BLOOD" which later became "RAMBO." At the same time, however, Bob Daly insisted on cash for "FIRST BLOOD," whereas he was willing to swap "REVENGE" for "CHARLIE PARKER."

"CHARLIE PARKER" was worthless to us, since after Pryor's autobiographical film, "JO JO DANCER," Columbia did not want to make another serious film with Pryor, but Guy McElwaine, as President of Columbia (and a friend), held me up two years while Pryor was doing "JO JO DANCER."

I appreciate your desire to replenish the coffers of Columbia's development account, but I think you should take into consideration that "CHARLIE PARKER" was worth nothing to Columbia while, on the other hand, Columbia has a chance of making something from "REVENGE." I am in the throes of trying to put together other projects for which Columbia would benefit, so please be assured that the welfare of your regime and Columbia's development account are utmost in my mind.

Awaiting your call.

RAY STARK

The convoluted path *Revenge* had taken on its way to Columbia was remarkable. And no less remarkable was the perseverance Ray exhibited during a five-year period to effect the film's arrival at the studio.

David might have gleaned the passion Ray had for *Revenge.* And he might have placed a value on the time Ray spent on the project. Furthermore, David would have been well advised to take note of the last line—"Awaiting your call"—for Ray was in fact doing just that.

But David chose to ignore the letter. And move on to things he deemed more important.

CHAPTER NINE

During the remainder of October, David Puttnam's days and nights were consumed by two activities—combing through the 120 projects in development at the studio and evaluating possible staff additions.

As far as the projects were concerned, David quietly canceled fifty films.

Personnel judgments, though more complex, at least were far fewer in number.

Long before any announcement was forthcoming, David's selection of Australian exhibitor/producer Greg Coote to head up Columbia's worldwide marketing division was being talked about all over Hollywood. The conversations centered on the rumor that David had authorized Columbia to buy Coote's Australian business for two million dollars.

The most often heard comment was: "David paid two million for a desk and a Rolodex. To an Australian."

The operative word was "Australian." Two million was not an amount that would have attracted much attention in Hollywood except for the growing perception that David Puttnam was ignoring qualified—and out of work—Americans in order to bring a foreign legion to Burbank.

Obviously that perception did not bother David, since he next brought in British film editor Jim Clark as senior production executive. Clark had served as editor on two Puttnam-produced pictures, *The Killing Fields*, for which Clark won an Oscar, and *The Mission*.

Considering David's constant harangues against "cronyism," Clark's appointment earned the new studio chief a wave of detractors who suddenly saw him as a hypocrite.

David's next choice also was viewed as contrary to his stand on cronyism. Lynda Myers, a former employee of David's Enigma Productions, was placed in the newly created position of senior vice president in charge of European creative affairs. She would be based in London.

October had been a bumpy month for David Puttnam. As the month neared an end, he was happy to board a plane for New York where he would attend the United States premiere of *The Mission* and—at least for a night—revert to his life as an independent producer hawking his wares at a theater.

The job might not pay as much as that of chairman/CEO of a motion picture studio, but it sure was a whole lot simpler.

It was déjà vu for David Puttnam when *The Mission* opened at Cinema I on Halloween night. His two highest grossing movies, *Chariots of Fire* and *The Killing Fields*, had both premiered at the Manhattan theater.

The Killing Fields opened November 2, 1984 and brought in $54,033 its first full week, while *Chariots of Fire* started at Cinema I on September 25, 1981 and garnered $70,488.

The Mission found $72,570 its first seven days in the Big Apple.

Like David's prior efforts, *The Mission* was being "rolled out," a term used to describe the gradual addition of theaters as a movie gains acceptance. In fact, the Warner Brothers plan was a classic example of such a distribution tactic.

After two weeks in New York, *The Mission* would open in one theater in each of the following cities: Boston, Chicago, Los Angeles, Minneapolis, Montreal, San Francisco, Seattle, Toronto, and Washington, D.C. At this point, the movie would be playing in ten venues.

On December 19, Warner Brothers intended to add fourteen screens in New York and six days later, on Christmas day, *The Mission* would be released to thirty-five more theaters around the country, bringing the total number to fifty-nine.

January 16 would see a large jump in play dates with 466 additional prints put into distribution. Finally, on February 6, yet another 495 screens would be added.

By the time the Oscars were announced on February 11, *The Mission* would be dancing across 1,020 screens.

The multitiered release described above is the exact opposite of what is known as "opening wide." Had *The Mission* opened wide, all or most of the 1,020 screens would have been booked for the Halloween debut.

While both distribution methods are used by motion picture studios, the strategy employed generally depends on the nature of the picture being released. *The Mission* was an anomaly.

The roll-out is usually reserved for the small "art" film with no major stars, while the shotgun approach is almost always used in the case of a big-budget picture with top names.

The reasoning is simple. Faced with having to recoup a substantial production cost, studios count on the magnetism of a stellar cast to draw a sizable first-week audience which can quickly replenish the company coffers. When tens of millions of dollars are at stake, Hollywood is loath to take a chance on word-of-mouth to build box office. Distribution executives feel it is much more prudent to open a star-laden big-budget motion picture as *wide* as possible.

Unfortunately, Warner Brothers found itself with a star-laden big-budget art film.

Although it cost $25,000,000 and boasted Robert De Niro and Jeremy Irons in lead roles, *The Mission* embraced the kind of socially relevant, historic story line not often seen in the megabuck genre.

Would hordes of people flock to see a drama about South American Indians and Jesuit Priests? Would audiences line up for a recounting of a two-hundred-year-old skirmish between Spain and Portugal?

In the big-budget category, the studio had recently found success with the $17,000,000 *National Lampoon's European Vacation*, a slapstick Chevy Chase comedy. Would a serious film like *The Mission*—at $8,000,000 more—generate a *higher* return than the inane farce which was *National Lampoon's European Vacation*?

Comparing two such disparate films might seem absurd, but the contrast serves as an illustration of the "Art versus Commerce" debate as it pertains to Hollywood.

In Atlanta, David Puttnam had told Coca-Cola that Columbia should not make movies based on the "lowest common denominator of public taste." Yet Chevy Chase lured $60,000,000-worth of ticket buyers to U.S. theaters with his pratfalls and silly facial contortions.

What would *The Mission* collect?

Variety appraised its box-office chances this way:

"Limited initial bookings . . . might well yield solid wicket action at the outset. After that, all bets are off."

The prediction proved to be right on the money. As *The Mission* opened wide, it fell flat, netting Warner Brothers $8,300,000 from U.S. film rentals. The American run of *The Mission* as measured against its cost turned up $17,000,000 *short*. Warners would have to try to recoup the rest from foreign and ancillary markets.

Warner Brothers did have a few mementos to show for its philanthropic endeavor involving *The Mission*. Reviews, for example, were often of the keepsake variety.

" 'The Mission' is a stunning and majestic film that seems already a prime contender for the Academy's Best Picture honor," gushed *The Hollywood Reporter*. ". . . a work of ascendant poetic accomplishment."

Indeed, *The Hollywood Reporter* was right. *The Mission* not only grabbed a Best Picture nomination, it pulled down six other Oscar nominations as well.

Ultimately, *The Mission* lost at the 1987 Academy Awards, giving way to *Platoon*. But a most graphic example of the David Puttnam filmmaking philosophy had played out in full view, with *every* element common to David's cinematic history intact.

The source material followed a familiar Puttnam pattern in that *The Mission* was a period piece. So did the story line, one which purported to teach a lesson.

Then there were the awards and critical acclaim. And finally, the modest box office.

However, *The Mission* did depart from David's previous projects in two significant ways. Its big-name cast and its big budget.

It was the first time the Hollywood notion of "bigness" had been interwoven with the David Puttnam concept of socially relevant cinema. In monetary terms, the mix was a disaster.

While *The Mission* ran its course, David set to work performing his duties as chairman/CEO of Columbia Pictures. Yet *The Mission* was far from being an unrelated event.

The performance of the picture did not alter David's resolve to produce films of historic and ethical value, but it did reinforce his aversion to bloated budgets and major stars.

During the remainder of 1986, David began assembling his first full slate of pictures, which he intended to announce after the holidays. He constantly read scripts, conducted long "pitch" meetings (where producers or directors would outline their concept for a movie), and viewed footage in an effort to fill Columbia's distribution system for the next twelve months. Despite his overcommitted schedule, however, David took the time to engage in his favorite pastime, talking to the press.

Hollywood journalists were overjoyed. Other studio heads—like Twentieth Century–Fox's Barry Diller or Universal's Tom Pollock, for example—made it a practice *never* to give interviews. David, on the other hand, made it a point to *always* speak to reporters.

Many felt that David's open-door policy with the media would end when he assumed control of Columbia Pictures. After all, speaking out as an independent film producer was quite different from making on-the-record statements as an officer of a public company.

Yet, his new position did not prevent him from being as accessible and controversial as ever. Often his comments seemed to bolt out of left field, making for a sizzling article.

One representative interview, in which David talked about his plans to make relevant movies at Columbia Pictures, took place at the end of October and appeared in the British trade magazine, *Screen International.* After expounding on the type of picture he found acceptable, David made two wildly controversial statements:

"I am not leaving the British film industry," David told *Screen International,* "in a very real sense the British film industry has left me."

He then went on to say that the British film industry had "the mentality of a Banana republic."

Inexplicably, David next attacked Cannon Films and its two copresidents, Menahem Golan and Yoram Globus. At the time, Cannon was making a strong bid to increase its presence in England via acquisition of British theater chains.

After blasting the Golan and Globus management style and denouncing their taste in films, David poked fun at the efforts of the Cannon coheads to extend the company's distribution base into the European market.

"Cannon is run by two men who spend their life on aeroplanes," David observed of the frequent trips the pair had made between Los Angeles and London.

Finally, David predicted Cannon would be out of business in a year.

The global motion picture community was stunned. Why would David Puttnam suddenly distance himself from the British film industry, an industry he had fiercely defended for years? And what possible reason could he have for making disparaging remarks about Menahem Golan and Yoram Globus?

Screen International was delighted, of course, because such rhetoric sells copies. It also generates an avalanche of letters to the editor. Two responses to the David Puttnam discourse were printed in the following issue.

One reaction came from Golan and Globus themselves. It was an open letter to David Puttnam.

"Mr. Puttnam," Golan and Globus wrote, "In response to your bizarre commentary in *Screen International*, especially to your 'prophecy' as to where we shall be one year from now, we were amused, and decided to invite you to a gracious dinner in a year's time to review where we both are (meaning you and us). However, in our generosity, we are prepared to extend the date to 24 months from now."

Another reader's retort published that week was written by British director Michael Winner, a former journalist who had joined the ranks of the film industry and gone on to direct a long list of motion pictures including the Charles Bronson action/adventure, *Death Wish*.

"David Puttnam," Winner conjectured, "is obviously auditioning for the roles of Alexis Carrington or JR Ewing. The remarks in your paper last week could not possibly come from the responsible head of a major motion picture company . . . Since I started writing about the film industry 37 years ago as a lovable lad of 14. . . , I have never seen such an unwarranted and disgraceful attack by the head of one company against the heads of another company."

And Winner said of David's "aeroplane" reference: "Only David can walk across the Atlantic. Lesser mortals have to take public transport."

But Winner's most pointed observation concerned David's views on what was and was not appropriate film fare:

"It is also rather quaint to suggest that a motion picture company can only distribute one type of movie, not mass entertainment pictures along with quality pictures. Historically, American companies have managed to do just that. David's new company, Columbia, managed to release films like 'Lawrence of Arabia' along with 'Confessions of a Window Cleaner.'"

The written repartee between David Puttnam and the three filmmakers indicated that, while the press was engaged in a love affair with the outspoken studio chief, the motion picture industry was not.

Meanwhile, David was popping up on a regular basis in the American media. Hardly a *day* went by when either *Variety* or *The Hollywood Reporter* or the *Los Angeles Times* didn't carry extensive quotes from the talkative David Puttnam.

On November 10, *Daily Variety* carried a page-one story by reporter Will Tusher with the headline: PUTTNAM VOWS TO PUT CO-LUMBIA ON IN-HOUSE DEVELOPMENT TRACK.

"Columbia Pictures will not be doing business as usual under the reign of David Puttnam," Tusher began, "and the chief casualties will be deal makers and phony producers."

Besides the content of the piece, there were many clues to the modus operandi of the new Columbia chairman/CEO. A telling paragraph illustrated just how far David would go to maintain a rapport with the media:

"Puttnam made it clear over the weekend that he does not mean to change his outspoken ways because he now heads a major studio. He served notice that his reputation for independence will not be put in mothballs simply because he has donned the uniform of chairman and chief executive officer."

Over the weekend? How many studio chiefs were accessible on Saturday or Sunday?

David used the *Daily Variety* opportunity to direct acerbic comments at various members of the Hollywood filmmaking community. Although he mentioned no names, the intended recipients of the remarks were obvious. Certainly, the following reprimand/

warning could have only been meant for CAA president Mike Ovitz:

"He [Puttnam] blistered Hollywood for 'shooting deals and not shooting movies.' In no uncertain terms, he let packagers know that they are not his cup of tea. . . . He said he has been appalled by the mind-set he has encountered in discussions of film-making the last few weeks. As a result, he asserted, Columbia plans to shift radically from prepackaged projects to in-house development."

David also took a swipe at big-name, big-price directors when he said:

"You get a screenplay and bring in a director who loves that screenplay—not someone who's out of work and needs the job, not someone who will do it because you offer him $2,500,000 and 10% of the rolling gross."

David chided producers as well:

" 'Unfortunately, what I've witnessed is that the film starts with a book, let's say, and a star—not necessarily the right star, but a book and a star.' . . . That kind of game playing, Puttnam made apparent, will be out under his rule at Columbia [and he] revealed a strong antipathy to what he perceives as the corruption of the role of the producer in Hollywood."

While denouncing agents, directors, and producers David noted that the current environment in Hollywood was "the reason there are so many lousy films around."

Understandably, Hollywood was not pleased.

A week later, David was back on page one of *Daily Variety*. This time, the article was the *lead* story, sporting a banner headline that spanned the entire page: PUTTNAM REFINES COL BLUEPRINT.

David had cohosted—with newly arrived Columbia president, David Picker—a press luncheon on November 17 at Hollywood's Le St. Germaine restaurant. Its purpose was to update the media regarding David's production schedule and to officially announce the appointment of Catherine Wyler as senior vice president of production.

Ironically, Catherine Wyler's career had received a big boost in 1986 from none other than Ray Stark, who provided her with seed money to develop a documentary entitled *Directed by William Wyler*, about her famous father, the late William Wyler.

Born in 1902, the elder Wyler had been a major force in the

motion picture industry for forty-five years, directing his first film, *Crook Busters*, in 1925. Over the decades he added classics like *Mrs. Miniver* in 1942, *Roman Holiday* (which he also produced) in 1953, *Ben-Hur* in 1959, and *Funny Girl* for Ray Stark in 1968.

The first few paragraphs of the *Variety* piece explained the new appointments and then turned to the subject of motion pictures.

"Puttnam said he has been given virtual carte blanche by parent company Coca-Cola on budgeting. He stated that he must obtain Coke approval only on budgets of $30,000,000 or more, but that he is on his own approving any project costing less. . . . [He] laid down budget parameters in which the most costly features would be made for $13,000,000 or under, and others would be price-tagged at $7,000,000 and under. . . . He deplored the fact that the average film the past year has cost $16,200,000—a rate of spending he called 'insane.' "

Then came the big finish, the David Puttnam kicker about the overpaid Hollywood creative community.

"On other subjects, Puttnam suggested multi-million-dollar deals with stars are due to be phased out over the next year. Puttnam vowed to craft future above-the-line deals which are 'miserly upfront, and generous on the back end' [and said] it is fair to ask high-priced actors and directors to share the risks if they wish to share in the profits."

Although the statement was comprised of just two sentences in a very lengthy story, the sentiment was the *only* one noticed and another tempest was touched off in the wake of the article. Yet, no one in Hollywood could bring themselves to respond in kind. Their aversion to the media was too ingrained, too long in the making, to suddenly start giving interviews. In a roundabout way, however, Hollywood did use the media to fight back.

Just before Thanksgiving, a Xerox copy of a quote David Puttnam gave to the *Los Angeles Times* in 1984 began circulating around town. It said:

"I personally do not believe I could do successful work outside my own native cultural environment. That's a pompous statement, but it's true. I just can't make those cultural transitions from England to Hollywood. I don't understand the way films are physically made here."

Across the top of the page, someone had written: This speaks for itself.

* * *

With his list of adversaries growing at an alarming rate, David Puttnam attempted to gain two allies: producers Don Simpson and Jerry Bruckheimer.

Since Columbia president David Picker had known Don Simpson from the days when Picker was president of Paramount a decade earlier, it was only natural that Picker make initial contact.

"David Puttnam is really interested in talking to you and Jerry," Picker told Don Simpson.

"You know we have an exclusive agreement at Paramount," Simpson responded, "with a year and nine months remaining on the contract."

Indeed, it was an agreement which had worked well, with Simpson and Bruckheimer in the midst of a hat trick of box-office bonanzas. *Flashdance* whirled off $36,180,000 in U.S. film rentals in 1983, *Beverly Hills Cop* had collared $108,000,000 in 1984, and *Top Gun* shot down $79,400,000 in 1986. *Beverly Hills Cop II*, scheduled for a 1987 release, ultimately generated $80,557,776 in rentals.

"I know about the agreement," Picker acknowledged, "and so does David. But he wants to talk about the future."

"Okay," Don agreed, "we'll listen."

A few days later, David Puttnam arrived at the small, inexpensive Thai restaurant he had chosen as the rendezvous point. Rushing in twenty minutes late, and without David Picker, David apologized for keeping Don and Jerry waiting, and then launched into his pitch.

"I can't tell you how much I respect you guys as filmmakers," David insisted.

After the opening pleasantries, David described his "agenda" at Columbia Pictures as it pertained to his self-imposed three-year time limit.

"Are you insane?" Don asked. "You won't even be able to get a project developed, produced, and released during that time."

"Well," David laughed, "I'm not a studio bloke, you know."

David's attitude was like that of a filmmaker who was "spying" inside studio walls, rather than the chairman/CEO of a major motion picture entity.

David next offered a condemnation of big-name stars, extolled the virtue of small films, and outlined his plan to turn Columbia into an "international" studio by making movies with foreign appeal. Don and Jerry listened, as they said they would, thanked

David for lunch, and headed back to Paramount.

"He's out of his mind," they said in unison as they left. "He's already failed."

The clear assessment of Hollywood's hottest production team—and they had a few hundred million in box office backing their appraisal—was that David Puttnam's approach to filmmaking was not workable.

And certainly not sensible.

CHAPTER
TEN

David Puttnam suddenly found himself operating under microscopic scrutiny. His every move was watched closely, not only by the creative community in general, but from 711 Fifth Avenue, New York, in particular.

One of the first signs that the Columbia Pictures management team had lost faith in its new chairman/CEO came when David finally turned down both of Marty Ransohoff's pending pictures, *Switching Channels* and *Jagged Edge II*.

At the time David was exercising his veto power, Marty Ransohoff happened to be in New York. During the course of conversation over lunch with Dick Gallop, Marty related David Puttnam's feeling regarding *Switching Channels*.

"Can you get me the script?" Dick asked. "I'd like to read it. Coca-Cola has a deal with Nelson Entertainment to cofinance twelve pictures. Maybe we could do *Switching Channels* under that arrangement."

The pact between the Entertainment Business Sector of Coca-Cola and Nelson Entertainment specified that the films designated under the agreement would be distributed by Columbia Pictures. Should Coca-Cola approve the *Switching Channels* script, David Puttnam would find himself in the position of releasing a movie he had previously rejected.

The saga of the *Jagged Edge* sequel was a bit more complicated,·

but the bottom line was the same. The powers in New York did not take David Puttnam's no for an answer.

In 1985, then studio chief Guy McElwaine had called for a follow-up to the successful *Jagged Edge* and Marty set out to develop a script.

In the midst of attempting to come up with a story line for the sequel, Marty had dinner with his son Steve at Spago.

"I'm having trouble finding the right idea for *Jagged Edge II*," Marty told Steve.

"I have an idea," Steve responded.

Steve, an attorney, described a possible scenario.

"Go home and put it down on five or six pages," Marty recommended.

Steve did so, signed with an agent, and made a deal with Guy McElwaine for the rights to the story.

But before the project got out of the development stage, McElwaine left the studio and David Puttnam succeeded him.

"I don't like sequels," David told Marty at a meeting in Marty's office. "But I have another idea. Let's do a *Jagged Edge Theater*. A film anthology with a different mystery-courtroom drama every year. Not sequels, but completely different pictures using *Jagged Edge* as a logo."

Since Marty had never done a sequel himself, he was not averse to the *Jagged Edge Theater* idea, and, in fact, expressed interest in the concept.

Unfortunately for Columbia, however, David, by turning down the sequel to *Jagged Edge*, effectively put Marty's script into "turnaround" and Columbia lost its *right* to do the sequel. Now that right rested with Marty Ransohoff and, had Marty elected to do so at that point, he could have taken *Jagged Edge II* anywhere he wanted while Columbia, short of litigation, could have done nothing about it.

Not wishing to engage in a protracted dispute, Marty agreed to bring *Jagged Edge II* back to the studio. A compromise was reached and the existing screenplay for *Jagged Edge II* was converted into a non–*Jagged Edge* courtroom drama with non–*Jagged Edge* characters and set for production as *Smoke* (later renamed *Physical Evidence*) under a three-picture deal Marty had with Columbia.

A short time later, Marty lunched with David Picker, the newly arrived president of the studio, and mentioned the *Jagged Edge*

Theater concept. David Picker responded by saying he didn't like the idea of a *Jagged Edge Theater;* rather he preferred doing a sequel.

With the chairman of the studio nixing a sequel to *Jagged Edge* while suggesting a *Jagged Edge Theater,* and the president of the studio nixing a *Jagged Edge Theater* but requesting a sequel, the saga of the development of *Jagged Edge II* was becoming as much a mystery plot as that of the original picture.

Fay Vincent, however, did not want to wait much longer for a resolution. Fay told Marty that Tri-Star chairman Victor Kaufman had approached him about doing a *Jagged Edge* sequel, and Marty responded by saying that Guy McElwaine, speaking for Weintraub Entertainment, had also expressed interest in *Jagged Edge II.*

"What do you think?" Fay asked Marty.

"If the sequel lies fallow," Marty said, "you're wasting an asset."

"I agree with you," Fay concurred. "Tell Puttnam, if he doesn't want to do *Jagged Edge II,* that's okay. We will do it with one of our other companies. But, no matter what happens, the company wants to exploit the asset."

Upon hearing this, David Puttnam relented. "Okay, Marty," he said, "we'll do it."

Thus, Marty began to develop yet another script for *Jagged Edge II.*

Although the bizarre events surrounding both *Switching Channels* and *Jagged Edge II* were indicative of the difficulty inherent in mounting motion pictures, the real point of the corporate jostling was that David Puttnam had been second-guessed. Not once, but twice.

While David's new decisions were being challenged, some of his prior commitments were coming under fire as well. Ben Bolt was having difficulty on the set of *The Big Town.* The director David had once described as "brilliant and talented" was now reported to be beleaguered and terrified. The picture began running behind schedule almost immediately and by early October it looked as if *The Big Town* would be going well over budget. Consequently, Marty Ransohoff notified the picture's completion guarantor, Film Finances, of this unsavory prospect.

Completion guarantors exist in Hollywood out of necessity, and the relationship between filmmakers and such entities is one of the love-hate variety.

The role of the completion guarantor is very simple: The guarantor issues a bond that indemnifies the studio from any future budget overages beyond a certain point. For this service, the guarantor requires two things: a fee equal to a percentage of a film's budget, usually between 5 and 6 percent, and a contingency buffer of 10 percent.

For example, if a film is set at $10,000,000, the completion guarantor *guarantees* that it will cost no more than that amount *plus* a $1,000,000 contingency. In other words, the studio pays the first 10 percent or, in this case, the first $1,000,000 over budget. In addition, the guarantor, having collected 6 percent ($600,000) as a fee, technically is not at risk until a $10,000,000 picture reaches the $11,600,000 mark.

Generally, the completion guarantor reacts *immediately* upon hearing of a problem on the set, so the 16 percent "cushion" usually provides time to rectify the situation before the financial ramifications extend to the guarantor.

Even with this safeguard, bonding films is not nearly as safe as it might sound. Most completion guarantors are involved with underwriting dozens of movies at the same time, representing an enormous potential risk. To minimize this risk, the companies "lay off" part of the downside. The mammoth insurance firm Lloyd's of London, for example, often takes on some of the completion guarantor's obligation. For a fee, of course.

Despite all the precautions, disaster looms each day of production, as the 1981 movie *Heaven's Gate* dramatically demonstrated. The Michael Cimino–directed film ran so seriously over budget (it wound up costing almost $40,000,000) that it literally dismantled a major studio, bringing United Artists to its knees. (The story was chronicled in a best-selling book by author Stephen Bach, *Final Cut*.)

While many outside Hollywood felt United Artists exhibited fiscal irresponsibility with *Heaven's Gate*, studios often find themselves in a no-win position when it comes to film production. If a $10,000,000 picture is only three-fourths done when the money runs out, what's a studio to do? It could refuse to fund the balance needed to complete the picture. But in that case, $10,000,000 is irrevocably lost, since studios obviously cannot release an unfinished film.

The alternative, however, is a treacherous path to take. Suppose the studio kicked in another $2,000,000 to wrap up production but, after that was used, the picture still wasn't in final form. What then? With $12,000,000 now invested in the project, there would be no other option except to add more to the budget. And more. And more. And more.

Thus, it quickly became clear to the motion picture industry that it was not prudent to undertake the financing of certain movies without some sort of insurance against a financial debacle.

Since the completion guarantor assumes open-ended risk when it bonds a picture, the guarantor reserves the contractual right to take over production if the film goes over budget and to remove any indulgent director in favor of one who will endeavor to protect the guarantor's interests. So as Marty Ransohoff conferred with Film Finances president Richard Soames regarding the predicament of *The Big Town*, first-time director Ben Bolt appeared to be a likely candidate for replacement.

"I've never had *three* directors on a film before," Marty told Richard Soames, "but there's a first time for everything."

Before Marty and Richard could formulate a plan of action, John Fiedler, the acting head of production at Columbia, contacted Marty.

"David Puttnam does not want Ben Bolt pressured," Fiedler informed Marty. "You shouldn't do that. David says young talent must be given a chance."

Marty reminded John Fiedler that *The Big Town* was being done under a bond and that there was a serious financial obligation to Film Finances to be considered.

The next day, John Fiedler called Marty again.

"Columbia Pictures," the studio executive told Marty, "will relieve Film Finances of its obligation."

Richard Soames was ecstatic. Even if he had been forced to replace Ben Bolt, Richard knew *The Big Town* would cost Film Finances money anyway. David Puttnam had given him just the out he wanted, but never dreamed he would get.

Negotiations were not over, however. Although Film Finances would be quickly removed from the financial front line after refunding 50 percent of the fee, Marty would still be faced with a ballooning budget upon which the studio would base any future payments. So Marty requested a "locked negative cost"—a ceiling on the amount Columbia would charge against him when calculating gross profit—and that figure was set at $10.5 million.

And so almost all those involved with *The Big Town* got exactly what they wanted. Film Finances collected a fee while extricating itself from an already over-budget film, Ben Bolt continued as director while freeing himself from the rigors of schedule and budget, and Marty Ransohoff was successful in placing a cap on his monetary base while escaping from a two-way squeeze being applied by Columbia and Film Finances.

David Puttnam, too, was happy with the resolution since it meant that he had survived yet another assault on his authority.

The only person or entity not benefiting from the arrangement was Coca-Cola. Coke was unceremoniously left with a multimillion-dollar tab.

For decades, the London-based law firm of Denton Hall and Burgin had been European counsel for Columbia Pictures. David Puttnam thought it was time for a change.

Without consulting the legal department, David dispensed with Denton Hall and retained British barristers Marriott, Harrison, Bloom and Norris to do Columbia's overseas legal work. Marriot, Harrison was a firm David knew well. After all, it was the firm he used personally.

Having been thwarted in his previous attempts to remove Warren Beatty from *Ishtar* and drop *Jagged Edge II* from development, David at last succeeded in executing a plan without being challenged by Columbia's senior management in New York. However, the shift in law firms probably went unchallenged because there were other items on David Puttnam's agenda, particularly those involving motion picture projects, which required constant vigilance.

When David greenlighted *Vice Versa*, a movie scripted by two British writers, it was not unexpected that somebody, somewhere, was not pleased. In this case, it was Victor Kaufman, chairman of Tri-Star Pictures.

The problem with *Vice Versa* lay in its plot, a comedy about a father and son who switch bodies, the father walking around with the mind of his son and vice versa. Unfortunately, Tri-Star was about to start production on a film with the identical story line, called *Like Father, Like Son.*

"Isn't it silly," Victor asked when he called David, "for both of us to be making the *same* movie?"

"Perhaps," David lectured, "but in filmmaking the story isn't everything, the *way* the story is told is everything. And Victor, I *passionately* believe in the *Vice Versa* script."

Realizing there was no way to convince David to abandon *Vice Versa,* Victor said, "Fine, David, but we are not coming out second. We plan to release *Like Father, Like Son* prior to *Vice Versa.*"

"It doesn't bother me if you come out first here," David remarked, "I don't think it makes much difference. But I would like to come out first overseas."

Was David really weighing American box office against foreign?

Victor quickly agreed.

So two movies with one plot started to roll toward the silver screen.

Despite the furor erupting over David's creative choices, the media in Los Angeles and New York continued to treat the new studio chief with kid gloves. Consequently, one of the first truly realistic articles about the budding controversy came not from either entertainment business hub, but from the city of Tea Party fame, Boston, Massachusetts.

Boston Globe writer Michael Blowen began his syndicated story with the following paragraph:

"One of the first images in producer David Puttnam's new film, 'The Mission,' is of a bearded Westerner tied to a cross by Indians and heaved into a churning river where, in several terrifying moments, he plunges to his death over the falls. Several Hollywood executives are expecting Puttnam to meet a similar fate as studio boss."

Blowen did allow that Puttnam might survive and "pull off a long shot" just as he did by "walking away with the 1981 Oscar for best picture with 'Chariots of Fire.'" But then Blowen noted that "while critics generally have praised Puttnam's work, his movies are not the chart-busting hits of the kind that tend to make a studio salivate over a producer's services" and added that the majority of David's films "trade profit for prestige."

Included in the piece was an in-depth interview. In typical David Puttnam fashion—that is, without even trying and perhaps without ever intending to do so—he managed to alienate a major star while making a point. This time it was Diane Keaton.

"We're going to try and do it a little differently. We'll make movies with Bill Forsyth and Pat O'Conner and without major stars. In a recent example, Bill had a movie at Warner Bros. with Diane Keaton. When she got shaky over some things in the script, she left and Warner Bros. dropped it. Now he's shooting it for us with Christine Lahti—an actress, I might add, who should have been in it in the first place."

The above statement prompted Blowen to write:

"The names like Lahti and Forsyth are not likely to send the executives of Coca-Cola, Columbia's parent company, dancing on Sunset Boulevard. They are surely not going to have Columbia run as if it were an art museum, right?"

Certainly, bottom-line-minded Herbert Allen did not envision Columbia Pictures as a factory for art films. And neither did Coke president Donald Keough. But a piece which appeared in the *Atlanta Constitution*, Coca-Cola's hometown paper, on December 15, clouded the issue for those who were trying to determine exactly what Coke management might be thinking.

Under the headline: No. 1 COCA-COLA IS FILM INDUSTRY'S TOP PROFIT-MAKER, was a story covering the appearance of Fay Vincent at a meeting with stock analysts. Since Fay was not only chairman of Columbia Pictures Industries but president of Coca-Cola's Entertainment Business Sector as well, readers had to assume that what he was saying was the gospel according to Coke.

Citing the performance of syndicated television shows *Wheel of Fortune, Facts of Life,* and *Silver Spoons,* Fay noted that overall entertainment profits were ahead by 33 percent. The executive said the Entertainment Business Sector would post operating profits of about $220,000,000 on revenue of $1.2 billion for 1986, up from $160,600,000 and $1.07 billion in 1985.

From the article, by staff writer Keith Herndon:

"Vincent . . . told stock analysts . . . that the division's [entertainment sector's] operating profits are greater than any of Coca-Cola's entertainment competitors.

" 'No one is remotely close to us in terms of earnings,' Vincent said.

"Last year, television operations accounted for almost 75 per cent of the sector's earnings, and company executives expect television to contribute an even greater percentage of earnings this year . . . however, emphasis on television production doesn't mean Coca-Cola intends to allow its movie division to languish. The company removed Guy McElwaine as head of the movie studio this past summer and replaced him with film producer David Putnam."

Putnam? One "t"? So much for the importance of Columbia Pictures and its British leader in the Deep South stronghold of a six-billion-dollar soft drink manufacturer.

The article continued with a series of quotes from Fay Vincent.

"We want higher earnings in that [film] division" Fay told the analysts, according to the *Atlanta Constitution*, "and we mean to have them."

Fay then described how he expected to squeeze those higher earnings from the motion picture arm of the Entertainment Business Sector:

"Vincent said Putnam intends to deploy a strategy of controlling overhead and avoiding major losses on individual films.

" 'The film division will produce somewhat lower-cost films,' he said, adding that attention paid to the foreign box-office will be greater.

" 'We will be making films with the taste and preferences of other countries in mind,' Vincent said."

Significantly, Fay's comments sounded like a recitation of the David Puttnam filmmaking credo.

Now Hollywood was confused. Did Coca-Cola *really* espouse David Puttnam's philosophy? Or was Fay—a former SEC attorney who had always freely admitted he knew nothing about filmmaking—merely repeating David's words by rote?

Did Coke condone Fay Vincent's remarks? Did Herbert Allen?

In the absence of an on-the-record clarification from Herbert Allen or Don Keough—which, by the way, never came—many assumed that the *Atlanta Constitution* article was tantamount to a strong endorsement of David Puttnam's filmmaking philosophy.

David Puttnam certainly felt it was.

With the attention of the Hollywood establishment now diverted toward Atlanta, Georgia, David used the welcome respite to finish putting together a slate of pictures based on his own personal tastes.

By the time David was through making deals, the Columbia Pictures commitment would total almost $300,000,000.

But there wouldn't be a dozen or so $20,000,000 pictures, which was the approximate makeup of previous Columbia slates. Instead, there would be more than two dozen films averaging under $10,000,000 each.

They are surely not going to have Columbia run as if it were an art museum, right?

Wrong.

As 1986 neared an end, screenwriter Howard Franklin began to wonder what was going on with *Someone to Watch Over Me*. Three months had passed since David Puttnam had assured him he would see rewrites of the script, but Howard had not seen a single page. Nor had Howard spoken with David since their meeting, so he placed a call to Columbia Pictures.

Later that day, Howard's phone rang and he heard a cheery greeting from a voice wrapped in a British accent.

"Hello, Howard," the voice said.

Perhaps Howard had been a bit pessimistic, but he never really expected a return phone call from David Puttnam, at least not that fast. In fact, for a moment Howard thought the caller was a hairdresser he frequented when in London.

"Why would he be calling me?" Howard wondered.

But then the voice identified itself.

"David Puttnam here. What can I do for you?"

Howard, a bit taken aback, composed himself and queried David on the status of the screenplay for *Someone to Watch Over Me*.

"Oh God!" David exclaimed. "Didn't anybody call you?"

"No. Why?"

"They've been shooting in New York for two and a half weeks."

For Howard Franklin, the experience with David Puttnam had been a bitter disappointment. Ironically, the man who kept insisting that new talent should be cultivated had just unceremoniously plowed him under.

CHAPTER

ELEVEN

In Hollywood, the Christmas season is just too long.

Since rigid union contracts specify huge salary premiums for holiday labor, the last week of the year generally is a series of nonshooting days. But with delivery dates and release schedules to be considered, those in the midst of production gnaw at their fingernails as they wait for January 1. And, since December is the month when there are few studio executives around to listen to pitches or read screenplays, the interruption is even more excruciating for the out-of-work filmmaker.

David Puttnam spent Christmas 1986 at his retreat in the English countryside. The new chairman/CEO mulled over possible projects for his first slate of movies and kept transatlantic phone lines buzzing. Plagued by anxiety and overcome with a sense of urgency, he was decidedly more preoccupied with wrapping up deals than he was with unwrapping presents.

The urgency was created by David's wholesale rejection of the Hollywood establishment. With many of Columbia's old-line suppliers of motion picture product shunted aside, there existed a need to replace them. Fast.

The anxiety was a product of David's indifference to the powerful. He knew that Hollywood, at least the most awesome segment, was aligned against him. Even with an apparent on-the-record endorsement from Fay Vincent in the *Atlanta Constitution*, David felt alone in his clash with conventional wisdom.

Thus, the slate of pictures became his obsession. Regardless of what happened to *him*, David reasoned that the slate would be his ultimate legacy.

But what should his legacy be? Certainly not commercial films. He had been too vocal in the media about his disdain for "the lowest common denominator of public taste." And what if he did make accessible movies but no one came to see them? What would be his excuse for selling out?

In this manner, the fear of failure precluded consideration of box-office potential. Subject matter, regardless of its mass appeal, became David's *sole* criterion for approving projects. Social relevance. High-minded ideals.

David Puttnam was determined not to submit to the "tyranny of the box office" or do anything that would contaminate his long-cultivated public image. After all, what would journalists think if their hero suddenly embraced Hollywood?

David had already seen the disappointment of *Los Angeles Times* reporter Jack Mathews over the Bill Cosby deal. Unaccustomed to criticism in print, David dreaded what might happen if he departed from the philosophy he had been so freely dishing out in the media.

David Puttnam *required* approval from the press. He worked very hard at obtaining it and then held onto it tenaciously. So, upon returning to Burbank early in January, the first thing he did was invite *Los Angeles Times* Arts Editor Charles Champlin to lunch. The very act itself (how many studio chiefs take reporters to lunch?) was ingratiating.

The result of the mid-day repast shared by David and Champlin was an article in which the prose sounded like it had been generated by David Puttnam's own publicity manager.

"He picks, characteristically, a small, low-budget, obscure, undiscovered ethnic restaurant where the food is marvelous but where he does not have to gaze upon or be gazed upon by other moguls or mogul seekers. The restaurant does not have a wine list, tablecloths or valet parking, only food and quiet.

"David Puttnam has broken more commandments of Hollywood executive decorum than anyone I can recall in the last quarter-century, and all of them were greatly overdue to be broken and discarded, starting with the Highly Visible Lunch."

By now, David had identified the Achilles heel of the average journalist: the fact that he was—at least economically—average.

What did newspaper reporters earn? Forty thousand? Fifty thousand? More? Less? Regardless of the precise salary, it could not accommodate a steady diet of expensive restaurants.

David's choice of restaurant, like his Audi, was a *statement*. In choosing a modest eatery and arriving in an Audi (a reporter couldn't drive around in a $160,000 Rolls-Royce either), David appeared to be on an economic scale near that of a newspaper employee. Of course, that wasn't true. David was a millionaire with a seven-figure salary.

The balance of Champlin's article provided the Hollywood establishment with what they perceived as strong evidence that David was a mass of contradictions.

First Champlin wrote:

"He is being handsomely paid by the Coca-Cola folks to run their Columbia operation. '*Very* handsomely,' he says with a faint smile, as if it were amusing but not crucial."

And then, later in the story, David was quoted as stating:

"When I lift my eyebrows about the asking prices [of stars, producers, directors, etc.], I'm told, very cynically indeed, 'It's the American way.' The American way? To price yourself out of the game?"

The dichotomy was duly noted. David could smile at his own compensation while, at the same time, begrudge the creative community a like reward.

"In Puttnam's view," Champlin went on, "being upfront about his salary and his term lets him make deals with no hidden agendas, no exchange of golden back-scratchers . . ."

Yet, a few paragraphs later—when Champlin reported on the progress of David's slate of pictures—many films gave the opposite impression.

"Meanwhile, Puttnam has picked up 'Housekeeping,' a new film by Bill Forsyth. . . . He is also acquiring 'Stars & Bars' by Pat O'Conner, who did the excellent drama, 'Cal.' . . . Ridley Scott is doing 'Someone to Watch Over Me' for the studio."

With a preponderance of David Puttnam associates signing deals at Columbia, it sure looked like "cronyism" to Hollywood observers.

Next, David seemed to provide an alibi for the eventuality that these films might not perform up to Hollywood box-office standards.

" 'But the point, the extremely significant point,' Puttnam says, 'is that what I earn will be exactly the same whether I deliver five more "Ghostbusters" (which is to say huge money-spinners) or fall flat on my face. In other words, I am allowed to fail.' "

Hollywood chuckled as David hung on his own verbal petard. But in New York, the reaction to another part of the article was far less giddy.

"If the Coca-Cola brass does ask for the extension, 'I will walk out of here on March 31, 1990.' That is the date he has circled in red on his mental calendar; he insists there will be no re-enlistment."

Immediately after reading the article, Fay Vincent placed a call to David Puttnam.

"David, I can't believe what you said about the three-year term."

"It's true," David retorted, "You know that."

"Yes, I know. But I never thought you'd talk about it publicly. David, I am very, very upset."

Fay Vincent had always been David Puttnam's anchor within the Coca-Cola hierarchy. But Fay realized that the water was getting too deep to keep his outspoken employee from drifting onto the jagged political reef which lay ahead.

David, too, came to a few realizations. He had alienated Hollywood. And he had just lost the support of Fay Vincent.

All he had left were his movies, his legacy.

And the media.

The first staff change at Columbia Pictures in the new year was one which pleasantly surprised Hollywood. A month before, David Puttnam had relieved John Fiedler of his duties as president of worldwide production. Fiedler had been one of a dwindling number of employees at the studio who had been brought in by David's predecessor, Guy McElwaine. Most of Guy's charges had long since departed.

The post of *worldwide* production president is a powerful one. The job requires day-to-day contact with filmmakers who have projects at a studio, so maintaining a relationship with that individual is helpful to producers.

Many in Hollywood feared that David would follow his past hiring practice and bring in a Briton to fill the vacancy created by Fiedler's exit. He did not. Instead, David promoted from within Columbia, upping executive vice president of worldwide production Fred Bernstein to president.

An entertainment business lawyer, Fred Bernstein began his movie industry career as a business affairs vice president at Polygram Pictures. He moved to Time-Life Films as head of business affairs before joining Columbia Pictures in 1983 as senior vice president, business affairs.

In Fred Bernstein, the creative community saw a friend. Someone who had been around town for a while and knew the power structure. Knew who was who. Knew the score.

But just as the key players of the Hollywood establishment were raising glasses to salute Bernstein's appointment, the new production president granted an interview to *The Hollywood Reporter* and spoiled the celebration.

"What we are going to be," Bernstein asserted, "is pro-active rather than reactive to the kinds of movies we are going to be distributing. We hope to take a very active role in all the early phases, rather than waiting for assembled packages to be dropped in our laps."

There was that word again. "Package." And here was another threat to the extinction of the concept. In fact, Bernstein's statement was nothing more than a paraphrase of the ideas advanced by his British boss.

It appeared that Fred Bernstein hadn't climbed the corporate ladder without picking up a few lessons in political savvy. In his new position, Fred was ready to implement the Puttnam party line.

On January 22, Hollywood learned something new about David Puttnam. They found out that the Columbia chief was more than willing to lend his time to a worthy cause.

David announced he would serve as honorary chairman of the American Cinematheque's second annual Moving Picture Ball to be held in February. The $250-a-ticket event was a benefit for the American Cinematheque and was given in honor of an individual in the entertainment industry who made a major contribution to the artistry of film. The 1987 recipient was Bette Midler.

From a public relations standpoint, David's offer to chair the gala could not have been more effective. The media reserved an inordinate amount of space to herald the selflessness of David Puttnam.

During the coming months, gestures like these served to elevate David to the status of saint in the eyes of entertainment business journalists.

As ardently as the media embraced David and his philosophy, the press had a rival in the affection department. Academia.

On February 16, the Los Angeles Film Teachers Association presented the British producer-turned-studio-chief with the Jean Renoir Humanitarian Award.

The award was particularly gratifying to David, an accredited film professor himself. David had periodically taught at Robert Redford's Sundance Institute and played an active part in many other educational programs devoted to cinema.

The honor bestowed on David Puttnam further enhanced an image which was already bigger than life. As usual, the media loved it. And, as usual, David found a way to take a swipe at Hollywood while basking in media adoration.

"There is in this room more love of film," David orated, "than on all the lots in Hollywood."

And Roland Joffe, director of *The Killing Fields*, was on hand to pour salt in the wound.

"David will see a way," Joffe shouted above swelling applause, "to change this town back to the warm, stylish cinema. It will once again become a place where we can hope and dream."

Between chairing benefits and accepting awards, David filled in two more pieces of his motion picture slate with *School Daze* and *The Big Easy*.

School Daze, by black filmmaker Spike Lee, had been developed by Island Pictures with an intended budget of $4,000,000. But a final analysis revealed that *School Daze* would cost closer to $5,000,000, an amount unacceptable to Island.

When Island decided not to proceed with the $5,000,000 *School Daze*, David stepped in.

The announcement of the deal generated the ironically misleading headline in *Variety*: 'DAZE' TOO RICH FOR ISLAND BUT OK AT COLUMBIA.

Actually, what was "too rich" for Island was "low-budget" for Columbia.

"Is Columbia Pictures on a bargain hunt?" Hollywood wanted to know.

If the budget of *School Daze* made David happy, the amount Columbia Pictures paid for *The Big Easy* must have made him ecstatic. *The Big Easy* cost the studio absolutely nothing to acquire. Zero dollars.

The picture found its way to Columbia when New Century/Vista Films relinquished its rights to distribute it for Kings Road Entertainment, the film's producer.

Under the new Columbia Pictures arrangement, Kings Road bore the entire production cost while Columbia agreed to pay at least $4,000,000 for marketing expense, known as "prints and advertising," or P&A.

Prints—the reels of film sent to theaters—cost about $1,200 each. Advertising, of course, varies with the media utilized and the duration or size of the ad.

Since P&A is an expense the studio must bear for every film it acquires, agreeing to pay for P&A was of no financial consequence. So David's deal was certainly advantageous on the cost side. But, as the old saying goes: "You get what you pay for." And there *was* a catch to *The Big Easy*.

For its outlay of zero dollars, Columbia received the right to United States theatrical distribution only. There would be no ancillary markets. No foreign. No video. No cable. No television.

Although David saved Columbia money, the studio didn't need to *save* money. It needed to *make* money.

It was a very important point. One that David Puttnam continued to miss.

Ghostbusters had become a synonym for "successful motion picture," and even David Puttnam himself had often used the title in that manner. Thus, the mounting of the sequel—*Ghostbusters II*—was a matter of heavy consequence to Columbia Pictures.

Former Columbia chief Frank Price, who had developed the original, put the *Ghostbusters* sequel into perspective when he told Herbert Allen: "It's like a huge check sitting in a drawer, waiting to be cashed."

Indeed, *Ghostbusters* was the most likely candidate for a sequel to come along in years. *Ghostbusters II* promised to duplicate the $220,000,000 plus in box office garnered by the original.

But David Puttnam, as Hollywood now knew, did not "like"

sequels. He didn't even like *Ghostbusters*, for that matter.

Notwithstanding David Puttnam's aversion to sequels, a major sticking point in mounting *Ghostbusters II* was Bill Murray's salary. Although negotiations had not reached the point at which a dollar amount was specified, Murray at the time commanded fees in excess of $5,000,000 a picture. David Puttnam wanted Bill to take more on the "back end," or profit side, and less on the "front end" or cost side.

Here again, David Puttnam was off the mark as far as Hollywood was concerned. If *Ghostbusters II* did anything near the box office of the original, a $5,000,000 salary would be cheap at twice the price. So why would David Puttnam be willing to give up profits in return for a couple of million dollars chopped off Murray's initial advance?

On the other side of the coin, why should Bill Murray assume any risk? After all, a few days before David Puttnam had told the *Los Angeles Times* that he was being paid "*very* handsomely" and added that his salary was not tied in any way to film grosses. ". . . I will earn exactly the same whether I deliver five more 'Ghostbusters' or fall flat on my face . . ."

Yet David expected Bill Murray to link his compensation to the eventual success of *Ghostbusters II* even though he had not structured his own employment agreement based on that criterion.

Thus, the "check waiting to be cashed" remained in the drawer as *Ghostbusters II* seemed doomed to remain on the negotiation table, bouncing back and forth like a very expensive Ping-Pong ball.

In the midst of this bizarre debate, David Puttnam cruised across the mountain from Burbank to act as the featured speaker at a British Chamber of Commerce luncheon being held at the Beverly Hills Hotel.

Before David agreed to address the group of fellow Britons, he made on incredible demand—incredible for David Puttnam, that is.

No press.

No press? The darling of the media *banning* reporters?

Understandably, Herbert Allen and Fay Vincent found great solace in David's condition. Maybe their new chairman/CEO was coming to his senses after all and finally realizing the damage that uncontrolled media exposure could inflict. Maybe David had at last come to understand the value of discretion as it pertained to public discussion of sensitive and controversial issues.

David Puttnam approached the podium to an explosion of applause.

"Before I begin, I want your cooperation on one matter. Everything I say today is off-the-record. There are no reporters here for a reason. I want to be totally uninhibited in my remarks. So, if there is anyone here who cannot accommodate my condition of confidentiality, I'd like to invite them to leave."

A hush fell over the room. With a set-up like that, *no one* was about to go anywhere.

One of the members of the audience was a young Los Angeles attorney named Tom Hansen. At the time, Hansen was a law partner with David Nochimson, an entertainment lawyer of prominence in general and of importance to Columbia Pictures in particular. Nochimson listed among his clients *Ghostbusters* star Bill Murray.

Although Tom Hansen was not British, he had been invited to attend the luncheon as a guest of a British attorney with whom he had a working relationship. Tom had been looking forward to the event with an itching curiosity. He knew that his law partner was having great difficulty in the *Ghostbusters* negotiations and he had heard many "colorful" descriptions of David Puttnam. So Tom was glad to have an opportunity to draw his own conclusions about the British producer-turned-studio-chief.

Tom Hansen regarded David's preamble regarding confidentiality as an odd opening, nothing more. And he felt that staying at the luncheon certainly did not constitute a condescension to David's request.

Having titillated interest in what he was about to say, David delivered a most innocuous address of recycled Puttnamisms. Hollywood was this, Hollywood was that. People in Hollywood were greedy. People in Hollywood had no taste.

So what? The audience had heard it all before.

Following his speech, David opened the floor to a question-and-answer exercise.

At first there were more observations than questions.

"David, I think what you're trying to do is *wonderful!*"

Applause.

"David, you're absolutely right about Hollywood!"

More applause.

"David, Hollywood has sorely needed someone like you to come along!"

Thunderous applause.

Next, a few questions, all of which David fielded with his usual flair and eloquence. And then . . .

"You've been very outspoken in your criticism of how highly paid many Hollywood stars are," an attendee noted. "Could you comment on that?"

"As you all know," David responded, "big upfront paydays are a drain on the financial resources of our industry . . ."

An ovation interrupted for a moment.

". . . especially since that outflow of money never comes back to the industry in a way that is beneficial. There are some film-makers—like Robert Redford—who do put back some of what they take out. Bob's Sundance Institute helps young filmmakers and that is a noble cause. After all, *people* are an important resource in the motion picture business. We who have done well owe something to those talented individuals who are struggling to be acknowledged . . ."

More appreciation from clapping hands.

". . . so it bothers me that many stars take the money and run, so to speak. You don't see people—for example Bill Murray—putting back any dollars made from *Ghostbusters*."

Hansen couldn't believe his ears. Wait until his partner David Nochimson heard this. Hell, wait until Bill Murray heard this!

David Nochimson frowned.

"He said what?!"

That night, Tom Hansen received a telephone call at home and related the story once again, this time to Bill Murray's agent, CAA president Mike Ovitz. Mike asked Tom to repeat *exactly* what David had said and to describe the precise circumstances under which the statement had been made.

"It wasn't part of his prepared remarks," Hansen explained, "and it didn't seem intended as an attack."

The following day, the "Bill Murray comment" was the hottest topic in Hollywood. Had he said it? Hadn't he said it?

"I *never* said it," David assured an exasperated Fay Vincent. "I categorically deny it. It is utterly untrue!"

"Well, okay, David. I believe you," Fay sighed. "But I really wish you would curtail all this public speaking and all these press interviews."

Two days later, the *New York Post* carried an item in its "Page Six" section—a section devoted to "inside" information about the rich and famous—and the Bill Murray comment was suddenly a "published report."

The next day, *The Wall Street Journal* printed a different account of David's speech. British attorney Nigel Sinclair, who had hosted the Chamber of Commerce affair, had been interviewed.

Sinclair classified the story as "absolute balderdash."

One of the readers of *The Wall Street Journal* that day was Herbert Allen. Another was Ray Stark.

During one of their daily phone calls, Ray asked Herbert in his best British accent:

"What does *balderdash* mean? Does that mean he said it or not?"

Herbert enjoyed a laugh over Ray's question, but he was painfully aware that the Bill Murray controversy was no laughing matter.

"Why doesn't David keep his mind open," Ray added, "and his mouth shut?"

In an attempt to defuse a situation that was rapidly getting out of control, David fired off a letter of denial to Bill Murray. But Bill Murray never did answer David Puttnam's letter and *Ghostbusters* became an apparition on the upcoming Columbia Pictures slate of films.

In the meantime, the 1987 Oscar nominations were announced. *The Mission*, with its box-office total of just $16,000,000, received a nod in seven categories, including Best Picture.

So it was that David Puttnam started off 1987 with his two most constant companions—personal glory and controversy—marching along beside him.

CHAPTER

TWELVE

If David Puttnam thought he had experienced adversity since disembarking in Burbank the previous autumn, he was sadly mistaken. He was about to encounter a two-hundred-year-old German baron named Karl Friedrich Hieronymus von Munchausen.

Baron Munchausen, for short.

And the convoluted story of the Baron would make the past six months look like a picnic.

Working within a hostile Hollywood environment—and under constant surveillance from New York and Atlanta—David quietly continued to compile his slate of films. Most deals were not announced by the Columbia publicity department, since David preferred to present the *entire* slate to the media at one time instead of issuing a series of press releases regarding individual motion pictures.

For one thing, David wanted the impact which would result from a weighty announcement chronicling two dozen films. For another, David was weary of the controversy which erupted every time he approved a project.

One movie, however, did not escape the attention of the media. Entitled *The Adventures of Baron Munchausen*, the film sparked a most incredible chain of events.

On March 10, *The Hollywood Reporter* noted that the project had landed at Columbia.

"Columbia Pictures is securing world rights to Terry Gilliam's $25 million 'The Adventures of Baron Munchausen' feature, *The Hollywood Reporter* has learned. . . . The deal was signed . . . between Columbia and 'Munchausen' executive producers Jake Eberts and Thomas Schuly and director Terry Gilliam. . . . The epic fantasy is likely to be the most expensive on Columbia chairman and CEO David Puttnam's first slate—unless problems with 'Ghostbusters II' are resolved in the near future."

David was annoyed at the story. If there was one film on his upcoming slate that he didn't want "leaked," it was *The Adventures of Baron Munchausen*. David felt, and he was right, that the project would raise too many questions.

Questions like:

Jake Eberts? Puttnam's old friend and former business associate? And by the way, isn't this his *second* film at Columbia, *Hope and Glory* being the first?

Twenty-five million dollars? What about Puttnam's stated preference for *low*-budget pictures?

And what about this Baron Munchausen? Who the hell is Baron Munchausen anyway?

Most of the questions were rhetorical, but one cried out for a response.

Who, indeed, *was* Baron Munchausen. And why was David Puttnam spending $25,000,000 to tell his story?

Baron Munchausen, dubbed "the greatest liar of all time," was a real-life character from eighteenth-century German history who had passed into folklore via his collection of outrageous tall tales about his travels.

Was this a character upon which to base a $25,000,000 movie? Jake Eberts thought so, as did Thomas Schuly and Terry Gilliam.

Unfortunately, so did Allan Buckhantz. And therein was a major problem, especially since Buckhantz claimed to be the rights holder to the story of the Baron.

By himself, Allan Buckhantz might not have been a consequential foe versus the likes of a corporation the size of Columbia Pictures. But Buckhantz had a business partner far bigger than Columbia could ever hope to be.

Buckhantz's partner was the West German government.

A Lithuanian concentration camp survivor, Buckhantz worked as a producer with Studio Hamburg—Germany's largest movie/

television production facility—before migrating to Hollywood in the early sixties. After a stint as a television producer, Buckhantz set up shop as a motion picture rights specialist and licenser.

Among the many titles controlled by Buckhantz were those in the UFA catalogue. And, among the many titles in the UFA catalogue was a 1942 motion picture called *Münchhausen*.

UFA (Universum Film Aktien Gesellschaft) was established in 1917 when several German film studios were combined into one large production entity. The German government assumed ownership of UFA in 1937 and used its facilities to produce Nazi propaganda. Despite the heavy hand of the Third Reich, UFA managed to generate entertaining movies that were not pointedly political, including *Münchhausen*, considered a masterpiece of special effects at that time.

After the war, the West German government established Transit Film GmbH to exploit the remake rights of the roughly one thousand movies in the UFA catalogue, and set up FW Murnau Stiftung, a foundation charged with the preservation of the films themselves.

Buckhantz's arrangement to license UFA remakes and ancillary rights was with Transit Film GmbH, and the government entity would share in the proceeds.

The alliance worked well and, in 1982, even generated a major motion picture. Buckhantz had placed the UFA picture, *Viktor und Victoria*, with MGM. Director Blake Edwards shot a new version of the old Hitler-era film entitled *Victor/Victoria* with James Garner and Julie Andrews. The result was $10,490,000 in U.S. rentals as Buckhantz and Transit collected respectable amounts of dollars and marks respectively.

But licensing titles was not what Buckhantz really wanted to do. He really wanted to produce films in general and one specific picture in particular.

As early as 1970, the Lithuanian television producer had been trying to mount a remake of *Münchhausen*. It was the "gem" of the UFA catalogue, the story of one of Germany's most colorful historic characters.

During the next ten years, Buckhantz endeavored to develop a script worthy of the Baron. Finally, in 1980, he felt he had the right screenplay and submitted it—along with three thousand storyboard illustrations—to Twentieth Century–Fox via Martin Baum at CAA. The studio never responded.

Undaunted, Buckhantz refined the script and began putting together independent financing.

Because Baron Munchausen is as well known in Germany as Santa Claus is in the United States, Buckhantz naturally sought money from German sources. By early 1984, he boasted that he had $20,000,000 pledged to the project.

However, much to his horror, Buckhantz awakened one morning to discover a *Daily Variety* article which proclaimed that Terry Gilliam would direct *The Adventures of Baron Munchausen* for Twentieth Century–Fox.

Reacting to the announcement, Buckhantz's attorney Stanley Caidin fired a letter off to Twentieth Century–Fox vice president of business affairs Jerome Sussman.

"As you are aware," Caidin wrote, "Mr. Buckhantz heretofore acquired exclusive worldwide re-make rights to the internationally recognized original UFA feature film based on the character and exploits of Baron Munchausen, released under the title, MUNCHAUSEN."

Caidin then referred to Buckhantz's 1980 submission to Twentieth:

"Mr. Buckhantz has heretofore delivered to you for review, partial documentation and historical background with respect to his acquisition of these rights and the extensive preliminary development work which he has undertaken and in which he has been engaged for the past 15 years. . . . He has employed the services of artists to create a series of full color drawings numbering in excess of 3,000, as a production design story-board."

And then Caidin couched the threat of a potential damage suit in his prose:

"In addition to the creative aspects involved in the development of the property, Mr. Buckhantz has been fully involved in undertaking to arrange financing of the film. . . . At the time of this development [Gilliam's deal with Twentieth Century–Fox], the parties had reached agreement and had intended to proceed with production of the film, based upon an approved budget of just under $20,000,000.

"The financing was available, had been committed, and the documentation was being drafted at the very moment of the announcement in Variety. As a result of the foregoing, the parties deferred signing of the financing documents. The matter has been placed on hold pending further developments."

Director Terry Gilliam insisted that his film would not utilize any information in the 1942 UFA picture and further asserted that the story of the Baron was public domain and therefore not subject to any copyright claim.

Apparently it was Caidin, not Gilliam, who made his point. The matter was settled abruptly when Twentieth opted not to continue with the development of *The Adventures of Baron Munchausen*.

Allan Buckhantz celebrated what he considered to be a victory and submitted a new *Munchausen* package to Columbia Pictures later that year. Again there was no response.

And again, in 1986, Allan Buckhantz encountered Terry Gilliam.

Word reached Buckhantz that new Columbia Pictures chairman/CEO David Puttnam was on the verge of greenlighting the Gilliam *Munchausen* project which was originally at Twentieth Century–Fox. This time, in addition to communicating with the studio, attorney Stanley Caidin corresponded directly with the man who had become the film's executive producer, Jake Eberts.

"Please be advised," Caidin opened his letter to Eberts of December 8, "that we are the United States counsel for Transit Film GmbH (hereinafter referred to as 'Transit') a corporation established and owned by the Federal Republic of Germany."

After outlining his client's rights in *Munchausen*, Caidin noted: "Any remake of the film undertaken by you, or anyone acting through you or under your authority, will be actionable."

And Caidin closed with: "Please be guided accordingly."

Yet Gilliam and Eberts persisted in their assertion that, although they recognized the sanctity of the 1942 UFA motion picture, the many existing accounts of the adventures of Baron Munchausen had long since passed into the public domain.

Indeed, the adventures of Baron Munchausen have been a favorite subject of filmmakers since the early 1900s. Besides the UFA film, the list of Munchausen movies includes *Baron Munchausen* (France, 1909), *The Hallucinations of Baron Munchausen* (France, 1911), *The Adventures of Baron Munchausen* (Italy, 1914), *The New Adventures of Baron Munchausen* (England, 1915), *The Adventures of Baron Munchausen* (England, 1927), *The Adventures of Baron Munchausen* (Canada, 1947), *Baron Munchausen* (Canada, 1948), *Munchausen in Africa* (Germany, 1958), and *Baron Munchausen* (Czechoslovakia, 1962).

Caidin continued his crusade to protect what he perceived as his client's rights in *Munchausen* the film and Munchausen the character, becoming totally immersed in the case. But that was not good enough for Allan Buckhantz.

Over Caidin's objections, Buckhantz began a barrage of letters to everyone from David Puttnam to Donald Keough. They were long, rambling communiqués, full of capitalized and underlined words, exclamation points and parenthetical observations.

When David Puttnam first saw one of Buckhantz's poison-pen letters he jumped from his seat and called David Picker and Fred Bernstein into his office.

"I have to wonder," David began, "whether or not we should get involved with this *Munchausen* mess."

Bernstein and Picker objected to David's sudden aversion to the project. They argued. And cajoled. And won.

"Okay, then," David allowed. "But before I make a final decision, I want this gone over by our legal department. And I want a damn good errors-and-omissions carrier. And an airtight completion bond."

An errors-and-omissions policy served a similar purpose to the completion bond in that both shielded a studio from open-ended liability. While the completion bond protected against budget overages, an errors-and-omissions insurance policy covered possible lawsuits regarding underlying property rights.

Columbia's legal department studied the *Munchausen* case and—in the meantime—more letters from Allan Buckhantz poured into Columbia Plaza East in Burbank and Coca-Cola headquarters in Atlanta.

Then, on March 10, *The Hollywood Reporter* story appeared.

As Allan Buckhantz compiled what he termed "exhibits" for the lawsuit he vowed he would serve upon Columbia Pictures if the studio actually began production of *Munchausen*, he received a letter from Ron Jacobi, senior vice president of legal affairs for Columbia Pictures.

March 12, 1987

Re: *"The Adventures Of Baron Munchausen"*

Dear Mr. Buckhantz:

We are in receipt of your recent communication concerning the above-captioned film project. Please be advised that Columbia Pictures is not a party to any agreement concerning this project. Please also be advised that we will not undertake any such project until

after we have investigated the rights involved and have determined
that we are free to do so without violation of the rights of any person.

Allan Buckhantz was stunned. Two days *after* a published report that Columbia had approved a Terry Gilliam–directed *Munchausen,* he received a written denial from a Columbia vice
president stating that the studio had no involvement in the picture.

David Puttnam paced in his office as a stream of phone calls
regarding *Munchausen* were duly recorded by his secretary. Most
were from reporters. Was *Munchausen* at Columbia or wasn't it?
That was the burning question of the day.

Of more consequence, a telex from Germany lay on David's desk.
It was from Karl A. Woerner, managing director of Transit Film
GmbH. Essentially, Woerner had wired David to inform him that
Allan Buckhantz was indeed representing the interests of the West
German government as they pertained to *The Adventures of Baron
Munchausen.*

First David had brought the wrath of Hollywood down around
him and now it appeared he had stirred up an ally of the United
States.

David shook his head and walked to the window. Across the
parking lot he spotted big block letters that spelled: RASTAR PRO-
DUCTIONS. It seemed that everywhere that David looked he saw
enemies.

It was dusk, almost dark, yet an eerie glow lit the rows of movie-
set facades which spread out around Columbia Plaza East. In fact,
it looked just like a horror movie outside on the back lot.

"Maybe the spirit of Baron Munchausen is haunting this deal,"
David mused.

But if the eighteenth-century ghost of Karl Friedrich Hieronymus von Munchausen really was wreaking havoc in twentieth-
century Burbank, the worst part about the whole thing was that
David couldn't even call on *Ghostbusters* to exorcise the increasingly dangerous apparition.

With one $25,000,000 project in the throes of insanity, David
thought about the other $25,000,000 picture which was becoming
a cause célèbre in Hollywood: *Ghostbusters II.* David was aware

of how anxious Coca-Cola was to utilize the asset and reasoned that he had better come to terms with the prospect of doing a sequel.

But how?

David wasn't about to soften his stand regarding Bill Murray's compensation because doing that would send contrary signals to his supporters and to the media. And it would certainly undermine his well-honed image.

What could he do?

Suddenly, an idea struck him that seemed to solve all problems at once. It was a brilliant stroke, David thought, a solution born of pure genius.

So when Bob Robinson, Columbia's executive vice president of worldwide business affairs, walked into David's office for a meeting, he found a smiling David Puttnam sitting behind his desk.

"Bob," David exclaimed, "I've got it! I've hit upon a way to get around the Bill Murray problem."

Since he had come in to confer with David on an entirely different matter, the reference to Bill Murray caught Robinson by surprise.

"What do you mean?"

"*Ghostbusters!*" David laughed. "I know what to do. I know how to solve this whole thing."

Bob was skeptical. "How, David?"

"With *black* ghostbusters," David exclaimed. "Bill Cosby in the lead and two other black ghostbusters! It's perfect. I launch the sequel *and* put Cosby to work on a second Columbia project."

David was enormously pleased with himself.

"So, Bob, what do you think?"

Bob Robinson wasn't sure how to respond. Here was the chairman/CEO of the studio absolutely exuberant about a motion picture. How could a business affairs staff member refute the idea?

While *Ghostbusters* had certainly been a major point of contention since David became chairman/CEO, it was just one of many issues which served to chip away at the morale inside Columbia Pictures. Bob Robinson had often described David's arrival at the studio as a "state of near euphoria," but now the word "disenchantment" seemed more appropriate. For the past several weeks, Bob had watched a dichotomy of attitudes develop between two distinct subsets of Columbia executives: those whom David had recently brought on board, and those who were in place at the studio when David took over.

To Bob Robinson, those executives who "bought David's program and philosophy" appeared to be operating in an intoxicating world of giddy approval. On the other hand, those executives whom Bob considered to be "more perceptive and knowledgeable" had begun to question the type of projects being put into development and production at the studio while other "assets" like *Ghostbusters II*, *Karate Kid III*, and *Jagged Edge II* were being ignored.

Now, David Puttnam had decided to exploit at least one of those assets: *Ghostbusters II*.

"It sounds interesting," Bob obliged.

"You think so? Really? You really think so?" David grinned.

Bob Robinson nodded but he knew that the concept was not exactly what Coca-Cola had in mind when they pressed for a sequel to the most successful film in Columbia Pictures' history.

On March 11, David Puttnam issued a proclamation which served to enhance his already godlike stature among the have-nots of the movie business. He had persuaded The Coca-Cola Company to bring its vast resources to bear on an effort to improve the hapless condition of undiscovered talent.

In Hollywood, of course, *everyone* has talent. In almost all cases, however, it is "undiscovered" talent. And all it needs is a "break."

David Puttnam was offering to provide that break. He had conceived and fostered a means by which aspiring directors could be groomed for such an exacting profession at the expense of Coca-Cola. It was dubbed the Discovery Program.

The trades played the news of the Discovery Program to the hilt. *Variety* obliged with a screaming headline and a reverent story: COKE WILL FUND PROGRAM FOR DEBUTING DIRECTORS.

"The Entertainment Business Sector of Coca-Cola, at the instigation of Columbia Pictures chairman David Puttnam, is funding a Discovery Program to enable professionals in other motion picture crafts to receive hands-on training as film directors."

Who could argue with such a noble statement of purpose? And oh what hope the Discovery Program would breathe into the breasts of the Hollywood huddled masses!

But the operative phrase in the opening paragraph was ". . .

at the instigation of Columbia Pictures Chairman David Puttnam . . ." Here was a man who put Coke's money where *his* mouth
was. A producer-turned-studio-chief who had not forgotten about
the struggling would-be filmmaker. Indeed, considering the reaction from the rank and file, David Puttnam was nothing less than
a messiah.

In fact, if a popular vote were held in Hollywood at that moment, David Puttnam would have been elected by a landslide.

But Hollywood does not operate on the principle of a popular
vote; it allows an electoral college to appoint the powerful, and
the delegates are Ray Stark, Mike Ovitz, Warren Beatty, and so
forth.

So the announcement of the Discovery Program did nothing to
close the gap between David and his Hollywood counterparts. If
anything, it widened it. Not that Hollywood had anything against
coming to the aid of fledgling talent, rather there were priorities
to be dealt with. David was chairman/CEO of a public company.
He wasn't supposed to be a philanthropist.

"What's he doing running around playing mentor," most key
players wanted to know, "when he still hasn't gotten back to me
on my screenplay?"

Immediately after founding the Discovery Program, David became involved in an equally worthwhile effort, yet one which was
no more beneficial to the Hollywood establishment.

Again *Variety* spread the word: ACCOMPLISHMENTS OF ENTERTAIN-
MENT SUMMIT HERALDED.

"The possibility of several Soviet-American joint ventures as
well as hopes for an exchange of talent were among the accomplishments heralded at a closing press conference yesterday by
the Entertainment Summit as the delegation of Soviet filmmakers concluded six days of meetings with industry representatives
in Los Angeles."

The article detailed the Soviet interest in aligning its filmmaking community with Hollywood. David Puttnam was the *only*
Hollywood studio chief quoted.

"Indicating that he would 'do everything to further the ends of
the Summit,' Columbia chairman and chief executive officer David
Puttnam said that specifically his company was 'actively pursuing one or two joint ventures' with the Soviets."

It was also reported that David planned to visit Moscow in the near future.

The refrain from Hollywood was identical to the one challenging David's role in the Discovery Program with the exception of one word: diplomat.

"What's he doing running around playing diplomat when he still hasn't gotten back to me on my screenplay?"

As Hollywood buzzed about mentor/diplomat David Puttnam, news of the fate of Marty Ransohoff's *Switching Channels* swept across town.

"CHANNELS" USES COLUMBIA'S SIDE DOOR, *Variety* declared, continuing with: "A Martin Ransohoff feature put into turnaround by David Puttnam shortly after he took over as chairman of Columbia Pictures is being reactivated by the Entertainment Business Sector of Col [*Variety* abbreviation for Columbia] parent Coca-Cola. . . . Puttnam could not be reached for comment."

Suddenly, the most accessible studio head in town was nowhere to be found. Yet, what could he have said?

It was by far David Puttnam's most embarrassing moment. And it gave the Hollywood establishment reason to feel vindicated in its belief that the outspoken British producer was ill-suited for the job of studio chief.

CHAPTER THIRTEEN

For David Puttnam, the month of March had come in like a lion and was going out like a lion. But he felt that the worst was finally over.

After weeks of last-minute negotiations in which some films were added and some were dropped, he was almost ready to unveil his new slate of pictures. He would be relieved to get that major event behind him and happy to focus Hollywood's attention on a lineup of movies while concentrating his own efforts on getting them made.

There was, however, one bit of nasty business which needed to be dealt with first: the termination of several development deals currently existing at the studio.

If David had learned nothing else during his seven months at the helm of Columbia Pictures, he had learned to read the scorecard. By now he realized that there was a group of favored filmmakers in Hollywood and doing or saying anything remotely offensive to this group was considered heresy.

Columbia had a host of members of this elite clique signed to production arrangements. But with his slate now complete, David had no room for "high-priced outside producers." As a result, some of Hollywood's most established filmmakers were in for a major surprise: a pink slip.

Certainly David knew that this would create a world-class furor, so he decided not to announce the terminations. He would just do it. Quietly. After all, the last thing he wanted was to have his new slate preceded by another controversy.

It almost worked. In fact, it would have worked except for the fact that the exit from Columbia by director Norman Jewison was already the hottest rumor in town.

Feeling he had no other choice, David spoke to *Variety* about Jewison's status at the studio.

"Columbia Pictures chairman David Puttnam yesterday confirmed," *Variety* reported, "that Norman Jewison is one of several producers whose multi-feature deals with the studio were permitted to expire before all the promised product could be delivered.

"A report that Jewison was severing his ties with Columbia over dissatisfaction with footdragging on his projects was disputed by Puttman. Puttnam said it was not Jewison who took the initiative, but that his pact expired Feb. 28. Puttnam said he did not elect to renew it, along with other similar arrangements that ran out.

"It is understood that Jewison and others fell casualty to the new Puttnam doctrine of avoiding costly outside commitments in favor of a new emphasis on more economical in-house production."

Although pressed for details on the other filmmakers whose services would no longer be required at Columbia, David wisely demurred. But most observers thought David had done enough damage even without further identifying the roster of rejects.

Clearly, David was not going to allow Norman Jewison to salvage his dignity by saying he "left" Columbia Pictures. The chairman/CEO made sure there was no mistake about the fact that the director was turned away from the studio gate, rather than it being the other way around.

The consensus in Hollywood was that it seemed a needless distinction to make, serving no purpose other than to further antagonize an already hostile creative community.

And the "costly outside commitments" versus "economical in-house production" comparison obviously did not endear David to the Hollywood establishment.

It became more than evident that some of the most recognized names in Hollywood would not be making films for Columbia Pictures.

Certainly not Ray Stark. Or Martin Ransohoff.

And now, of course, Norman Jewison.

But Hollywood did get a laugh out of the article, despite its serious implications.

The date *Variety* told the entertainment world that David Puttnam would drop Norman Jewison from the Columbia production rolls was appropriate, many chuckled.

April Fool's day.

The following morning, April 2, David Puttnam stood before a mob of curious reporters and outlined a diverse package of twenty-five motion pictures which would keep Columbia's production and distribution divisions fully occupied over the next two years. Thirteen films had been previously announced—or ferreted out by the media—and twelve were brand new. In addition to the core of twenty-five, a few surprise films were hinted at, and one—which had been previously announced—was *not* on the schedule.

At David's side were Columbia president David Picker, president of worldwide production Fred Bernstein, executive vice president of production Michael Nathanson, and Thomas Rothman, executive vice president and assistant to the president.

"The films I am about to announce," David began, "are films we all can be proud of. The filmmakers involved in bringing these pictures to Columbia are as responsible, diligent, and as perfectionistic as we are."

David paused as reporters scribbled away in their notebooks.

"What's important," David continued, "is that we're trying to put together a company which mirrors what filmmakers want."

David Picker interjected: "Hopefully, filmmakers who share our enormous passion for movie-making will discover that there is a home for their passion."

And David Puttnam added: "I want to be a company that understands filmmakers' needs. A company that first and foremost understands that filmmakers are human beings."

Reporters, of course, have a "creative" rather than "business" orientation, so the two Davids were not challenged when they talked about "what filmmakers want" as opposed to what stockholders might expect. It would be distinctions like this which would continue to distance David Puttnam from the Hollywood guard.

David next addressed the cost aspect of his slate and explained how the average production budget had been kept to a minimum because of his emphasis on in-house development and his aversion to high fees. He pointed out that this average was $10.7 million, $4,000,000 less than the norm for previous Columbia regimes.

Then the chairman/CEO told the gathering exactly how he intended to disburse the staggering sum of $270,000,000.

The purpose of a press conference is to announce something previously unknown. It was not unusual, then, that many film titles in David Puttnam's first slate of pictures were totally unfamiliar.

However, it *was* unusual to see so many unfamiliar names.

In place of major stars and prominent Hollywood filmmakers, the cast and crew of the new Columbia Pictures lineup included a preponderance of outsiders. Many of the directors and actors tapped by David Puttnam enjoyed a respected reputation within the boundaries of their own country, but not in Hollywood.

Consequently, as David went through the list of films, most journalists, unless they were certified film buffs, seemed puzzled. Often, when a producer or director was mentioned the expression on most faces asked: "What has he done before?"

"What's he done?" is an important question in Hollywood, in that it places a project in perspective. With millions of dollars at stake, a "track record" provides evidence of the wisdom of making a production deal. A studio chief can point to past films as justification for his decision. If a movie fails at the box office, the "track record" is quickly evoked. Thus, to a studio chief, "track record" translates as "insurance." Many an executive has salvaged his career in the wake of failure because—even though a picture flopped at the theaters—the *reasoning* behind the decision to make the picture was inarguably sound.

Meanwhile, those filmmakers who did not get a green light on their own projects can say: "No wonder he got the deal. He has a *track record*."

So, familiarity is an important political concept in Hollywood. It is vital for survival of those in power and a comforting rationalization for those who walk the streets of Beverly Hills with unsold screenplays under their arms.

This convoluted idea, of course, is the essence of *Catch-22*, a hopeless situation wherein one needs to have done something of consequence in the past in order to do something similar in the future. Yet, the whole world, not just Hollywood, works in such a manner. Anyone who has applied for a job, whether that job be waitress, accountant, salesman, or plumber, and been told: "You just don't have enough experience," can attest to that fact.

David Puttnam, however, apparently made his decisions concerning the slate without regard for such conventions. He chose filmmakers using just one criterion: his own taste.

What did David Puttman's taste dictate?

To start with, almost half his slate boasted British talent.

Sylvie's Ark—originally called *Housekeeping* and destined to be renamed *Housekeeping*—would be directed by Briton Bill Forsyth. Although David had logged this film onto the Columbia schedule a few weeks before, the press conference was the first official word of its arrival at the studio.

Hope and Glory, directed by Briton John Boorman, used World War II as a backdrop.

There was *Someone to Watch Over Me*, an action/thriller from British director Ridley Scott, scheduled for an October 2 release. *Someone to Watch Over Me* would be the first film released by Columbia which had been entirely developed by David Puttnam.

Toys, the story of an ex-military type who finds himself in charge of his brother's toy company, placed Briton Iain Smith in the executive producer's chair.

The New Adventures of Pippi Longstocking would be directed by Englishman Ken Annakin, while English actor Daniel Day Lewis would headline in *Stars and Bars*, a movie being produced by David Puttnam's former partner, Sandy Lieberson. (A brief description of *Stars and Bars* sounded much like David's encounter at Coca-Cola headquarters in Atlanta: "A comedy about an Englishman sent to Georgia.")

Two British writers, Dick Clement and Ian Frenais, contributed the father/son switch farce, *Vice Versa*, and young Briton Ben Bolt had earlier been brought in to direct Marty Ransohoff's bit of 1950's Americana, *The Big Town*.

Then there was the coup de grace: *Leonard Part 6*.

David had selected British director Paul Weiland for the big-budget feature from America's favorite television personality, Bill Cosby. And he placed fellow-Briton Alan Marshall at the top of the production hierarchy, naming him executive producer of the comedic takeoff on private detectives. During the past few weeks, rumbles of discontent had emanated from the set of *Leonard Part 6* on a daily basis.

Beyond the British element, socially relevant cinema was well represented.

The Beast of War (later shortened to *The Beast*) related the drama of a Russian soldier in Afghanistan who begins to question the Soviet invasion, ultimately joining forces with the Afghans. Since the Soviet involvement in Afghanistan was not the most prevalent topic of conversation around the United States, *The Beast* seemed destined to limited appeal.

The cast of *The Beast*—all unknown—also portended a difficult time at the box office. However, it could have been a much different movie. It could have had a major star.

Actor Kevin Costner, certainly a hot name in Hollywood, approached David when he heard about *The Beast* a few months before. Although he had been mentioned by Ray Stark regarding *Revenge*, the *Revenge* project had come to a halt following David's letter to Ray in which he suggested that the film be done by other producers.

As it happened, the Afghan/Russian conflict held a great deal of importance in Costner's overall view of world politics. Besides that, Costner was a good friend of director Kevin Reynolds, who was set to direct *The Beast*. Consequently, Costner obtained a copy of the script, read it, and rushed over to Columbia Plaza East to see David Puttnam.

"I want this role," Kevin insisted, referring to the lead part of the Russian soldier.

To most studio heads, having an actor the status of Kevin Costner volunteering to do a film would be looked upon as manna from heaven. But David didn't see it that way.

"Kevin, I'm sorry, you're just not right for the role."

"What do you mean, 'not right'?"

"You're too much of a sympathetic character."

Costner responded incredulously, waving the script: "That's what you want in this screenplay. That's the way the character is written. You *want* the audience to be sympathetic."

"Yes," David replied, "but I simply can't see you in the part. All I can say is that I'm driven by my passion for films. I see *The Beast* a certain way. You're a wonderful actor, but I just don't see the role as a Kevin Costner role."

"You don't have a monopoly on passion," Costner remarked as he left.

Thus, *The Beast* went into production without Kevin Costner or any other name recognizable to the American moviegoer. Instead, names like Jason Patric and George Dzundza would fill the credits.

Next up on the Puttnam slate was *True Believer*, the story of an aging down-and-out civil rights attorney battling social injustice.

Three films inherited from the Guy McElwaine era were given tentative summer release dates: *Rites of Summer*, obviously a summer movie; *Roxanne*, a Steve Martin comedy drawing upon Cyrano de Bergerac, produced by Dan Melnick; and *Ishtar*, the $40,000,000 picture starring David's oldest enemies, Warren Beatty and Dustin Hoffman.

David had little to say about the Elaine May–directed *Ishtar* because, incredibly, he had *refused to see it.*

"It's a non-event for me," David had repeatedly told stunned executives as he continued to bypass screenings of the film.

Besides Dan Melnick with *Roxanne*, others in the Hollywood establishment had found their way onto the slate of pictures via Guy McElwaine. Taylor Hackford with *La Bamba*, a biographical cinematic treatment of the short life of fifties pop star Richie Valens. And Marty Ransohoff added a second movie to *The Big Town*, entitled *Smoke* (later renamed *Physical Evidence*).

Other films included *The Far Side*, based on the Gary Larson comic strip of that name; the previously announced pickups, *The Big Easy* and *School Daze*; *Punchline*, a drama relating the human side of standup comics, starring Tom Hanks and Sally Field; *Little Nikita*—directed by actor Richard Benjamin with Sidney Poitier in the lead—about a boy who learns his parents are Russian spies; and *Vibes*, described as a "psychic comedy" and marking the acting debut of rock singer Cyndi Lauper.

Also revealed was the signing of a three-year pact with Jane Fonda and her first effort for Columbia Pictures, a comedy called *Flawless*. Ultimately, *Flawless* would be postponed in favor of an update on the old genre of Westerns, a movie named *Old Gringo*.

David even told the congregation of reporters that two sequels were in preproduction: *Karate Kid III* and *Ghostbusters II*.

"What about the problem with Bill Murray?" someone wanted to know. David skirted the question, choosing not to reveal his plan to proceed with an all-black cast.

Conspicuous in its absence was *The Adventures of Baron Munchausen*, as legal problems over the rights issue had delayed the signing of a production deal with Jake Eberts.

There was another Jake Eberts–backed picture absent, though not conspicuously. It was called *Me and Him,* and it was the story of a talking penis. Since the media did not know of its existence and it had not been finalized at the studio, the film had not yet become a controversy.

So there it was, the long-awaited David Puttnam slate. A grab bag of plots and a mixture of Puttnam-inherited and Puttnam-approved pictures.

The most extraordinary two aspects of the slate were its low cost-per-film average and its reliance on British filmmakers. Both facts were duly noted by the media the following day.

COL OUTLINES FIRST SLATE UNDER PUTTNAM'S PRODUCTION TEAM, *The Hollywood Reporter* stated across page one. TWO-YEAR COLUMBIA LINE-UP, was *Variety*'s page-one banner, with a bank that said: AGGRE-GATE $269.5 MILLION PRICETAG ON STUDIO'S FIRST OVERALL PLAN UNDER PUTTNAM. And British-based trade magazine *Screen International* chimed in with: PUTTNAM PEPS UP COLUMBIA WITH $270M PRODUC-TION SLATE PLAN.

The *Variety* piece focused on the cost aspect of the slate, *The Hollywood Reporter* highlighted the quality and relevance of the films, and *Screen International* boasted about the "substantial amount of British talent" among the filmmakers.

Other articles, too, alluded to philosophy when analyzing the slate. Terms like "reasonable budgets," "important statements," and "classy cinema" were used to describe Columbia's lineup. Nowhere was the phrase "potential blockbuster"—or anything even akin to the phrase—employed to qualify a single picture.

Another point missed in the media coverage of David Puttnam's slate involved the modest budgets. David had declined to go into specifics on a per-picture basis, so—while the press focused on the $10,700,000 *average* per picture—no one was aware that some films, *The Big Easy,* for example, was acquired by Columbia at a cost of zero dollars, dramatically decreasing the average budget.

But the philosophical debate was now moot. David Puttnam had committed $270,000,000 of the studio's cold hard cash on a potpourri of pictures which reflected his own tastes and the tastes of his executive team. That being done, it was counterproductive to argue whether David was right or wrong. A commitment had been made, and a very large commitment at that.

All that really mattered now was whether or not Columbia Pictures was going to take a bath, or come out clean.

David, on the other hand, couldn't lose. Financially, his contract was clear. No matter what happened at the box office, he would still be paid in full.

More significantly, David Puttnam had done *exactly* what he said he would do that morning in Atlanta, Georgia, at Coke headquarters. And he had the avid support of the Hollywood populace as well as the entertainment business media firmly behind him.

Although it seemed David was taking a gamble that the American audience would embrace such an eclectic slate, it really was no gamble at all; rather it was a win-win situation for the chairman/CEO from Britain.

It was Coca-Cola that was taking a gamble. At twenty-five cents a pop on the wholesale market—about twelve cents profit—the soft drink maker would have to sell over *two billion* bottles of Coke to offset $270,000,000 should the new lineup of pictures fail at the box office. Add a requisite couple of hundred million for prints and advertising, and Coke might have to ship out *four billion* units of fizzy caramel-colored liquid to pay for David Puttnam's slate.

Needless to say, Coke had a great deal riding on David Puttnam's taste in motion pictures. The scary thing was that David had cooked up a whole new filmmaking formula.

And no one around Coca-Cola had to be reminded of the last time the company had introduced a "new formula."

In New York, Fay Vincent and Herbert Allen were getting frequent updates from David as well as from various agents and attorneys representing key talent. And, way down south in Atlanta, Georgia, even Coke chairman Roberto Goizueta and Coke president Donald Keough had become preoccupied with casualty reports from Hollywood.

David was painfully aware of the damaging word-of-mouth circulating around the Columbia management triangle—Los Angeles—New York—Atlanta—and was therefore happy that Roberto and Don were on their way to Los Angeles for the annual Coca-Cola corporate dinner.

It was to be a formal affair, a gala event. But most important to David, he would have an opportunity to sit down face-to-face with the two high-ranking Coke executives. Always brilliant in one-to-one encounters, David *knew* he could allay the fears of Roberto and Don while, at the same time, reinforcing their crumbling confidence in his ability to function as Columbia's chairman/CEO.

The day Roberto and Don arrived, however, they did not call David Puttnam.

David sat in his office watching morning turn to afternoon and then to early evening. He had answered a hundred phone calls. But not one from Don or Roberto.

A bit concerned, David headed home, slipped into his tuxedo and boarded a limousine for Beverly Hills.

When David arrived at the China Pavilion for Coke's big event, he discovered—for the first time—one very disconcerting fact. Although he envisioned the post of chairman/CEO of Columbia Pictures to have some special and exalted place in the hearts of Roberto Goizueta and Donald Keough, he quickly found out that he was given no greater consideration than the chairman/CEO of any other Coke division. In other words, someone like the head of bottling operations in Zambia was just as important—maybe even more important—to the two chief executives. So David received no outpouring of warmth when he strode into the room.

But the reaction of Roberto and Don to David's arrival seemed to David to be more than just corporate cool. The pair from Atlanta appeared to be distant and uninterested in what David had to say. It was not apathy, rather a strained cordiality.

Perhaps in an effort to mend fences, David dwelt on the progress of *Leonard Part 6*. The Bill Cosby extravaganza had just gone into production and David spent an inordinate amount of time extolling the virtues of Cosby as an actor and writer. After all, singing the praises of a man who was a Coca-Cola spokesman had no downside.

But Roberto and Don were unimpressed. Even sweeping endorsements of America's number-one television star did not thaw the frigid atmosphere between David and the Coca-Cola contingent. The momentum of the avalanche of trouble David had triggered during the previous eight months was too compelling to turn aside.

The isolation of David Puttnam was now complete. First the Hollywood establishment. Then Herbert Allen. Next Fay Vincent.

And now Roberto Goizueta and Donald Keough. There was, in fact, no one in the chain of command above David who would continue to support him.

For all practical purposes, David Puttnam's tenure at Columbia Pictures was over.

CHAPTER
FOURTEEN

In a business community as small as that of the motion picture industry, most confrontations eventually come back to haunt you. Such was the case regarding David's media melee with Menahem Golan and Yoram Globus, the copresidents of Cannon Films. The "haunting" was indirect, via Warner Bros., David's former home as an independent producer, but it was nonetheless a haunting.

The evocation of the Cannon ghost occurred when Columbia Pictures and Warner Bros. decided—actually, it was David Puttnam and Warner president Terry Semel who did the deciding for their respective companies—to discontinue a sixteen-year international codistribution relationship.

Since 1971, product from the two studios had been released in Europe by Columbia-Warners Distribution Ltd. On May 1, that partnership came to an end.

Three ironies existed in this dissolution.

Primary was the fact that the codistribution arrangement had done very well for almost two decades, only to finally fall apart when two close friends, David Puttnam and Terry Semel, were in charge of maintaining it.

The second irony was the effect of the breakup: an immediate drop in the number of available films for Columbia's European product flow. Now on its own overseas—without the security inherent in the Columbia/Warners tie—Columbia Pictures would be *forced* to take a more aggressive posture in Europe, something David had repeatedly said he wanted to do.

Finally, it was supreme irony that one of the reasons Warner Bros. elected to go solo in Europe was its recent alignment with Cannon Films. Warners had not entered into a codistribution plan with Cannon, but the studio had done something just as effective. Coinciding with the Columbia-Warners termination, Warner Bros. had purchased an option to buy half of Cannon's interest in its 525-screen European theater circuit for $50,000,000.

The significance of the option was that 525 screens represented a huge block of European theaters and, in Europe, to a much greater degree than in the United States, those who control theaters control box office.

An amusing observation regarding the Cannon option appeared in *Daily Variety*.

"Should Warners at some point elect to exercise its two-year option," *Variety* said of the potential purchase by Warners of an interest in the Cannon theater circuit, "the dissolution [between Columbia and Warners] could prove to be an added plus. In theory at least, under those circumstances, Warner products could enjoy favored treatment on Cannon overseas screens vis a vis competing Columbia features."

What was amusing?

Simply the idea that—all other things being equal—Warner Bros. didn't already enjoy a "favored treatment" by Cannon, even without actually buying half interest in Cannon's European theater chain.

After all, given a choice between a film from Warner Bros. and a film of exactly the same box-office appeal from Columbia Pictures, which might Menahem Golan and Yoram Globus elect to exhibit?

Would it be the Warner movie? Or the movie from Columbia, a company run by a man who had openly blasted them in print?

On May 15, the day that *Ishtar* was finally released, David was not in the United States, he was in France. But it wasn't a snub of the premiere of the Warren Beatty/Dustin Hoffman movie which took him there, it was the Cannes Film Festival.

Each year, the global motion picture industry converges on the small town in Southern France to enter its celluloid wares in the festival's cinematic competition. Once a major affair which could launch a film into the stratosphere of box-office grosses with the presentation of a prestigious award, Cannes, by 1987, had become a social gathering place, rather than the site of an event with meaningful ramifications.

The era of electronic media—home video, cable, etc.—brought with it a stripping of the mystique of motion picture marketing. Promoting a motion picture was now a complicated and sophisticated endeavor, requiring a great deal more imagination than merely offering a laundry list of honors as a lure to the potential audience.

In fact, Cannes 1987 was like a grand old dowager once of great wealth and dignity, now clinging only to dignity, her brocade dress a bit tattered. As her youth had deserted her, so had her suitors: the movie moguls who in previous years had shamelessly doted on her and begged her adoration. Now just one admirer, David Puttnam, sat at her knee, for he was the only Hollywood studio head in attendance.

In addition to its normal agenda, the 40th Cannes Film Festival had designated May 15 as "British Day." It was a gesture by the worldwide motion picture industry to recognize the cinematic efforts of the United Kingdom.

And on that evening, a special dinner had been scheduled to pay homage to the illustrious career of legendary English actor Sir Alec Guinness.

Sir Alec had earned a Best Actor Oscar in 1957 for his role in *The Bridge on the River Kwai* and appeared in such classic films as *Oliver Twist, Lawrence of Arabia, The Rise and Fall of the Roman Empire, Doctor Zhivago*, and *Star Wars*, in which he played the benevolent master of the "force," Obi Wan Kenobe. In 1959, he was knighted by Queen Elizabeth.

The fact that the Sir Alec Guinness affair was scheduled on "British Day" made it even more special. And the planned attendance of two members of the British royal family—the Prince and Princess of Wales, Charles and Diana—added to the luster. It was the toughest ticket in Cannes that year, and perhaps the most sought-after invitation in the forty-year history of the festival.

Among the speakers selected to address the distinguished guests were His Royal Highness Prince Charles and, as many joked, His Royal Highness David Puttnam.

Festival officials—well aware of David's affinity for controversial turns of phrase—beseeched him not to say anything even vaguely combative.

"Remember," they said, "Charles and Di are here. And not only that, this is an occasion to honor a knighted member of the motion picture industry, not to express personal opinions."

The message was straightforward: a perfectly innocuous speech would be perfect, thank you. *Please!*

Given David's reputation for candor, few in attendance really believed that the presence of royalty would deter him from speaking his mind. So—even though he started his monologue with high praise of Sir Alec—anticipation in the audience grew with each sentence. It was like hearing a time bomb ticking away, knowing it was going to explode, but having no idea at what point.

When would David launch into his now-familiar attack on Hollywood? When would he get to the part about Hollywood being a godless place? After all, with British royalty hanging on his every word, how could he resist?

But David surprised everyone. He didn't say one disparaging word about Hollywood. Not one word. Instead, he reserved his criticism for another locale.

England.

Looking down on the smiling faces of Charles and Di, David raged about the inadequacy of the British film industry. By the time he was finished, he had delivered a thorough condemnation of the state of cinema in his homeland.

The irreverence of Britain's most well-known filmmaker—on "British Day" of all days—came as quite a shock.

Following David to the podium was Prince Charles.

"Why is it I'm always asked to speak at these affairs?" the Prince asked as he looked out over the stellar crowd. "Quite frankly, I'm rather bored with the sound of my own voice."

Prince Charles did not appear to be very happy. After David's diatribe, it was hard to blame him.

The next day, in a special Cannes issue, *The Hollywood Reporter* described the evening thus:

"Columbia Pictures chairman David Puttnam blasted the British Cultural Ministry and government bureaucracy for its attitude of complacency with respect to the sagging British film industry here Friday, kicking off a series of speakers at the Royal Gala honoring Sir Alec Guinness for a distinguished film career that spans 40 years.

"Acknowledging that he had been asked to address only non-political issues in the presence of Their Royal Highnesses the Prince and Princess of Wales, Puttnam nonetheless expressed his concern about the British film industry's current propensity to " 'view itself from the back of the queue.' "

Two days later, Monday May 18, *The Hollywood Reporter* again carried an account of the Sir Alec Guinness dinner, this time in more detail and this time sporting the front page headline: COL'S PUTTNAM BLASTS BRIT OFFICIALS AT KICKOFF OF GALA.

It is hard to shock Hollywood, but this story did it.

If Hollywood was a despicable place and the British film industry was at "the back of the queue," what was left?

Ray Stark came up with what he thought was a plausible explanation.

"Since he has problems with both America *and* England," Ray conjectured, "maybe all those months he spent in the South American jungle doing *The Mission* ruined him for civilization."

Back in the United States, *Ishtar* was being greeted with empty theaters. The film had opened on 1,115 screens but was pulling in abysmal box-office numbers. Understandably, Warren Beatty and Dustin Hoffman were furious.

As Warren and Dustin saw it, David Puttnam was responsible for the poor showing of their motion picture. Throughout production, the press had reported the film's cost overruns and troubles on the set with alarming regularity. Even more alarming was the accuracy of the reports, as if they were "leaked." Whoever was the Columbia "source"—and based on the detail of the information, there appeared to be no question that there was indeed an inside informant—Warren and Dustin were certain it was David Puttnam.

Notwithstanding the relative quality or appeal of *Ishtar*, the continuous barrage of negative press certainly diminished its chances of success.

Not only did Warren and Dustin realize this, but so did the rest of the movie business. The *perception* was that David Puttnam was continuing his vendetta against his two old adversaries and had notched a convincing victory at the cost of $50,000,000.

It may not have been the case, but, remember, in Hollywood, perception is everything.

***

Considering the above truism, the next several decisions made by David Puttnam seemed suicidal. In rapid-fire succession during June, the chairman/CEO signed production pacts with a whole new series of British filmmakers and former associates, starting with Ben Bolt.

Bolt, upon finishing *The Big Town*, his *first-ever* feature film effort as a director, was presented with a "first look" deal and given offices and staff on Columbia's Burbank lot. It was a particularly puzzling move in that a director whose *only* picture had *not even been released* was tapped by fellow Briton David Puttnam for an expanded relationship at Columbia Pictures. Consequently, the best credit the media could manage when writing about Bolt's arrangement with the studio was "British-born Bolt is a graduate of the National Film School in London and has directed episodic television."

The next British bombshell detonated in Hank Grant's column in *The Hollywood Reporter*, which carried the following item:

"Sir Richard Attenborough is no longer reeling from the not so succe$$ful movie version of 'A Chorus Line.' My Columbia Pics spy Onda Lotalot reports that honcho David Puttnam's tagged him to a two-pic pact."

A week later David appointed Uberto Pasolini to the post of production vice president. Pasolini had slipped onto the Columbia payroll as one of David's assistants shortly after the British producer became chairman/CEO. At the time, Pasolini's background was not generally known. By elevating his assistant to vice president status, however, David opened up a can of wriggling worms.

Working as an investment banker in England in 1984—a position he had held for twelve years—Pasolini left banking to join David Puttnam as a production assistant on *The Killing Fields*. He subsequently worked with David on several other pictures, ultimately serving as assistant director on *The Mission*.

From banker to studio vice president in three years! Hollywood felt only two things could possibly account for such a dramatic turn of events.

Enormous talent.

Or cronyism.

At the same time, David made a marketing decision which was as stupefying as his choice of personnel. He may have had a perfectly reasonable basis for the action, yet the *perception* was that David had gone from aggressive destruction of the Hollywood establishment to vengeful kamikaze assaults.

David reduced the number of screens for the opening of Dan Melnick's *Roxanne* from 1,058 to 847, a drop of 211.

As usual, David couldn't wait to share this information with the media, so he spoke to *Variety* about his rationale for the reduced *Roxanne* release. After quoting David as saying, "You pays your money and you takes your choice," *Variety* continued:

"Puttnam revealed that the decision to cut back on opening day prints was based on 780–790 advertised 'sneak' previews across the country . . . 'It played very strongly in all the areas we thought it would, and where we extended outside into downtown locations, we were having problems.' "

Hollywood read the phrase ". . . we were having problems . . ." as overt sabotage.

To most filmmakers, seeing a studio head say *in print*, well before its scheduled release, that a film was "having problems," was outrageous and irresponsible since theater owners were particularly sensitive to any negative indication regarding a movie. Certainly, the expectation of box office that exhibitors may have held for *Roxanne* could only have been diminished by the less-than-confidence-instilling appraisal by David Puttnam. And the marketing and distribution departments of Columbia Pictures must have felt undermined at the very least.

It is not likely that David Puttnam really intended to ambush *Roxanne*, even though he did inherit it and even if it was produced by one of the Hollywood old guard. Yet, if sabotage wasn't his intention, the only other explanation for such a public remark was that David just wasn't using his head in discussing Columbia product with the press. Either way, the beleaguered studio chief had driven another nail in his professional coffin and accelerated the advent of his now-rumored demise.

The ghost of Baron Munchausen surfaced again on June 24 at the World Exhibitors' Symposium in Munich. Erich Mueller, Columbia Pictures European production chief, announced that the $25,000,000 picture was set to roll at the studio.

This contradicted a conversation Mueller had with Transit Films president Karl Woener a week before in which he told Woener:

"Columbia Pictures has no intention of proceeding with *Munchausen.*

Immediately following Mueller's statement to the symposium, another denial that *Munchausen* was a go at Columbia was issued by Ron Jacobi.

At this point, there had been *two* announcements and *three* denials regarding the picture. Quite appropriate for the saga of a character known as "the greatest liar of all time."

The truth was, Fred Bernstein and David Picker were working very hard to bring *Munchausen* to Columbia. However, the rights issue raised by Allan Buckhantz—which was compounded by the involvement of the West German government—rendered the deal far more delicate than the typical project.

Ron Jacobi had been correct about the status of *Munchausen* on both occasions. *Munchausen* was *not* at Columbia Pictures, simply because the film had not yet cleared all the legal hurdles necessary to satisfy David Puttnam.

In fact, the already convoluted *Munchausen* situation had become even more convoluted on June 7 as a result of a telex from Transit Film to David Puttnam. In that communication, Transit informed Columbia that yet another entity was aligning itself with Transit and Allan Buckhantz: the estate of Dr. Erich Kaestner. Kaestner was the author of a series of books on Baron Munchausen and the screenwriter of the 1942 UFA picture. So now it was Columbia Pictures versus Allan Buckhantz, the German government, *and* the estate of one of Germany's most revered writers.

And as if that was not enough, there was another complication: money.

David's autonomy in the selection of motion pictures had one very specific constraint. He had a ceiling of $30,000,000 per project. Beyond that figure, David was required to gain approval from the Columbia executive committee.

The problem was, David *knew* that *Munchausen* would cost much more than that. His experience as a producer told him that the $25,000,000 budget tendered by his friend Jake Eberts was far from being realistic.

Jake Eberts also knew that the budget was well under what the film would actually cost. So did David Picker and Fred Bernstein.

The trick was to limit Columbia's liability and find someone else to take the financial fall. Which was the reason completion guarantor Film Finances was brought in to cover the contingency of costs overruns.

That done, the last piece in the *Munchausen* puzzle would be to secure an errors-and-omissions policy, shielding the studio from potential lawsuits stemming from the copyright claim. But in order to find an insurance carrier willing to underwrite an e&o policy, Columbia had to convince the carrier that the story of Baron Munchausen was truly in the public domain.

Thus, in mid-June, there was still a great deal of legal maneuvering necessary to clear the way for Baron Munchausen's arrival in Burbank.

In view of this fact, the March 10 article in *The Hollywood Reporter* and the June 24 statement by Erich Mueller appeared overzealous and certainly premature.

And with all the other projects floating around Hollywood in search of a home, the single-minded pursuit of *The Adventures Of Baron Munchausen* by Picker and Bernstein seemed very odd indeed.

On June 26, shooting finished on *Leonard Part 6*. During the course of six weeks of production, several incidents almost turned the film into an outright and unfinished disaster, most stemming from the fact that the first feature film by America's favorite comedian was being directed by a Briton and produced by a Briton. Alan Marshall, David Puttnam's coproducer on *Midnight Express*, was in charge of the production while Paul Weiland, who had *never* done a film before, was sitting in the director's chair.

It seemed incongruous that David could express his deep commitment to *Leonard Part 6*—he chose every opportunity to update Coca-Cola on the status of the film—while at the same time entrusting the interpretation of Bill Cosby's decidedly American humor to a pair of British filmmakers, one of whom was a complete novice in the feature film department.

Adding to the risk was the presence of former Columbia president Steve Sohmer as executive producer. While Sohmer had lured Cosby to the studio just prior to David's appointment, he had never before produced a motion picture, proving that sometimes a golden parachute can deposit someone in a mine field.

The reason David Puttnam chose Alan Marshall—their previous relationship—appeared obvious. But David's rationale for selecting Paul Weiland defied explanation. Weiland's experience was limited to directing British television commercials and he could not have been considered a wise choice by any standard in view of the enormity of *Leonard Part 6*. It boasted an enormous star, an enormous budget, and an enormous importance to Coca-Cola.

Despite a torturous time on the set in which Cosby and Marshall clashed at every turn, *Leonard Part 6* somehow wrapped and left its San Francisco location for postproduction in Burbank.

At this point, no one—not Alan Marshall, not Paul Weiland, not Steve Sohmer, not Bill Cosby, and certainly not David Puttnam—had any idea at all what would emerge.

As the Hollywood summer grew hotter, so did the controversy engulfing David Puttnam. The worsening situation, however, did nothing to stop David from speaking out in the media.

For example, on the day that Erich Mueller was making his *Munchausen* proclamation, David Puttnam was making proclamations of his own as a guest speaker at a luncheon held in commemoration of the twenty-fifth anniversary of A&M Records.

"Put your beliefs on the line" David shouted hoarsely as he neared the end of a rousing speech, "and have the courage to take risks . . . We need to trust our audience . . . It is our jobs to turn our respective mediums into a responsible influence . . ."

It was David's most philosophically flavored address to date, his most idealistic content. The media, of course, devoured the message like hungry disciples.

PUTTNAM TALK TOUTS SOCIAL RESPONSIBILITY, *The Hollywood Reporter* blared on page one.

The story noted David's comments regarding "artistic creativity and responsibility" and pointed out that the studio chief "repeatedly stressed the importance of balancing the 'sinister cliche of bottom line' with socially responsible art."

While doing nothing to turn the group of music moguls into idealists, David's address did accomplish one thing. A new phrase, "sinister cliche of bottom line," became a part of the growing vernacular of the legion of David Puttnam supporters.

CHAPTER

FIFTEEN

Nero fiddled while Rome burned. David Puttnam flew off to Moscow while Hollywood simmered.

On July 1, the chairman/CEO of Columbia Pictures arrived in the Soviet capital for a series of talks regarding Russian-American coproductions.

In interviews from the USSR, David revealed that Columbia would be involved in two cooperative projects, *Glasnost*, to be produced and directed by John Boorman, and *Chernobyl*, set as a Stanley Kramer production. In addition to the Soviet pictures, David announced that two other deals had been made. One with Czechoslovakian filmmaker Jiri Menzel and the other with David's favorite "pound for pound" director, Hungarian Istvan Szabo.

With Hollywood still reeling from the quartet of newly announced movies, David followed—two days later—with word on yet another project. The head of the Union of Soviet Filmmakers, Elem Klimov, would direct a Columbia feature film based on a novel by Soviet writer Mikhail Bulgakov, entitled *The Master and Margarita*.

There was a deep sense of betrayal in Hollywood. Certainly David's efforts were noble, but with names like Ray, Marty, Warren, and Norman missing from the Columbia production roles, it was incomprehensible that names such as Jiri, Istvan, Elem, and Mikhail would replace them.

In New York, the mood was one of absolute bewilderment.

Herbert Allen was not focused on what David did creatively, but he damn well cared about the administration of the studio. Feeling that Columbia had hired an executive rather than an ambassador, Herbert wondered what the hell David Puttnam was doing in Moscow with all the problems erupting in Hollywood.

When David returned to California in the middle of July, he was viewed as a conquering hero by the media. He briefly basked in the praise heaped upon his Soviet tour and then got back to the business of running the studio and making motion picture deals.

Exhibiting incredibly bad timing, David immediately signed British producer Iain Smith to produce a $20,000,000 picture entitled *Seven Years in Tibet.*

The climate existing at the time was such that every move David made was dissected from every possible angle. It did not escape Hollywood's attention that Smith had been associate producer on three of David's previous pictures, *Local Hero, The Killing Fields,* and *The Mission.*

Even though it appeared that time was running out, David Puttnam continued to forge ahead, making wholesale changes along the way. On July 21, Columbia unwrapped a brand new marketing division, dubbed "Worldwide Marketing Group." Its president would be none other than former David Puttnam associate, Austrialian Greg Coote.

In addition to his six-figure salary (the exact amount was never divulged), Coote would be paid $1,500,000 (another number which was never officially confirmed) as compensation for leaving his production company, Roadshow, Coote & Carroll, behind in Australia.

The loud buzz about Greg Coote's deal had the same effect as pouring salt in an already gaping wound. And even more salt was poured into that wound the following day as *Daily Variety* offered David Puttnam's thoughts on the function of the Worldwide Marketing Group.

The headline—COLUMBIA ESTABLISHES NEW WORLDWIDE MARKETING GROUP—was descriptive enough, but a teaser above the head really drove home the point: INT'L APPROACH.

"A major step," *Variety* said, "in implementing the international approach pledged by David Puttnam when he became chairman of Columbia Pictures last September was completed yesterday when the company's domestic marketing division was officially scrapped to make way for a new Burbank-based global entity, the Worldwide Marketing Group.

"First to be designed for a global sell will be the platformed release of John Boorman's 'Hope and Glory,' followed by the first wide-breaking release under the new marketing design, Ridley Scott's 'Someone to Watch Over Me,' ticketed for international release Oct. 2."

Many readers were less than thrilled. Nothing—not the president of the group, not the product, not even the marketing thrust of the new division—had anything to do with Hollywood.

An already disgruntled creative community translated the article like this: First David brings in an Austrialian; then the Australian is charged with marketing two pictures by British directors. Worse yet, the chairman/CEO, the marketing group president, and both directors are all longtime friends.

The all-encompassing and all-important position of worldwide marketing chief historically went to a seasoned American who had a full and working understanding of Hollywood motion pictures and the best way to exploit them. Once again, David Puttnam had strayed from the conventional path, and, in doing so, shed the armorlike protection offered by precedent.

Although he had begun to suspect as much, the first time David Puttnam came to the realization that he was in serious trouble occurred in early August when he traveled to Atlanta for a meeting at Coke headquarters. When David walked into the conference room, he found Herbert Allen sitting there waiting for him.

David assumed that Herbert had traveled to Atlanta on his account but he had not. In fact, other than Robert Goizueta and Don Keough, few people were privy to the true purpose of Herbert's visit: the conclusion of negotiations on a merger which would see Columbia Pictures combine with Tri-Star Pictures to form an entirely new entity called Columbia Pictures Entertainment.

The secrecy was necessary and required by law in that the Securities and Exchange Commission has strict regulations governing inside information. *No one*—other than those who *needed* to know—would be informed of the planned merger until it had actually taken place.

One of the decisions made in Atlanta earlier that week was that Victor Kaufman, chairman of Tri-Star Pictures, would be installed as president of the newly formed Columbia Pictures Entertainment. Victor, a forty-four-year-old former Wall Street attorney and professor at the University of California Law School, had joined Columbia Pictures as assistant general counsel in 1974. A year later he was named general counsel, was appointed vice president in 1976, and became senior vice president in 1979. In 1983, after serving briefly as executive vice president of Columbia Pictures Industries and vice chairman of Columbia Pictures, he founded Tri-Star Pictures and became its chairman/CEO.

Since there was no room at the top for *two* chief executives, the merger would necessitate a change in David Puttnam's status at the studio. What that status would be had not yet been decided, so David's arrival was certainly propitious. Although he was unaware of the pending merger and would not be so informed that day, at least David would have a chance to state his case in front of the entire Columbia Pictures power structure in a sort of ad hoc job-performance review.

"Hollywood is a despicable place!" was David's opening line.

"If it's so despicable," Herbert shot back without hesitation, "why did you ask to work there?"

After a grueling hour of explanations, David, tired and frustrated, turned to Don Keough.

"Look, I have to do what I think is right. I don't want to have to wake up every morning, look in the shaving mirror and say, 'I wonder if Don likes me?' "

Don couldn't believe what David had just said. It was not even remotely appropriate for a meeting at this corporate level.

Herbert Allen stared at David for a long moment.

"You have every right to make whatever pictures you want," Herbert noted. "However, since you announced your retirement in three years, you have no right to tamper with the franchise of Columbia. That franchise includes our library, sequels, people we want to do business with in the future, and the infrastructure of the company. These will be working assets long after your three years are up. Had you not announced your retirement, this would be a completely different subject."

David, like a cat, had seemed to have nine lives during the previous eleven months. It is hard to say when he used up the other eight, but this clearly was the ninth.

***

The next warning bell went off as David prepared to fly to Montreal in late August for a luncheon honoring Garth Drabinsky. Drabinsky, a Canadian native who headed Cineplex Odeon, the largest chain of theaters in the world, would be named "The Renaissance Man of Film" by the Montreal World Film Festival.

Knowing that Don Keough would be attending the festivities, David placed a call to Atlanta to ask Don if they could spend time together while they were both in Canada. Don was unavailable, so David left a message.

Don never returned the call.

Concerned, David proceeded to Montreal and encountered Don Keough and Dick Gallop. Don and Dick were cordial, but nothing more. What had started as the benefit of the doubt for David Puttnam had turned into just plain doubt.

But the final blow came when, after lunch, David noticed that Don and Dick were nowhere to be found. In fact, they had left the gala without so much as a good-bye for the Columbia chairman/ CEO.

In late September, David made a decision that cost Columbia Pictures several million dollars.

Hard Knox, a picture starring Sidney Poitier and Donald Sutherland, was about to begin production under the supervision of producer Walter Mirisch. Mirisch, sixty-six, had produced a long list of Hollywood classics including *The Fall Guy* (1947), *The Magnificent Seven* (1960), and *In the Heat of the Night* (1967). He had served as executive producer on *West Side Story* in 1961 and had mounted a recent series of contemporary films such as *Scorpio* in 1972, *Gray Lady Down* in 1978 and *Same Time, Next Year* in 1978. In addition, Mirisch, like Ray Stark, had been the recipient of the coveted Irving Thalberg award presented to him in 1973 by the Academy of Motion Picture Arts & Sciences (the Oscar people) for outstanding achievement in cinema.

After greenlighting the development of *Hard Knox*, David Puttnam brought in British director John Mackenzie and then supervised two major rewrites of the script. When the picture itself became a "go" on May 15, it seemed logical to assume—considering David's deep creative involvement—that he was firmly behind the project.

Then, without warning, David canceled it. He provided no explanation to Walter Mirisch. He simply canceled it.

Unfortunately, *Hard Knox* had gone into a "pay-or-play" situation. Which meant that even though Columbia would *not* be doing the picture, Sidney Poitier, Donald Sutherland, and others *would still be paid.*

"Pay-or-play" is a contractual concession insisted upon by most major stars, directors, and producers. Obviously, those in demand must block out time for a project, thus removing themselves from consideration for other projects which might be going on simultaneously. To protect themselves from arbitrary last-minute cancellations, key players require a studio to *guarantee* payment after a certain date has passed, whether or not the film is ever made.

Hard Knox—though it never went before the cameras—cost Columbia Pictures $4,500,000. Sidney Poitier received $1,000,000 and Donald Sutherland $750,000, with the balance either charged against development costs or distributed among other personnel who had pay-or-play provisions in their contracts.

Yet it was not the money which fueled anger about the abrupt end of *Hard Knox*, it was David Puttnam's seemingly callous treatment of respected producer Walter Mirisch. And, since Mirisch had always espoused the *same* filmmaking philosophy as David Puttnam, the cancellation seemed all the more capricious.

In the biography of Walter Mirisch contained in *The Film Encyclopedia* (Putnam, 1979), author Ephraim Katz observes of the production entity founded by Mirisch in 1957:

"The company soon gained a reputation for its quality of production and for its policy of allowing creative freedom to independent producers and directors whose pictures it financed."

Obviously, there were others in Hollywood who felt a commitment to making quality motion pictures and fostering creative talent. The difference seemed to be that they implemented their philosophy quietly like Walter Mirisch rather than with fanfare like David Puttnam.

And there was one other difference.

The "art" Walter Mirisch and the Hollywood establishment produced for the enjoyment of the audience made a great deal of money for the stockholders too.

At the same time David Puttnam slammed the door on *Hard Knox*, he opened the gate for a picture which had been knocking around the studio for months. Finally, after several false starts, *The Adventures of Baron Munchausen* officially became a Columbia project. Sporting a budget of $25,000,000—of which Columbia would finance $20,500,000—the film would be shot in Rome, five thousand miles away from the watchful eye of the studio.

The approval of *The Adventures of Baron Munchausen* was a puzzling development. Already embattled because of his earlier decisions involving past associates, David chose to ignore the rumblings in Hollywood and give a "go" to a movie backed by his old friend, Jake Eberts. Furthermore, the cost to Columbia far exceeded the $12,000,000 figure David had pledged would be the most expensive production during his term and even surpassed the $16,000,000 amount he had once classified as "insane."

David Puttnam, outspoken crusader against cronyism and big budgets, had succumbed to both in one stroke.

As the Columbia/Tri-Star merger progressed from concept to reality, it became increasingly difficult to contain word of the event since a growing number of executives fell into the "need-to-know" category each day. Of course, the more people who knew about the combination of companies, the greater the possibility of an ill-timed leak to the media. So, when the multibillion-dollar deal was finally concluded on the evening of August 31, all concerned were relieved that a transaction of such mammoth financial proportions had been executed in the absence of rumor and speculation.

The merger would serve two purposes, one practical and one related to accounting.

From a practical standpoint, much redundancy would be eliminated as both Coca-Cola subsidiaries would now utilize one rather than two administrative hierarchies. But it was the accounting ramification which was the most intriguing aspect of the metamorphosis.

Coke would transfer its ownership in Columbia and Tri-Star to its stockholders and, via a complicated exchange of securities, wind up with a 49 percent equity position in the new entity, Columbia Pictures Entertainment. The effect would be to remove the entertainment business sector of Coca-Cola's operations from the balance sheet and shield an otherwise consistent income statement from the volatile performance of motion picture distribution.

The combination complete, all that remained was to make the

announcement as quickly as possible, so Donald Keough planned a press briefing for the following day. He would invite a small number of reporters to 711 Fifth Avenue and fulfill his obligation as president of a public corporation to immediately disclose any significant change in the financial structure of Coca-Cola.

One of the four journalists summoned to Coke's New York headquarters was me. My name is Charles Kipps. On the day Donald Keough prepared to issue a statement regarding the merger, I was starting my third week at *Variety* as a writer covering the film industry. The brief period I had been on *Variety*'s staff proved to be relatively routine, a time of orientation, and nothing of consequence had occurred. But that changed on the morning of September 1 at 11:00 A.M., with a phone call.

"Mr. Kipps," a pleasant female voice said, "can you be at 711 Fifth Avenue at one o'clock?"

"Yes, I can. May I ask why?"

"It's for a special briefing by Mr. Donald Keough," she replied matter-of-factly. "Please be prompt."

Donald Keough entered the eleventh-floor conference room with two Coca-Cola executives at his side: corporate communications vice president Carlton Curtis and senior vice president/chief financial officer Doug Ivester.

"We've asked you here today," the Coke president began, "to announce the merger of two Coca-Cola subsidiaries—Columbia Pictures Industries and Tri-Star Pictures—into a new company, Columbia Pictures Entertainment."

As Don Keough spoke, Carlton Curtis handed out press kits which contained a detailed description of the complex transition.

"Victor Kaufman will head the new company," Don Keough said.

"What about David Puttnam?" a reporter asked.

Don Keough deferred to Carlton Curtis.

"David Puttnam will remain in his post," the Coke executive stated.

When I returned to *Variety*, I was surrounded by a curious group of colleagues. No one, however, inquired about the details of the combination of two major Hollywood studios. Instead, there was just one question:

"What did they say about David Puttnam?"

I couldn't believe how the British transplant had captured the imagination of the American press corps, especially journalists as jaded and street-wise as the *Variety* crew.

"They said he would remain in his post," I replied.

Indeed, it did appear that David Puttnam had miraculously survived the Columbia/Tri-Star embrace. Following a breakfast meeting a few days later with his two bosses, Don Keough and Roberto Goizueta, David emerged with the impression that his job was secure.

The media quoted David as saying he had "every intention" of completing his term and had been given "assurance" by Keough and Goizueta to that effect. However, when asked how and when he was apprised of the merger, David's answer contained a subtext which indicated his continuing tenure at Columbia Pictures might be far less a certainty than he proclaimed.

"I found out about the merger," David remarked, "by reading it in the newspapers."

While this revelation seemed damning enough, there was a more pointed clue to David Puttnam's future hidden within the mechanics of the merger. The British producer who had caused such controversy during his first year in Hollywood was about to enter his second year as chairman/CEO of a company which, technically, no longer existed.

David Puttnam (Laura Luongo/Peter Borsari)

From left: Roberto Goizueta, chairman of The Coca-Cola Company; film producer Ray Stark; Donald Keough, president of The Coca-Cola Company; Wall Street investment banker Herbert A. Allen of Allen and Company, Inc. The four men were key players in the David Puttnam/Columbia Pictures saga.

David Puttnam clutches the Best Picture Oscar for Chariots of Fire *as the film's director, Hugh Hudson, straightens his tie. (Peter Borsari)*

David Puttnam with David Picker (left) and Dan Melnick (right). Puttnam brought Picker in as president of the studio, but severed ties with independent producer and former Columbia Pictures president Melnick, even after Melnick's box-office hit Roxanne. *(Peter Borsari)*

Dustin Hoffman and Warren Beatty in Ishtar, *a $50-million picture that David Puttnam refused to see. (Courtesy of Columbia Pictures)*

Bill Cosby sits atop an ostrich in the box-office turkey Leonard Part 6. *(Courtesy of Columbia Pictures)*

Richard Vuu as the young Emperor Pu Yi in The Last Emperor. *The film won all nine of the Academy Awards for which it was nominated, including Best Picture. (Courtesy of Columbia Pictures)*

Ray Stark, Omar Sharif, and Barbra Streisand at the 1968 premiere of Funny Girl.

The late John Huston, legendary director/writer/ actor, with his close friend Ray Stark. Huston directed four pictures for producer Stark, including Night of the Iguana *(MGM/Seven Arts, 1964),* Reflections in a Golden Eye *(Warner Brothers/Seven Arts, 1967),* Fat City *(Columbia, 1972), and* Annie *(Columbia, 1982).*

Ray Stark receives the Irving G. Thalberg Memorial Award, bestowed for "a lifetime of achievement in film." The special Oscar was presented by Kirk Douglas at the 1973 Academy Awards ceremony.

Producer Marty Ransohoff (left) and actor Robert Loggia on the set of Jagged Edge. *David Puttnam, who repeatedly said he did not like sequels, refused to approve* Jagged Edge II. *(Courtesy of Columbia Pictures.) (Inset) This photo of Ransohoff adorned a giant billboard near Spago, the famous Hollywood watering hole. Since David Puttnam eschewed trendy restaurants, he may have been spared Ransohoff's steady stare. (Courtesy of Martin Ransohoff)*

Don Safran with Dolly Parton on location in Louisiana during the filming of Steel Magnolias, *a movie produced by Ray Stark for Tri-Star Pictures. (Zade Rosenthal. Courtesy of Tri-Star Pictures)*

Actor John Neville strikes a pose as Baron Munchausen. Cost over-runs and litigation plagued the production of the film. (Courtesy of Columbia Pictures)

Left to right: Bill Murray, Dan Aykroyd, Ernie Hudson, and Harold Ramis in a scene from Ghostbusters II, *a movie that did not find its way onto the David Puttnam slate of films due to Puttnam's aversion to sequels. (Courtesy of Columbia Pictures)*

Kevin Costner and Madeline Stowe in a scene from Revenge. *David Puttnam aborted the development of the picture, which was brought to Columbia Pictures by Ray Stark, but, after Puttnam's departure, Dawn Steel reactivated the project. (Courtesy of Columbia Pictures)*

David Puttnam and his wife, Patsy, share a Coke at the premiere party for La Bamba. *(Peter Borsari) (Inset) David Puttnam in a pensive mood, his tenure as studio chief coming to a close. (Laura Luongo/ Peter Borsari)*

Columbia president Dawn Steel (left), who succeeded David Puttnam at the helm of Columbia Pictures, is pictured with Columbia Pictures Entertainment president Victor Kaufman and his wife, Loretta. (Courtesy of Columbia Pictures)

PART II

CHAPTER

SIXTEEN

On September 13, David Puttnam flew to Canada for another in a seemingly endless lineup of annual film festivals held throughout the world. This one boasted the somewhat ambitious name, Toronto Festival of Festivals.

It was unusual for a studio chief to attend such an event and, in fact, David was the only Hollywood chairman/CEO in attendance. But the circus atmosphere surrounding his arrival had more to do with the uncertain status of his title than the title itself. The question dominating hundreds of hushed conversations was: How much longer can David Puttnam survive? Consequently, it was no surprise that a full house was on hand when David stood before the festival's Trade Forum to deliver the keynote address.

Instead of launching right into his speech, however, David waited for the applause to abate and then made a request.

"Please do not report my remarks out of context," he asked.

Most in attendance were surpised. Never before had David come so close to chastising the media. Actually, it wasn't really an invective, but, coming from David Puttnam, it was an extraordinary plea.

That said, David began his remarks with a denunciation of the Canadian motion picture industry, insisting that Canadian filmmakers didn't believe in themselves and looked to the United States for their creative spark.

"The U.S. is not the problem," David boomed, "and it cannot supply the solution."

By now, David had developed a knack for choosing the most effective venue for specific verbal assaults. He chastised Britain when in Britain and Hollywood when in Hollywood, perhaps realizing that no one could get too worked up if he interchanged location and harangue. After all, who would care if he attacked Hollywood or Britain while in Canada?

Later in his remarks, David used a broader brush and embarked on yet another reworking of his familiar criticism of the overall quality of motion pictures.

Despite the warmed-over content, David's speech was filled with renewed eloquence and freshly minted admonishments. He insisted that the filmmakers were ruled by the bottom line, which he termed an "ugly phrase," and needed to develop a system of values.

"Artists and those who work with them," David suggested, "have a moral responsibility to the audience."

It was an audience David said had "put up with drek for the past twenty years."

The reaction, as always, was a resounding standing ovation. David then descended from the stage and conducted an impromptu press conference with a group of appreciative journalists.

"I've got a big decision to make," David responded when asked whether or not he would continue in his current capacity at Columbia Pictures, "and I've not made it yet."

A few days earlier David told journalists that Coca-Cola had assured him he was still chairman/CEO despite the merger. Now he was saying he wasn't so sure he wanted the job.

Yet, with two years left on his contract and millions of dollars of compensation hanging in the balance, why would David resign? Wouldn't it be better to be fired, at least from a monetary standpoint, and exit Columbia with a huge contract settlement? After all, Coca-Cola was clearly unhappy with the British filmmaker, and, considering the merger, that scenario seemed likely anyway.

Regardless of who would be making the "decision"—David Puttnam or Coca-Cola—one thing seemed certain.

The sun was about to set on "British Columbia."

***

Three days after announcing he had a "big decision" to make, David Puttnam returned to Hollywood to host the seventh "Reel Truth" session, a monthly affair at Columbia in which secretaries, accounting clerks, and junior executives were invited to meet producers, directors, actors, and high-level studio brass. A Cinderella seminar, "The Reel Truth" brought the commoners together with royalty, giving the unheralded Columbia Pictures support staff an opportunity to rub elbows with the celebrated filmmakers for whom they performed their forty hours a week of labor.

In fact, the "Reel Truth" gatherings were very effective in evoking an above-the-call-of-duty effort from the nameless faces whose ordinary lives had intertwined with the rich and famous. It made them feel important. Or, as David liked to put it, it made them "part of the process."

Ever since March 10, when David conceived and introduced "The Reel Truth," there had been backlash from the Hollywood establishment. Many of the old guard felt it was a waste of time for David to be playing hero to a bevy of secretaries. Others, however, and this even included a few of David's enemies, allowed that the seminars seemed to be helpful in promoting a positive attitude around the Columbia office complex. This appeared to be true, as "The Reel Truth" took on an almost religious significance at Columbia Plaza East.

Each "Reel Truth" had a similar format. David would begin the evening with a brief speech and then screen a new Columbia film. After the screening, one or more of the filmmakers or actors involved in that motion picture would be on hand to answer questions from the audience.

On this particular evening, director Ridley Scott's *Someone to Watch Over Me* was on the agenda, the *first* movie resulting from David Puttnam's sole input. All previous releases during David's first year had been inherited, but not *Someone to Watch Over Me*. David had sought the project, brought it to the studio, and nurtured it through production. It was all David Puttnam. And it was to be his flagship motion picture, leading the way for the rest of his slate.

When the film ended, David brought director Ridley Scott to the front of the room.

"Ridley and I have known each other—and started working together—twenty years ago," David said. "When we were both four."

The audience laughed.

"I think, without doubt," David added, "he's one of the half-dozen finest filmmakers in the world. And so, without further ado, as they say in these kind of situations, I'd like to introduce my friend and your colleague, Ridley Scott."

Ridley opened with a brief statement about the development of *Someone to Watch Over Me* and then fielded questions.

"Your movie was fabulous," a young blonde smiled, "and I just wanted to ask you if you could tell us anything about the production design."

Ridley answered in his *very* English accent:

"To me it's very important how a film looks . . . to do posh is quite difficult . . . If you aren't really used to what is New York at that level, unless you've set foot through a door and seen it several times where you can absorb it without overdoing it, you know, so it's *just* enough, is really tough. In a funny kind of way, it's a lot easier to do working class and things like that, in Queens . . ."

This was fascinating stuff, a top director explaining the inner workings of filmmaking.

When Ridley finished his revealing twenty minutes of responses, David took the microphone again.

"I'll tell you a story. How Ridley and I first worked together on feature films because it happens to involve our president here. About ten, eleven, twelve years ago, I was able to produce a film with Alan Parker called *Bugsy Malone*. And the last bit of money— quite a small sum of money, I might add—came from Paramount Pictures and its then president, David Picker.

"David came to see the film at the Cannes Festival—I guess about 1975 or '76—and hadn't seen it before and was very, very nervous as to what he might encounter.

"It was a particularly bloody Cannes—I mean there was a surfeit of films of an extremely violent nature—and second to last film of the festival was *Bugsy*—for those of you who know it, it was bloody in its own way but not quite as bloody as the other films.

"And it's fair to say it was the phenomenon of the evening— quite extraordinary success. And David and I were walking down the steps behind Mr. Parker who was being cheered out of the hall.

"David said: 'Look, you got any other guys like Parker?'

"So I said: 'Well, yes, as a matter of fact.'

"He said: 'Well, who?'

"I said: 'A man I've been working with called Ridley Scott. We've been developing a couple of screenplays.'

"And he said: 'Can I meet him?'

"I said: 'Absolutely!'

"So I phoned Ridley—went straight back to the hotel—phoned Ridley, and lunchtime the following day, on the beach at Cannes, the three of us had lunch.

"And we pitched David on the scripts we had. We had one enormously elaborate film—his eyes glazed over as soon as we started talking about it—so we gave up on that one. We described a script that we liked very, very, very much, indeed, about the gunpowder plot. And we described a script that we quite liked called *The Duellists*.

"So David said: 'What's the gunpowder plot film going to cost?'

"And we said: 'Well, that's going to cost about a million eight.'

"And he said: 'So what can you do *The Duellists* for?'

"And I knew by the question, it better not be a million nine.

"So I said: 'Well, we can make *The Duellists* for a million dollars.'

"He said: 'I prefer that one!'

"So, for those of you who think the film industry's done by people who sit around holding the bridge of their noses and dreaming of art, *The Duellists* got made exactly on that basis.

"And thanks to David, Ridley and I were able to further our careers. It was Ridley's first feature. He then went on to do *Alien*, which I was silly enough not to get involved in.

"You know me," David Puttnam laughed as he concluded. "Retreat from capital."

Why did Columbia employees adore their chief executive? How could they help it? What other studio head would take the time to stand before his staff and deliver "inside" anecdotes?

Next, David informed the group that he had come up with a way to honor Frank Capra, a filmmaker whose name epitomized the golden era of Hollywood and who had been a driving force in the formative years of Columbia Pictures.

Frank Capra had been a contract producer/director—that is, tied to one studio—at Columbia. He began his epic career in 1918 and over several decades was responsible for pictures like *It Happened One Night, You Can't Take It with You, Lost Horizon, Mr. Deeds Goes to Town, Mr. Smith Goes to Washington, Arsenic and Old Lace,* and *It's a Wonderful Life.*

Eventually, as studios lost their stranglehold on creative talent, Frank Capra began producing and directing films for motion picture distributors other than Columbia. But he remained forever associated with the studio, and was looked upon as an important figure in the history of Columbia Pictures.

"This studio," David began, "I think from its early times, has been a filmmaker's studio. And I don't know whether it's chicken or egg, whether the man created the studio or the studio created the man, this studio, even today, is synonymous with the name Frank Capra.

"It's been something I've been wrestling with ever since I arrived here—discussed it with David [Picker] any number of times—and about six months ago I asked Frank Capra, Jr., if he'd be happy about us making some tangible demonstration on the part of the studio towards his father. Towards what his father meant to the studio—the truth of the matter is, none of us would be here today if it hadn't been for him, without any doubt at all, let's not kid ourselves—an attempt maybe to redress some of the damage that was done during considerable years of neglect, I think particularly during the fifties and sixties, when what Frank had done for the studio wasn't fully realized or recognized.

"The upshot of all that is Frank's come along tonight. His father is really quite ill as I'm sure he'll tell you, unfortunately he can't be with us. Frank Capra, Jr., is here tonight and it's my incredible pleasure to present him with something, in a moment, with something we've been developing for a long while. But before we do that, we're going to run—Hollace Davids has put together, at enormous expense—some clips to remind you of exactly what Frank Capra did do for the studio."

Once again, David exhibited a thoughtfulness which endeared him to those around him. Hollace Davids was the director of video services at Columbia, a job which entailed supplying various cinematic compilations—such as the Frank Capra montage of film scenes—for official Columbia functions. She was also responsible for arranging the videotaping of events like "Reel Truth." In fact, her video crew was present in force on this night, capturing the proceedings for posterity. Having the chairman/CEO mention her name in front of her Columbia colleagues certainly must have been a satisfying and thrilling experience for Hollace Davids.

After the moving picture scrapbook of Capra classics, David addressed his employees:

"The marvelous thing about film is that it's ten times more eloquent than anything you could stand here for five hours and say. I mean that's what the man did for the studio and that's what the man did for the world. We're just damn lucky to have the Columbia lady on the front of the movies."

Looking out into the room David said, "Frank Capra, Jr.!"

Frank, Jr., made his way to the microphone amid resounding applause.

Frank, Jr., had followed his father into the entertainment business, working both in television (*Gunsmoke*, *The Rifleman*, etc.) and in motion pictures (*Born Again*, *The Black Marble*, *An Eye for an Eye*). He also served as president of Avco Embassy Pictures for one year, assuming that post in July 1981 and resigning in May 1982.

"For everything his dad did for us," David proclaimed as he handed Frank Capra, Jr., a statuette of the "Columbia lady," Columbia's trademark female form, "and everything we'll try and do for his dad in years to come."

"Thank you very, very much, David. It's a great pleasure for me to take this award and take it to my dad in Palm Springs. As you know, he's really not able to be here. I'm sure all of us join together in feeling it's too bad he isn't because I'm sure he really would have loved to have seen it.

"Also, thank you very much for including a few films that were not Columbia films in there. That was very nice of you. For all of you and everyone who was involved in this award—but especially to David Puttnam, thank you very much."

Applause—lots of it—followed the brief acceptance speech by Frank, Jr.

Inarguably, David's formal recognition of Frank Capra's contribution to the growth of Columbia Pictures was a noble gesture. Certainly it was long overdue. Frank Capra was a prominent pioneer in motion picture history and a forefather of Columbia Pictures. There were no controversial opinions about Frank Capra;

rather an outflowing of respect and affection.

Most executives, preoccupied with the forward progress of their own careers, never would have even thought of taking a fond look backward at the career of a filmmaker who had long since ceased making pictures. But to David Puttnam's immense credit, he alone, a Briton, had deemed it appropriate to honor a great American filmmaker. It was a compassionate act, but, undeniably, it was also a *popular* one.

Notwithstanding the genuine nature of the act itself, the presentation of an award to such a revered figure in Hollywood history placed David Puttnam within the glow of admiration stirred up by Frank Capra's vast cinematic achievements. There was a subliminal *association* inherent in David's praise of Frank Capra.

But Frank Capra *is* Hollywood, representing its very essence, and to pay homage to such a legendary figure in a non-public forum could easily have been construed as self-serving.

Just like a series of scenes from a movie which are designed to have a certain cumulative effect, on this evening, an *actual* sequence of events—the screening of *Someone to Watch Over Me* and the award to Frank Capra—resulted in the audience feeling *good* about David Puttnam.

While David may not have consciously thought of the seventh "Reel Truth" seminar in dramatic terms, as a filmmaker, he must have *sensed* its dramatic elements.

"When Hollace and I originally organized tonight," David said, his voice softer and suddenly serious, "I was going to give you a rah-rah speech about what a lot we'd achieved, and that it wasn't nearly enough, and what a lot more we'd have to achieve. I guess both are true.

"But the last month for all of us—or three weeks for all of us—have been very trying and very difficult and life's like that sometimes. It's been a bit like Pearl Harbor in trying to gather ourselves back together again.

"Anyways, the upshot of all this is, there's a piece that's going to appear tomorrow, and I wanted to read this to you first, if I may."

CHAPTER
SEVENTEEN

David Puttnam looked down at a piece of paper, cleared his throat, and began to read.

"The Entertainment Business Sector of The Coca Cola Company announced today that David Puttnam, Chairman and Chief Executive Officer of Columbia Pictures, a division of the EBS Unit, and Victor Kaufman, Chairman and Chief Executive Officer of Tri-Star Pictures, Inc., have met concerning Mr. Puttnam's relationship with Columbia following the anticipated combination of the Entertainment Business Sector with Tri-Star.

"During that meeting, Messrs. Puttnam and Kaufman agreed that in view of this anticipated combination and Mr. Puttnam's original and irrevocable decision to vacate his post no later than the summer of 1989, it would be in the company's best interest to plan for an orderly transition now."

So it was that David Puttnam, standing at a podium in Columbia's Screening Room 12, performed his last official duty as he quietly read from a press release which announced his exit from the studio. He spoke without expression, his British accent lending a peculiar detachment to the words. There was no hint of the impassioned and eloquent delivery which had become his trademark. There was no fire in his voice.

In about a minute—the time it took to issue the tersely written formal statement—the walls of the motion picture fortress David had vowed to build crumbled in around him.

His audience was stunned. At first there was a spreading puzzlement, as if David had uttered a group of vaguely related phrases strung together in some cryptic fashion.

"No!" a woman cried out. It was a discordant wail, an involuntary sigh echoing both disbelief and realization in the same measure.

There were sobs of despair. Streaming tears. Dazed expressions.

He waited a moment and then continued.

"Both men stated that, in their view, this approach would most properly facilitate the organization's long-term goals, and allow a settled structure for the newly combined company. Mr. Puttnam will remain as Chief Executive Officer until the consummation of the combination and at that time, or shortly afterwards, relinquish his position. During the interim, they stressed that they will work together in planning for a smooth transition, and one that works in the best interest of Columbia and the filmmakers with whom the studio is presently working. During this period, Mr. Puttnam will specifically supervise the production, marketing and distribution of the bulk of the motion pictures previously committed to.

"Victor Kaufman indicated that he will consider a number of candidates to fill Mr. Puttnam's position following completion of the combination, but no decision has at present been made. Both Mr. Kaufman and Mr. Puttnam stated that because Tri-Star expects shortly to file a proxy statement concerning the proposed combination, neither would be making further comments concerning this announcement in the near future."

David laid the release aside and smiled faintly as he surveyed the group of colleagues who had come to participate in what everyone thought would merely be another installment of "The Reel Truth."

"Well," David sighed, "obviously it's not—I hope it's not thrilling for you—I'm not delighted. But it's correct. What the statement says is absolutely accurate.

"I came to the conclusion at the weekend that it's not right in any way, shape, or form to put you all through two or three months of uncertainty while this particular situation gets sorted out and then put you through the entire thing all over again in sixteen or seventeen months when I go back to England."

On such an occasion as a resignation, few aspects of the decision can be tied in neat bundles or explained away with a phrase. But here, David's frequent past references in the media about "walking out the door in March, 1989" provided a marginally plausible explanation for what appeared to be an incomprehensible act.

David had always vowed he would leave in three years. Now, it sounded as if he was indicating that, considering this "irrevocable" time limit he had placed upon his term as chairman/CEO, he was just doing the studio and its employees a favor by making his exit a few months early. He was merely hastening the inevitable, that's all.

"I think it's sensible and correct," David stated, then added with a bit of melancholy, "I mean, obviously I'm sick to my stomach, because one thing, when I came over here I didn't ever reckon on was—thanks to Frank Capra and all of you—falling in love with this lady [the Columbia trademark]. That was never part of my plans. So . . . uh . . . it's a bad day."

David seemed on the verge of breaking down, his voice cracking slightly. He took a deep breath and exhaled.

"But, what is most important," he pointed out, "is this studio, and the fact that it continues into the future. For me, this studio is a little like—this is not a joke, sadly—a bit like Poland. An awful lot of people over the years have thought they owned it, and it continually gets knocked backwards and forwards and sideways by continuous invading forces."

David spoke kindly of his successor.

"Victor has a real opportunity—a real opportunity—to stop that happening ever again. And, in order to consolidate the studio, make it work, make it prosperous, and make it all the things that you and I would want it to be, he needs time and a very clear run. And it's up to all of us to give him that."

And then he turned his attention to chronicling the accomplishments of his brief tenure.

"I'd just like to talk about a couple of things I'm very, very proud of. During the past year, we've given opportunities to the following directors: Ken Kwapis, Tina Rathbone, David Selzer, Agnieszka Holland, Brian Gilbert, Paul Weiland, Doris Dorrie, Spike Lee, and Paul Golding.

"You've seen none of their films, but I've seen most of them, or, in one or two cases, not a lot yet. But they're all remarkable. And all of those careers will irrevocably—using that word again— will have started at Columbia. And all of them will be tied forever to Columbia in the way that Frank Capra is tied forever to Columbia. And, no matter where they work, they started here and, thanks to you, and David [Picker], Freddie [Fred Bernstein], and the rest of us, they had their shot.

"So, it isn't just Ridley's film, which I am unbelievably proud of—and a dozen other features that will appear in the next year— it isn't just the movies, it's the filmmakers, and at the end of the day, this business is about filmmakers, not about corporations. It's about filmmakers and our ability to serve them."

David sifted through some notes on the podium and then continued.

"I didn't really know what to do, so what I've done, if you don't mind, is read you a speech, ironically, a speech I prepared a month ago, and that I gave in Toronto on the weekend. And I'll just read you an extract from the end, because it sums up everything I feel."

Again the now-former chairman/CEO began to read:

"Twenty years have sped by, during which a select few people and nations have imagined themselves part of a special creation.

"It would be well for many of us—perhaps especially we in the motion picture industry—to seriously consider restating our commitment to what benefits the rest of the human race. This is not intended as an idle criticism because my primary discontent is specifically reserved for myself."

David appeared to be back in form as far as his speech-making prowess was concerned.

"In criticism lies also the responsibility for action. I find myself, almost by accident, an example of a man, who, in confrontation with himself, realized that you have to put your beliefs on the line. On the bottom line, if you will.

"To me it was a challenge to attempt the work at which I'm now engaged. To some I came to whisper at dragons and tilt at windmills, and therefore should be easily unmounted and defeated. But the truth is, I'm neither St. George nor Don Quixote, I'm just a European motion picture producer who crossed the Atlantic to ask a few questions and possibly seek a different way forward and present another point of view, and, maybe, based on my experience, offer some practical suggestions for change.

"Do I have all the answers as some believe I think I do? Of course I don't. But I do plead guilty to strong beliefs, to faith in the individual vision, informed by craft and purpose. To a passion for my craft and the process of its growth into an art form which is capable of uniting, in peace, the family of man of which we're all a part."

Next, David offered what sounded like his personal David Puttnam credo.

"I believe in the future of film artists who are prepared to show sensitivity to the real needs of society. I believe absolutely in those arts which aid our mutual understanding and which question any diminution in the quality and/or the meaning of our lives.

"For sure, the answers lie not in the stars, but in ourselves. Perhaps we can offer a new vision to old eyes and a different path to creativity and even profit in our business, by incorporating the best of the traditional past into a new and viable dream. A dream secured by real faith in talent and a courage to risk."

By now, tears were streaming down almost everyone's face. A few male executives bravely fought back emotion, but just barely.

"I think that Abe Lincoln had it right when he said: 'We hold the power and bear the responsibility, old and young alike, in what we give and what we preserve, that we shall nobly save or meanly lose the last best hope of earth. The way of it is plain, peaceful, generous and just. A way which, if followed, the world will forever applaud and forever bless.'

"These are wonderful words, but they're more than mom and apple pie, they're a challenge. They represent a challenge to all of us, but most particularly to we who can loosely be described as the creative community.

"To paraphrase Bernard Shaw, some look at what is and ask why, but we should look at what might be and demand why not."

David studied the audience.

"Well that's what we tried to do in the past year. Uh . . ."

The British producer swallowed hard, a blink away from crying.

". . . Sometimes we failed and sometimes we succeeded. I think probably we succeeded more often than we failed.

"What you've got to do for me and the company in the next months, and maybe years, is allow the movies we made to speak for themselves. Because no matter what machinations or changes or anything else that anyone dreams up that can do anything other than help Columbia, at the end of the day, we make movies. And the movies we make are our *only* ambassador.

"So I *beg* you, work truly hard on the films we finished, on the films we conceived, on the filmmakers we've worked with, on the filmmakers who are going to rely on you to carry on. And you'd be doing me the greatest favor you could possibly do me."

David's eyes glistened.

"I've had the most wonderful year. A year—I could never have believed it—a few months ago, up to three or four months ago—I was wondering really if I'd ever made the right decision, but in the last few months it's got fabulous and Patsy and I will take home a bunch of memories I'll never ever ever be able to forget or thank you enough.

"Obviously, there's a thousand people I should thank specifically, but if I start, I'd never finish. So, tonight, instead of me, I'm going to ask David Picker to wrap things up and . . . uh . . ."

His voice choked by an evening-long battle against breaking down, David finished just in time.

". . . thanks a lot for hearing me out."

There was an awkward moment as everyone hesitated, unsure what to do, then a spontaneous standing ovation which seemed to last forever.

David Picker raced to the front of the room and embraced his former boss.

David Puttnam, who had held on and remained relatively composed throughout the evening, started to come undone. Tears—denied for the last half hour—finally filled his eyes.

"I was doing very well in the composure stakes till just now," he laughed hoarsely.

Picker appeared confused and certainly unprepared for what was going on around him. It was obvious that the Columbia president had little notice regarding what was to occur that evening.

"As you probably gathered from David's words earlier in the evening," Picker began, "lives and paths cross. The story about *The Duellists* is one of hundreds of examples. Wherever we go in the world, we find people whose lives we've affected. And, of course, David has affected all our lives. I'm here because *he's* here. Many of you are here because *he's* here. And, in turn, many of you are here because *I'm* here."

Everyone in the room knew that David Picker's words contained a basic truth about Hollywood, one that David Puttnam had often challenged. Cronyism, even under the administration of its most vocal critic, was alive and well at Columbia Pictures as many employment decisions over the previous year had been made in large part due to past relationships.

So—the next day—youthful sentimentalists bemoaned their great loss, while grizzled veterans banged out a new résumé as fast as they could.

When I arrived at *Variety* the morning of September 17, it was obvious that something big had happened. Several reporters were huddled together in what looked like a wake.

"David Puttnam resigned," I was told.

Variety had "scooped" the competition with the story of David Puttnam's exit from Columbia Pictures. Reporter Will Tusher had been invited to attend "The Reel Truth" seminar the night before.

"Hold the presses," Tusher grinned as he headed for Burbank and *Daily Variety* editor Thomas Pryor did just that.

Throughout David's tenure at Columbia, Tusher had written extensively about the chairman/CEO. More significantly, Tusher's stories were always kind, even laudatory on occasion. So David knew that the best he could hope for in a media recount of his resignation would be a Will Tusher article.

When David Puttnam arrived in Burbank in 1986, he found a Hollywood press corps which was suffering like a group of suburban housewives, locked in a loveless marriage with the motion picture industry. Although well provided for financially—indirectly, in this case, through the mega-advertising budgets of major studios—reporters elicited little genuine affection from studio executives. By showing a modicum of respect for this respect-starved army of writers, David Puttnam was able to kindle and sustain an ardent media affair.

Will Tusher, who had been with *Daily Variety* for eleven years, switching from *The Hollywood Reporter* in 1976, was one of David's favorite reporters. And *Daily Variety* editor Thomas Pryor, generally considered to be the most powerful entertainment business editor in Hollywood, was also an object of David Puttnam's public relations strategy. Pryor, who was seventy-five years old, had been at the helm of *Daily Variety* for thirty years, having served as an editor of *The New York Times* before moving west.

The one-two knockout of Will Tusher and Tom Pryor by Britain's most charismatic film producer resulted in *Daily Variety* being labeled a "Puttnam publication" by an angry Hollywood establishment. The battle lines had been drawn, and, as Hollywood saw it, *Daily Variety*, with its senior writer and exalted editor hobnobbing with the enemy, had aligned itself with the "Puttnamites."

The Will Tusher–David Puttnam relationship did have its final reward, however, in the form of an exclusive on the resignation speech. *Daily Variety* played the story across page one with the banner headline: COL'S PUTTNAM DROPS A BOMBSHELL.

Underneath the head was the further explanation: EXEC SAYS HE'LL GIVE UP STUDIO REINS WHEN MERGER BETWEEN TRI-STAR, CPI WRAPS.

"David Puttnam," Will Tusher reported, "last night stunned a group of some 200 studio employees attending a pre-planned monthly seminar by disclosing that he will be giving up his post as chairman and chief executive officer of Columbia Pictures."

From there, Tusher gave a blow-by-blow description of what had happened the night before at "The Reel Truth," offering the *only* eyewitness account of the seminar.

But Will Tusher's article, despite its proprietary look at the actual speech, was not the only piece regarding David Puttnam's resignation to appear on the morning of September 17. *The Wall Street Journal* headlined a report by Laura Landro with the blunt statement: COLUMBIA ASKS DAVID PUTTNAM TO LEAVE POST.

The bank, a large-type sentence which further defines an underlying story, stated: COCA-COLA UNIT PRESIDENT HAD ALIENATED PRODUCERS AND STARS, SOURCES SAY.

Landro's piece did not contain a single on-the-record quote.

"Company executives denied comment," Landro wrote. "Mr. Puttnam did not return calls."

But the article did offer a great deal of information on the negative aspects of David Puttnam's term, something rarely seen in the media.

On September 18, the rest of the newspaper world caught up with *Daily Variety* and *The Wall Street Journal*.

Los Angeles Times writer Jack Mathews, who had written an open "fan letter" to David Puttnam a year earlier, reported the resignation in a story tagged: COLUMBIA'S PUTTNAM RESIGNS POST.

"Reached Thursday," Mathews reported, "Puttnam said he would stay on only until the Coca-Cola Co.'s previously announced merger of Tri-Star and Columbia studios is completed and a successor has been named."

The Hollywood Reporter's Claudia Eller filled in the blanks under the headline: PUTTNAM ERA ENDS AT COL. AS STUDIO HEAD STEPS ASIDE.

"I don't look at this as a defeat in any way, shape, or form," David told Claudia Eller. "I look upon it in some ways as an unfortunate conjunction of events over which I had absolutely no control."

Will Tusher, too, filed a story on September 18, but, having already broken the news of David Puttnam's exit from Columbia the previous day, the piece was a follow-up interview with the former studio chief.

The *Daily Variety* headline looked like this: KAUFMAN PLEDGE: NO IMMEDIATE POST-PUTTNAM COL EXEC-SUITE CHANGES SEEN.

"Puttnam has told his handpicked lieutenants," Tusher revealed, "that CPE president Victor Kaufman has pledged 'there will be no changes in the foreseeable future' and that all incumbent residuals of the Columbia executive suite will get their opportunity 'to prove their worth.' "

With KAUFMAN PLEDGE emblazoned across the page, the casual reader might have gleaned that Victor Kaufman had agreed to maintain the status quo at Columbia Pictures. The actual text, however, indicated something quite different. Victor Kaufman had not spoken to *Daily Variety* at all. Instead, it was David Puttnam who related that Victor Kaufman had "pledged" to do something.

The article next addressed the terms of David's departure from the studio. "Meanwhile, an amicable settlement has been reached on Puttnam's aborted 3-year contract. . . . While Puttnam balked at elaborating on dollar signs or other details, in London a top Coca-Cola executive and a top Columbia executive said he will be returning to the United Kingdom with a cool $3,000,000 in consolation money, the payoff of his contract."

Laura Landro's article in *The Wall Street Journal* had mentioned a settlement as well, but, in that case, the settlement was within the context of David Puttnam being fired and therefore made sense.

In Tusher's story, the allusion to a settlement followed David's insistence he had resigned. In fact, David even struck back at *The Wall Street Journal*'s speculation that he had been terminated by Coca-Cola.

Noting that "a published report Sept. 17 quoted unidentified sources as saying Puttnam was asked to resign," Tusher continued:

". . . Puttnam called the article false from 'top to bottom,' including allegations that he alienated top talent—among them Bill Cosby, Warren Beatty and Dustin Hoffman."

Perhaps even more interesting than the content of the stories was the insight into David Puttnam's multitiered treatment of the media. Certainly David was aware that his resignation was big news and he meted out the story in varying degrees.

Daily Variety's Will Tusher was invited to attend the September 16 "Reel Truth" seminar. *The Hollywood Reporter*'s Claudia Eller and the *Los Angeles Times*'s Jack Mathews, though not guests at the seminar, were provided interview access by David the following day. *The Wall Street Journal*'s Laura Landro, however, was shut out completely.

This layered level of accessibility to David Puttnam coincided precisely with the relative support these writers had previously exhibited in print.

Will Tusher was the clear winner, having frequently filed favorable stories about David Puttnam. Second place in the pro-Puttnam contest fell to Jack Mathews, his open "fan letter" in the *Los Angeles Times* giving him the edge over *The Hollywood Reporter*'s Claudia Eller. Finishing last was *The Wall Street Journal*'s Laura Landro, who had been among the first reporters to point out David Puttnam's unorthodox behavior in Hollywood.

Other stories followed, including an analysis by *The New York Times*'s Aljean Harmetz on September 28.

Calling the "real truth" about David Puttnam "opaque," Harmetz raised the question: "Did he resign by choice or was he pushed?"

Harmetz didn't offer an answer, rather she described the series of events involving David's term and let the reader decide for himself.

The piece concluded with a comment pertaining to David's adamant assertion that Victor Kaufman had assured him his staff would remain in place at the studio after he was gone.

"Hollywood regarded his belief in such assurances as another example of his naivete."

Following David Puttnam's departure, it looked as if the media was careening toward an all-out fight over whose version of the facts were correct. This impending war was evidenced by the volley which had occurred—very visibly—in print.

The Wall Street Journal said David was fired and alienated top talent, according to "sources."

Daily Variety challenged *The Wall Street Journal*'s version of events, indicating David quit and did nothing of consequence to annoy the Hollywood establishment, according to David Puttnam himself.

And *The New York Times* challenged *Daily Variety* by pointing out that David was naive as far as his staff's chances of survival, according to "Hollywood."

With *The Wall Street Journal*, *The New York Times*, and *Variety* squaring off, reading a newspaper promised to be a more exciting experience during the next few months.

All the reader had to do was figure out who was telling the truth.

"Sources." "Hollywood." Or David Puttnam.

Just as David Puttnam's term at Columbia Pictures had been controversial, so too was his exit from the studio, as inconsistent "facts" began to surface in the wake of his resignation. Most basic among these contradictory elements of the story were the precise circumstances surrounding the decision that David would step down as chairman/CEO. When, exactly, was that decision made and who actually made it?

David himself placed the timing of the decision when he said during his speech at the "Reel Truth" seminar that he had chosen to "relinquish his position" following a weekend meeting with Victor Kaufman, the new president of Columbia Pictures Entertainment. Yet, this did not correspond with comments he made at the Toronto Festival of Festivals on Sunday night about "having a big decision to make." Obviously, that "decision" had already been made.

The only conclusion one could draw from David's statements was that he was no longer chairman/CEO at the time of his address in Toronto but he opted to announce his departure in a more appropriate location, Burbank, in front of a more sympathetic audience, his employees.

Discerning just who made the decision was a more difficult task.

Although David insisted he had *resigned*, it is not standard practice in corporate America that an employee quits *and* receives a
financial settlement. Thus, rumor of the ample severance package
which Columbia would provide its outgoing chief executive seemed
to indicate David was asked to leave.

Did David Puttnam resign or was he fired? The question sparked
another heated debate in Hollywood, demonstrating that the
British producer seemed unable to do anything without creating
a major dispute.

CHAPTER

EIGHTEEN

The thing that struck me as most peculiar about David Puttnam's brief tour of Hollywood was the absence of on-the-record quotes from anyone other than David Puttnam. Ray Stark, for example, had only done *two* interviews since 1958, one pertaining to a Teamsters Union problem on *Annie* and the other about art. Likewise, a scrapbook of press clippings of Warren Beatty quotes wouldn't even require a page. And it seemed that Herbert Allen would be more comfortable with losing his vast fortune than speaking "on-the-record" with a reporter.

Such was the relationship between Hollywood and the media when David Puttnam became chairman/CEO of Columbia Pictures. Imagine the delight of journalists when they discovered a studio chief who not only spouted an endless stream of on-the-record quotes, but joined in the sport of "Hollywood bashing" as well.

But with David Puttnam on his way out of Hollywood—along with his colorful media dialogue—the entertainment business press corps turned once again to "sources."

During the next two weeks, the media post mortem on David Puttnam's abrupt resignation continued unabated. With each article, I grew more and more fascinated by the increasingly disparate recounting of "facts" and wondered if the *actual* story could ever be discerned. At the moment, I was working on an article pertaining to just *one* facet of the David Puttnam saga, *The Adven-*

tures of Baron Munchausen, and that in itself was a major investigative task.

As I placed various calls regarding *Munchausen,* I learned—quite by accident—of the existence of an extraordinary item: a video tape of David's resignation speech.

Naturally, I was curious about the tape, especially when I was told that, although all seven "Reel Truth" seminars had been taped, this particular video was different in two respects. First, an extra camera, three instead of two, had been added on the night of September 16. And second, David Puttnam himself had edited the final version.

An Oscar-winning filmmaker editing a seminar tape! Now I *really* had to see it.

For the next two days I concentrated my efforts on locating a copy of the tape and convincing someone to send it to me in New York. When the video finally arrived, I went straight into the den and planted myself in front of a television set with the VCR humming away.

The opening credits read:

"THE REEL TRUTH"
The Columbia Process
Seminar #7 9/16/87
Featured Movie:
"Someone To Watch Over Me"
46:00 Minutes
September 28 1987

At first, I was puzzled. Nothing so far had indicated that the skilled hand of a master filmmaker was at work. Camera angles were static: usually straight-ahead shots of David or Ridley Scott.

When a young blonde asked Ridley a question about *Someone to Watch Over Me,* there *was* a cut to a long shot of the girl. And when David handed Frank Capra, Jr., the award, there was a quick "two-shot"—a term used to describe the presence of two people in the same frame—in which they shook hands.

Yet nothing particularly creative or unusual had occurred on screen. Certainly nothing worthy of the producer of *Chariots of Fire.*

Then David Puttnam started his resignation speech and suddenly the images came alive.

It is safe to say that what I saw was the most spectacular bit of footage *ever* to come out of a business seminar. For the next three or four minutes, David Puttnam proved, at least to me, that editing is the essence of cinema. Here he was working with video tape instead of expensively produced 35 mm film. And he was not even given the luxury of having countless takes to pore over during the edit. Yet he was able to pull together a most convincing and emotional sequence.

Of course, he *had* written the script.

There are many verbal languages in the world but only one *visual* form of communication. The universal nature of cinematic language was best illustrated during the silent movie era when Hollywood exported its motion pictures around the world without any alteration necessary. Charlie Chaplin's antics, for example, needed no elaboration whether the viewer was in a theater in Cleveland, Ohio, or in a theater in Paris. Chaplin exemplified the old adage: "A picture is worth a thousand words."

In fact, many filmmakers during the silent era chafed when sound arrived on the scene, arguing that cinema was a *visual* art form and insisting that audio would be a corrupting influence on the purity of motion pictures.

Sound, of course, came roaring across movie-house speakers in 1927 with the first "talkie," *The Jazz Singer* starring Al Jolson, from Warner Brothers. (Actually, the first picture with synchronized sound was the 1926 *Don Juan*, also from Warner Bros., but the film's soundtrack carried only music, no voices.)

But, as important as sound is to motion pictures, it is only half—perhaps one quarter—of the filmmaking equation. It is the sequence of *images* which really tells a story.

David Puttnam himself had alluded to that fact during his speech when he said, "The marvelous thing about film is that it's ten times more eloquent than anything you could stand here for five hours and say."

The resignation video provided ample testimony to David's statement. As dramatic as the "live" event must have been, the cassette displayed *more* drama than could have been experienced by a member of the audience. When David spoke the words "relinquish his position," those in attendance must have had their eyes riveted on the chairman/CEO. The tape, on the other hand, moved from image to image.

Neither did media accounts convey the spirit which was skillfully edited into the video tape. I had seen many newspaper renditions of the resignation and had even been sent a copy of the press release David read to his employees that evening. Yet nothing captured the poignant moment like the video tape David Puttnam had so carefully constructed. Perhaps the only way to adequately describe the interplay of words and images that danced across my television screen is through the written language of film: the screenplay.

FADE IN ON

DAVID PUTTNAM. MEDIUM SHOT. He is standing at a podium and looks a little like a college professor with his full beard and conservative suit. Although he is in his mid-forties, his collar-length hair is streaked with gray. He seems nervous, as if something terrible is about to happen. But suddenly he smiles and everything appears to be okay.

>   DAVID
> I was going to give you a rah-rah speech about what a
> lot we'd achieved, and that it wasn't nearly enough, and
> what a lot more we'd have to achieve. I guess both are
> true.

DAVID stares off for a moment, collecting his thoughts, trying to make sense out of something which, to him, is senseless. The smile has disappeared and now the ominous feeling is back. Even stronger than before.

>   DAVID (continuing)
> But the last month for all of us—or three weeks for all of
> us—have been very trying and very difficult and life's like
> that sometimes. It's been a bit like Pearl Harbor in
> trying to gather ourselves back together again. Anyways,
> the upshot of all this is, there's a piece that's going to
> appear tomorrow, and I wanted to read this to you first,
> if I may.

CUT TO

DAVID. LONG SHOT. He looks alone on an otherwise empty
stage and the more distant point of view makes him appear
smaller, more vulnerable. He picks up a piece of paper from the
podium and clears his throat.

PAN TO

An AUDIENCE. The screen, from top to bottom, corner to corner, fills with people. As the camera slowly moves across dozens
of concerned faces, DAVID begins to read.

> DAVID (*OVER*)
> The Entertainment Business Sector of the Coca Cola
> Company announced today that David Puttnam, Chair-
> man and Chief Executive Officer of Columbia Pictures . . .

HOLD ON

Several WOMEN. All of them are young and attractive.

PULL BACK TO REVEAL

A small SCREENING ROOM.

> DAVID (*OVER*)
> . . . and Victor Kaufman, Chairman and Chief Executive
> Officer of Tri-Star Pictures, Inc., have met concerning
> Mr. Puttnam's relationship with Columbia following the
> anticipated combination of the Entertainment Business
> Sector with Tri-Star. During that meeting, Messrs. Putt-
> nam and Kaufman agreed that in view of this antici-
> pated combination and Mr. Puttnam's original and
> irrevocable decision to vacate his post no later than the
> summer of 1989, it would be in the company's best inter-
> est to plan for an orderly transition now.

Members of the AUDIENCE turn and look at each other in
disbelief. Soft whispers swell into a collective hum.

> FEMALE VOICE (*OVER*)
> (anguished)
> No!!

The cry of the woman silences those around her. There is no sound for a moment, then DAVID continues.

> DAVID (*OVER*)
> Both men stated that, in their view . . .

CUT TO

A pretty BRUNETTE. CLOSE UP. She is holding her face in her hands, obviously in shock.

> DAVID (*OVER*)
> . . . this approach would most properly facilitate the organization's long-term goals . . .

CUT TO

A different BRUNETTE. MEDIUM SHOT. She has tears streaming down her face.

ZOOM TO

The BRUNETTE's FACE. EXTREME CLOSE UP. She wipes away her tears, but it is a futile exercise. More tears follow. She looks miserable, shaken.

> DAVID (*OVER*)
> . . . and allow a settled structure for the newly combined company. Mr. Puttnam will remain as Chief Executive Officer until the consummation of the combination and at that time . . .

CUT TO

A blond WOMAN and WOMAN with dark hair. MEDIUM TWO SHOT. They are sitting side by side and seem to be leaning on each other for support. They stare straight ahead. The WOMAN with dark hair is crying. The blond WOMAN shakes her head "No," and, as she does . . .

ZOOM TO

The BLONDE. CLOSE UP. Her eyes begin misting over. Finally, a tear forms and falls onto her cheek. The tear catches the light, sparkling like a tear on the face of a fairy tale character. Cinderella, perhaps, at midnight.

> DAVID (*OVER*)
> . . . or shortly afterwards, relinquish his position. During the interim, they stressed that they will work together in planning for a smooth transition, and one that works in the best interest of Columbia . . .

CUT TO

Another teary-eyed BLONDE. EXTREME CLOSE UP. Her face taut, her lips trembling. It is almost unbearable to look at her, to see her pain displayed so publicly at such close range.

> DAVID (*OVER*)
> . . . and the filmmakers with whom the studio is presently working.

PAN TO

A BRUNETTE. Her dark hair frames a pale white face and red eyes.

HOLD ON

The BRUNETTE as she breaks down.

> DAVID (*OVER*)
> . . . During this period, Mr. Puttnam will specifically supervise the production, marketing and distribution of the bulk of the motion pictures previously committed to. Victor Kaufman indicated that he will consider a number of candidates . . .

CUT TO

The profile of a very young and certainly attractive WOMAN with brown hair. Her eyes are red, her mouth open in astonishment.

> DAVID (*OVER*)
> . . . to fill Mr. Puttnam's position following completion of the combination . . .

CUT TO

Yet another pretty BRUNETTE. CLOSE UP. She takes her hand and brushes tears from her eyes.

> DAVID (*OVER*)
> . . . but no decision has at present been made.

A giant TEAR—clearly visible—runs down the BRUNETTE'S cheek.

> DAVID (*OVER*)
> Both Mr. Kaufman and Mr. Puttnam stated that because Tri-Star expects shortly to file a proxy statement . . .

CUT TO

A MAN. CLOSE UP. His jaw is stiff and he swallows hard. He is near crying. He fights back emotion.

> DAVID (*OVER*)
> . . . concerning the proposed combination, neither would be making further comments concerning this announcement in the near future.

CUT TO

A STRAWBERRY-BLONDE wearing glasses. CLOSE UP. Through the lenses, tears can be seen forming in the corners of her eyes.

> DAVID (*OVER*)
> Well, obviously it's not—I hope it's not thrilling for you . . .

PAN TO

Another WOMAN. She appears horrified at what she is hearing.

> DAVID (*OVER*)
> I'm not delighted.

PAN TO

A dark-haired MAN. You can almost hear him thinking: "I will *not* cry . . . I will *not* cry . . ."

> DAVID (*OVER*)
> But it's correct. What the statement says is absolutely accurate.

CUT TO

DAVID. CLOSE UP. He is forlorn. He looks abandoned. Very sad.

> DAVID
> I came to the conclusion at the weekend that it's not right in any way, shape, or form to put you all through two or three months of uncertainty while this particular situation gets sorted out and then put you through the entire thing all over again in sixteen or seventeen months when I go back to England.
>   (after a beat)
> I think it's sensible and correct. I mean, obviously I'm sick to my stomach, because one thing, when I came over here I didn't ever reckon on was—thanks to Frank Capra and all of you—falling in love . . .
>   (pointing off screen)
> . . . with this lady. That was never part of my plans. So uh . . . it's . . .
>   (looking down at the floor)
> . . . a bad day.

FADE OUT

The tape, of course, continued through David Picker's speech, but at this point there were no more cuts, just static head-on shots.

I snapped off the VCR and pondered what I had just seen. It truly was an incredible piece of tape, an unexpected insight into both the "The Reel Truth" seminar and into the mind of David Puttnam. It seemed obvious to me that if an Oscar-winning producer, indeed, a chairman/CEO of a major Hollywood studio, would spend time editing a video tape, then there had to be a desired effect associated with that effort. There had to be a point which he wished to make.

David Puttnam might have accomplished his exit from Columbia Pictures quietly and without controversy. Instead, he left behind a parting shot: a visual sequence of crying women played over the audio of his resignation.

Yet, as it turned out, it wasn't a parting shot at all.

It was an opening salvo.

CHAPTER

NINETEEN

Within twenty-four hours after David Puttnam's resignation, the term "legacy" became the new buzzword in Hollywood.

David's supporters predicted that his "legacy" of films would vindicate the ex-chairman and prove that Coca-Cola's decision to relieve the British producer of his duties was an ill-advised and premature action. Of course, David *insisted* he had *resigned*, but that didn't seem to matter to his legion of fans when advancing this argument.

On the other hand, David's detractors made derisive remarks about the "legacy" David Puttnam left behind.

Neither side had to wait very long for the first round of what was certain to be a very long and bloody bout. On October 2, Columbia Pictures released Ridley Scott's *Someone to Watch Over Me*.

Unfortunately, what *Someone to Watch Over Me* needed and didn't get was someone to watch it. After a strong opening week, the film dropped off the edge of the charts, ultimately bringing in just $9,700,000 in U.S. box office, with $3,900,000 of that amount accruing to Columbia.

While Puttnamites charged that Columbia had purposely sabotaged *Someone to Watch Over Me*, the facts of distribution negated that argument.

The only power a studio has is to "open" a picture. If the initial weekend of release is strong, that provides ample evidence that the distribution and marketing team has done its job by attracting an audience. Whether the audience stays or abandons the film is then entirely up to the power of the film.

Considering its $16,800,000 cost and its prints and advertising budget of $10,000,000, the studio was $22,900,000 in the hole on *Someone to Watch Over Me* before $3,900,000 in foreign and ancillary revenue reduced that deficit to $19,000,000.

So, for those who were keeping track, the score was now: Hollywood establishment, 1. Puttnamites, 0.

As other films in David Puttnam's legacy were being prepared for release, *The Adventures of Baron Munchausen*—after several delays—finally started principal photography in Rome on October 10. A press release announcing the occasion was dispatched from Columbia Pictures.

Two lines in the press release nettled Hollywood.

". . . starring distinguished British stage actor John Neville . . ." stirred up the festering nationality issue, while ". . . worldwide distribution . . . with the exceptions of Italy, Germany, and Austria" generated howls of disbelief.

Columbia Pictures, or, more specifically, David Puttnam, had agreed to pay more than $20,000,000 for a movie about a famous figure from German history—a man who was *only* known in Germany—and yet the studio had *no rights* in that territory. Certainly, Germany might have been considered a safety net for the expensive motion picture simply on the basis that even if it flopped everywhere else in the world, it would at least have an audience in Munich.

Another aspect of the *Munchausen* project which generated heated debate was the contractual status of the film at Columbia Pictures. Was it an in-house production or a negative pickup?

Essentially, the difference between the two is one of ultimate liability. With an in-house production, the studio is *directly* responsible for the completion of the picture and the payment of fees to actors, crew, producers, directors, and other people or entities connected to the project. If the movie doesn't turn out the way it was intended, the studio only has itself to blame as well as a constant celluloid reminder of its miscue.

Conversely, in a negative pickup deal, the studio contracts with an outside production firm and agrees to buy the picture only on delivery of a completed "negative" and only if that print corresponds exactly with what had been spelled out in the initial agreement. Furthermore, the agreement specifies a price which will be paid by the studio regardless of what the cost of production actually was.

The negative pickup arrangement is advantageous to the studio in that it *limits* the cash outlay to whatever had been previously agreed upon. In the case of *Munchausen*, the amount was $20,500,000.

A major portion of a negative pickup contract dictates that the studio has script and cast approval. *Every* page of the script *must* be shot exactly as approved. Even the slightest deviation gives the studio just cause for citing a breach of the agreement.

Consequently, independent producers who have such a deal are religious in their adherence to the contract. Just in case the studio doesn't like the finished product—which, by itself, is *not* sufficient justification for refusing to "pick up" a picture—the producer endeavors to make certain there are no "loopholes" which would enable the studio to leave him holding the film canister.

The delineation between in-house and negative pickup arrangements is sharply defined. In theory, that is.

Although negative pickup arrangements were designed to provide limited liability when dealing with external independent productions, there was another aspect of the deal which held even more appeal for studio management: freedom from stringent union agreements. Studios are signatories to precisely worded documents which require them to closely adhere to certain labor parameters, while independent producers have more latitude in hiring personnel. Hence, the hybrid deal, seemingly a contradiction, wherein the studio is actually *committed* to release the picture but the contract specifies the project as a "negative pickup." Consequently, the production can be done in a more relaxed and less expensive manner than if it were labeled "in-house." As a result, the terms "pickup" and "in-house" became less a descriptive qualifier and more a matter of semantics. (Even though this maneuver runs contrary to the spirit of existing union agreements, it does not run contrary to the substance. It's all *very* legal and certainly a testimony to the ingenuity of film industry attorneys.)

Thus the confusion over *The Adventures of Baron Munchausen.* Although Columbia was calling it a "pickup," the studio was treating it like an "in-house" project. It was an important distinction to make, especially in view of David Puttnam's departure. Was there a possibility the studio could refuse to "pick up" the picture?

For the moment, there was no reliable answer to the question.

Of course, it was frequently pointed out over coffee at the Polo Lounge that *Munchausen* was a Jake Eberts deal. And Jake Eberts was a David Puttnam friend. Therefore, *Munchausen* was probably, despite what Columbia called it, a guaranteed "in-house" deal.

While the creative community chattered away about *Munchausen*, none of those speculating about the film had a vested interest in the project. Consequently, their observations were purely academic. One man, however, did not speak from a detached point of view. Nor did he calmly discuss *Munchausen* over breakfast. Instead, he flew into a rage at the mere mention of the German baron's name.

Allan Buckhantz saw the start of filming on *The Adventures of Baron Munchausen* as a major defeat. He had been lobbying for months to reach some sort of compromise with Columbia Pictures regarding a licensing arrangement on the picture, and felt he was making some progress in that direction.

Proof that Allan was obsessed with *Munchausen* madness came in the form of his volumes of correspondence.

A case in point was a *thirteen*-page letter he fired off, on August 21, to then-chairman/CEO David Puttnam.

"Difficult, however," Allan wrote to David, "is getting through the British style 'LABYRINTH' you have seemingly managed to instill within Columbia Pictures which, in the end, will be a 'legacy' both Columbia Pictures and its 'Parent' will be left to deal (cope) with long after you're gone."

Note that "legacy"—even before David resigned—had become an amorphous word which could either connote future promise or past failure.

"NOW COME ON . . . !" Allan continued. "GET OFF IT, *PUTTNAM*! The fact(s) is (are): COLUMBIA PICTURES . . . has been *deceptive, evasive, circumventive*, etc., thus maybe cunning— from Columbia's point of view—but not very smart I say . . . please *Mr. Puttnam* . . . DON'T MAKE ME LAUGH! If anything, THE JOKE IS ON YOU . . . *NOT ME!*"

Later in the letter, Allan made reference to the first and only time he and David had met. David was acting as executive producer of *The Pied Piper* in 1972 and Allan was the general manager of the motion picture production facility, Studio Hamburg, where the film was being shot. According to Allan, David had fallen into arrears and attempted to "double talk" his way out of settling the account. It was a story Allan loved to tell, a story in which he boasted that he almost "pulled the plug" on David Puttnam. Now, fifteen years later, he refreshed David's memory too.

> You should recall that I, in no uncertain terms, told you that unless the Past Due funds were paid by 12:00 NOON, the next day, I would, indeed, and *personally* "pull the plug" at "lunch break." As you are sure to recall, you caused payment *In Full* the following morning at approximately 10:30 A.M. by Bank Transfer.
>
> (As if yesterday), I recall that look on your face and vividly remember a/your statement (or something to the effect):
>
> ". . . I don't get mad . . . I get even." I cannot help but feel that your latter month's and day's actions are of vindictive nature at an eventual *immense cost* to others . . . ultimately the "Parent"—The Coca-Cola Company—itself and its Stockholders.
>
> But then . . . it's not your money . . . is it? . . . I wonder . . . "at what price Glory comes."

Significantly, Allan Buckhantz was accusing David Puttnam of risking millions of Columbia's money in a convoluted plot to settle an old score.

Had this been the only communication between Allan Buckhantz and Columbia Pictures, its thirteen pages would have been weighty enough. But it was just one item in a relentless barrage.

In addition to the August 21 letter, the following small sampling is indicative of the frequency of Allan's poison-pen letters:

August 4: A *seventeen*-page tome directed at the Columbia legal department.

August 22: *Seventeen* more pages of what Allan termed a "Damage and Loss Evaluation."

September 3: Addressed to Roberto Goizueta and Donald Keough, a scathing *seven*-page tirade.

September 16: Two more pages to Roberto and Don.

September 17: Three pages to Victor Kaufman.

September 20: Three additional pages to Victor Kaufman.

It went on and on. And on.

Besides the alarming regularity of the paper flow and the venomous nature of the prose, there was another aspect to Allan's letters which was even more disturbing to those who received them.

The bizarre way in which they were written.

Although Allan spoke English well in his rasping German accent, he seemed unable to write a normal-looking business letter. In addition to the liberal use of capital letters and exclamation points, some communiqués even contained *numbered lines* as did Allan's August 4 note to the Columbia legal department:

1) The *unequivocal* fact(s) is (are)—
2) the issue(s) and matter(s) in progress is (are) subject to *various*
3) (International) *Law(s)* and is not limited to determination(s) under
4) U.S. Law(s) only; in essence; it is especially subject to GERMAN
5) *and* ANGLO-SAXON LAW(s).

With *Someone to Watch Over Me* dying at the box office and *The Adventures of Baron Munchausen* promising to explode into litigation, the "legacy" everyone kept talking about began to look more like a debacle than anything else.

On a bleak October morning, I walked into *Variety* to find a telex on my desk from the West German government-owned Transit Film. It was sent by Transit president Karl A. Woerner, date-stamped Munich, and addressed as follows:

IDENTICAL TO:
1) ROBERTO GOIZUETA, CHAIRMAN, THE COCA-COLA CO.
2) DON KEOUGH, CHAIRMAN COLUMBIA PICTURES ENTERTAINMENT
3) VICTOR KAUFMAN, PRESIDENT-CEO COLUMBIA PICTURES ENTERTAINMENT
4) KENNETH LEMBERGER, COLUMBIA PICTURES, LEGAL DPT.,
5) CHARLES KIPPS, VARIETY, NEW YORK
6) CC: MARTIN BAUM, ALLAN BUCKHANTZ, STANLEY CAIDIN

I stared at the document for a moment. Why was I listed as an addressee? I had written two previous stories for *Variety* about the *Munchausen* mess and was working on a third, but I was an *observer*, not a participant in the drama. For some reason it made me nervous to be cast among a group of corporate executives locked in a major controversy, especially when that controversy involved a foreign government.

The telex stated in part:

"We have taken notice and are thus taking issue with Columbia Pictures Executive Personnel identifying our product, the Universum Film AG (UFA) motion picture 'The Adventures Of Baron Munchausen' (1942) as Nazi oriented propaganda with which Columbia Pictures does not wish to associate itself or be identified with . . . Equally, to identify Mr. Buckhantz, a former concentration camp inmate, to allegedly further such material is unheard of."

Nazi propaganda? I wondered what bizarre twist the David Puttnam saga had taken now.

A call to Allan Buckhantz revealed that his attorney, Stanley Caidin, had told him that Ronald Jacobi, senior counsel for Columbia Pictures, had said that Columbia had no intention of becoming involved with *The Adventures of Baron Munchausen* because it was filmed in Germany under Nazi supervision. This, of course, angered Allan *and* the West German government.

There appeared to be no limit to reverberations from one brief year in the life of British producer-turned-studio-chief David Puttnam.

While Hollywood waited for word on who would replace David Puttnam, Columbia Pictures Entertainment president/CEO Victor Kaufman announced that instead of filling the vacated post, the post would be *eliminated*. Although Hollywood joked that the move was a knee-jerk reaction to the performance of the previous chairman/CEO, it actually was part of an overall plan to streamline the corporate structure of the newly combined Columbia/Tri-Star entity.

At the same time, CPE revealed that David Picker would leave Columbia Pictures and return to independent production, a euphemistic way of saying Picker had been fired. Taking over for Picker would be Paramount's president of production, Dawn Steel.

Dawn Steel had joined Paramount in 1978 as director of merchandising and marketing, was promoted to merchandising and marketing vice president in 1979, and became vice president of production in 1980. In 1983, she was elevated again, this time to senior vice president of production, and subsequently was named president of production in 1985. Her rise at Paramount had been spectacular with *Flashdance, Footloose, Top Gun, Star Trek IV, Beverly Hills Cop II, The Untouchables*, and *Fatal Attraction* included in the films she had championed at the studio.

Most significant among her credits were *Star Trek IV* and *Beverly Hills Cop II*. At least it was clear that she had nothing against sequels.

Running a major studio is an awesome task in itself, but following the most revered *and* the most hated studio head in recent Hollywood history was a difficult proposition for Dawn Steel. She hadn't hesitated when the Columbia job was offered, but, by mid-November—after she had a chance to fully examine the state of things at the studio—reality came thundering in around her. Not only was it her responsibility to develop her own slate of films, she was also charged with completing and nurturing David Puttnam's "legacy."

Exacerbating the situation for Dawn Steel was the lingering affection for David Puttnam expressed by journalists. Indeed, much of the commentary was filled with praise for the fallen British hero.

Dawn Steel was in a no-win situation as far as David's projects were concerned. Even if she *was* able to create a string of box-office sensations out of the "legacy," she would merely be providing proof that David's ouster was a mistake. On the other hand, if the pictures failed miserably, she would be blamed for not properly promoting David's projects.

Thus, the Dawn of a new era at Columbia Pictures was overcast with billowy clouds of controversy even before it began.

CHAPTER
TWENTY

Despite the fact that gaining an on-the-record account from the Hollywood establishment was beginning to look like an impossibility, I placed a call to Don Safran at Rastar Productions. Since I was in the midst of a running story on *The Adventures of Baron Munchausen*, I told his secretary—in response to the standard question: "Does he know what this is regarding?"—that *Munchausen* was the purpose of my call.

"*Munchausen?*" Don laughed.

Don knew Allan Buckhantz and had often spoken with him about *Munchausen*.

"I've been doing a series of stories on the film and . . ."

"I've seen them."

". . . and I thought you might be able to shed some light on what's going on."

"Me?" Don seemed surprised. "I'm sure I don't know any more than you've already been told by Allan."

"What about Ray?"

"Ray? Ray doesn't have anything to do with *Munchausen*."

"Yes, but he is a consultant to Columbia. And he does have a great deal of influence at the studio. I thought he might . . ."

"Ray may discuss some policy and overall aims with Columbia but never advises them on projects. He's spent his career avoiding studio bureaucracy and details. He has his own company to run."

"Can I at least meet with him?"

227

"He doesn't have much confidence in the media and would rather not give up his time."

"Well, anyway, Don, thanks for taking the call."

"Sorry I couldn't have been of more help. I don't mean to sound like we're inventing the stealth bomber, but Ray prefers being a private person."

"Maybe we can get together one of these days," I said in closing. "Are you coming to New York any time soon?"

"Let me see . . . I'll be in New York in a couple of weeks . . ."

We arranged to meet at the Parker Meridien Hotel on West 57th Street.

Although Don Safran insisted Ray Stark had very strong feelings about talking to the press, I felt that meeting with Don might be a start in changing that stance. At least Don could tell Ray about my interest in doing an interview with him.

Even if the meeting with Don didn't ultimately lead to Ray, Don and I had a very good reason to get together anyway: He was in charge of the marketing of Rastar's pictures and I was a writer for *Variety*.

But I was determined that our association extend well beyond that limited sphere.

Before Don Safran traveled to Manhattan, Allan Buckhantz breezed in and out of town on his way to Germany. He arrived at *Variety* nattily dressed and caressing his ever-present cigarette, an unfiltered Pall Mall. His hair was combed backward and fiercely intent eyes peered out through steel-rimmed glasses.

Allan and I spent two hours talking about *Munchausen* before he boarded a plane and continued on to Munich. But I now had a face to attach to a disembodied telephone voice. And I had met a walking, talking character from the David Puttnam saga.

On a bitterly cold December night—the kind of night that makes Californians consider never coming back East—Don Safran landed at New York's Kennedy Airport and made his way to the Parker Meridien Hotel.

"What kind of weather is this?" Don said as he emerged from the elevator.

Don, fiftyish with wavy brown hair, was dressed in a dark suit but had forgotten to bring a coat. He was still dealing with the trauma of walking out of the airport and into a blast of arctic air.

During the course of our conversation, I found out that Don was himself an ex-journalist, having served as entertainment editor for the *Dallas Times-Herald* before moving to Hollywood in 1978. He entered the entertainment business via the television industry, writing scripts for several *Happy Days* episodes and acting as associate executive producer of the *Blue Thunder* series. In 1980 he wrote a film called *Homework* starring Joan Collins and then joined Rastar in 1982, where he now serves as senior vice president of marketing.

"I'm thinking of doing an article for *Variety*," I told Don, "on the David Puttnam year at Columbia."

Don smiled. "You might want to prepare for it by watching *Rashomon*."

Don was referring to the film which explored the fact that many people can view the *same* incident while drawing completely *different* conclusions.

"Did you tell Ray Stark I wanted to see him?" I asked Don.

"After you called, I passed on your request. I don't think it's going to happen though. As I told you before, Ray rarely talks to the media."

"I've only been at *Variety* six months. Does that count as the media."

"Semi-media," Don laughed.

We talked for a while about our respective backgrounds and the movie business before Don's daughter Dona arrived for dinner.

On the way home that night, I felt one step closer to Ray Stark and one step closer to the rest of Hollywood as well.

As the holidays approached, most of the film industry began its yearly slowdown. Many executives, but not Allan Buckhantz, were "out until the first" according to their secretaries, and many pictures, but not *The Adventures of Baron Munchausen*, began a short sabbatical.

By Christmas, Allan Buckhantz had sued Columbia Pictures for $80,000,000 in a libel action regarding the "Nazi propaganda" statement and then withdrew it because he became convinced that Columbia attorneys would use his deposition in the libel case to build a defense in his threatened copyright infringement lawsuit.

Meanwhile, *The Adventures of Baron Munchausen* continued to soar over budget and bog down with seemingly endless delays in Rome, causing Sean Connery to remove himself from the troubled project.

As is always the case in out-of-control productions, problems cause other problems causing still more problems. Sean Connery had contracted to play the role of a headless moon man, specifying a "window" of time in which he would shoot the sequence. In other words, because Connery had other commitments, his agreement stated that he would start and complete his part during a certain three-week period. The picture became so hopelessly behind schedule, however, that it was impossible to schedule Connery during the planned time frame. So Connery, well within his right to do so, bowed out.

Unfortunately for director Terry Gilliam—and particularly for producer Jake Eberts and completion guarantor Film Finances—Sean Connery was on a "pay-or-play" status. Thus, the delays in Italy cost the producers $500,000 they could ill afford for an actor who would not even be in the film.

On February 9, 1988, David Puttnam, having been rejected by one Fortune-500 company—Coca-Cola—was honored by another—the Eastman Kodak Company—when he received the Second Century Award for outstanding contribution to the motion picture industry.

"The medium is too powerful and too important an influence on the way we live," David said when accepting the award, "to be left solely to the tyranny of the box office, or reduced to the lowest common denominator of public taste."

Although the audience did not realize it, the line was from the statement of film-making philosophy David had presented to Roberto Goizueta and Don Keough in Atlanta a year earlier.

Roland Joffe, director of both *The Killing Fields* and *The Mission*, was on hand to offer a testimony to his former employer, given in the guise of a fable in which El Inglés, an avowed Los Creativos (David Puttnam), rode into battle against the forces of El Vested Interest (the Hollywood establishment). El Inglés, Joffe related, was supposed to be backed by the Seventh Cavalry from Atlanta (Coca-Cola), but was defeated when the Seventh Cavalry turned on El Inglés as well.

Joffe's tale was humorous, but the most unusual aspect of the luncheon was David's subdued delivery of a noncontroversial speech. The former chairman/CEO leaned heavily on philosophy instead of resorting to verbal assault. Yet David didn't convey a sense of having given up. Rather it seemed as if he were biding his time, waiting for a more strategic platform from which to launch an offensive.

At the end of February, I flew to Los Angeles for the American Film Market, a frenzied convention of movie buyers and sellers. The films vended at the yearly AFM are predominantly of the "B" variety with independent American filmmakers seeking video outlets and theatrical distribution in foreign territories.

Before leaving New York, I let Don Safran know I was headed west and questioned him once more about the possibility of meeting with Ray Stark and again he said he would check with Ray. So, when I arrived at the hotel, the first call I made was to Rastar Productions.

"I'm afraid nothing has changed," Don informed me.

A few days later, however, something happened which changed everything. Something which reopened all the wounds inflicted during David's term at Columbia Pictures. Something that united the Hollywood establishment in collective anger.

On the morning of February 26, a limousine was dispatched with a peculiar cargo and an even more peculiar mission. Instead of a human occupant, the stretch Lincoln carried a manila envelope as it wended its way toward the residence of Ray Stark. Inside the envelope was an advance copy of the April issue of *Vanity Fair* magazine. Inside the magazine was a story entitled "Hollywood Knives" by *Vanity Fair* editor-in-chief Tina Brown.

Before opening the envelope, Ray sat for a minute recalling the circumstances surrounding his acquaintance with Tina Brown. A mutual friend had introduced them, and Ray had made it clear to Tina at the time that any conversations they might have would be of a social nature and certainly *off-the-record*. Subsequently, Ray spoke to Tina often, not feeling it necessary to censor his words. But then, on January 10, 1988, the *Los Angeles Times* Calendar section carried a piece that heralded the upcoming *Vanity Fair* article as describing "how Ray Stark 'got' David Puttnam." Ray immediately responded by sending Tina a letter advising her of the *Los Angeles Times* item and reiterating the fact that all his conversations with her had been as a friend and, of course, confidential.

"I am concerned," Ray wrote. "I have never talked to the press about Puttnam. Yes, I have talked to you, off the record, as a friend. We talked at length on the telephone a while ago and, as a good friend which you have always been, I perhaps opened up more to you than I normally would have. I know that confidentiality will be honored. However, if you have any questions on what you believe should be clarified, you certainly may check with me."

Two days later, Tina Brown wrote Ray and countered by saying that she was "preparing a piece that is a psychological evaluation of mistakes that were made." Furthermore, Tina insisted that her article "could certainly not be headed 'How Ray Stark Got David Puttnam,' " and added that she had "no idea" why the *Los Angeles Times* would characterize her upcoming story in such a manner.

"Dear Tina," Ray wrote back immediately, "How very thoughtful of you to have eased my concerns."

Now, however, Ray faced an actual copy of *Vanity Fair*. He flipped through the pages until his eyes fell on the title: "Hollywood Knives."

The implication was unmistakable. "Hollywood Knives." The kind that stabbed David Puttnam in the back.

Under the title, a teaser asked the questions: "What is the real story of David Puttnam's tumultuous year as head of Columbia Pictures? Why did half of Hollywood, from Ray Stark to Warren Beatty, set out to get him?"

Then came a shocking opening paragraph:

"The day David Puttnam resigned as chairman of Columbia Pictures, after just one year in the job, the Hollywood producer Ray Stark came on the phone to accept an invitation to a *Vanity Fair* party. 'Well, darling, it's a bad day for Rule Britannia,' he commented genially. 'Your compatriot turned out to be a real asshole, didn't he? He should go off and be a professor somewhere.' "

CHAPTER
TWENTY-ONE

When David Puttnam criticized Hollywood during the late seventies and early eighties as an independent British producer, the Hollywood establishment took little notice. After all, at that point, David was a continent and an ocean away.

Later, when he continued to preach the evils of the American film industry while chairman/CEO of Columbia Pictures, Hollywood reacted a little more violently. With British guns being fired right in their own territory, the danger seemed more clear and present. Yet, the reclusive creative community remained entrenched in their bunkers, not engaging in open warfare, waiting instead for what they knew would be an inevitable retreat by the brash British invader.

But when David Puttnam started to put words in their mouths, as he did in "Hollywood Knives," well, that's where they drew the line. Until then, David's attacks had been ambiguous rather than personal. "Producers" were greedy. "Hollywood" was a despicable place. "American movies" were all bad.

Now, however, in *Vanity Fair*, David named names. And gave his version of *both* sides of private conversations.

For a group of people who *never* talked to the press, seeing themselves quoted was bad enough. Seeing themselves quoted *secondhand* was just too much to bear.

For example, *Vanity Fair* detailed a meeting between Ray Stark and David, as related by David:

Stark: "I want to know once and for all: am I making pictures at Columbia?"

Puttnam: "It will all depend on the script."

Stark: "Don't be a smart ass—what's it got to do with the script?"

There were many other cases of David playing ventriloquist. Bill Cosby was quoted according to David. So were Herbert Allen, Roberto Goizueta, and Don Keough.

Besides David's recollections, there were two other aspects of the article which outraged the key players in the drama.

One was the tone of Tina Brown's observations.

"Two Puttnam projects," Tina noted, *The Last Emperor* and *Hope and Glory*, were nominated for Best Director. It was ironic for Bertolucci [*The Last Emperor* director] since, after Puttnam's departure, Columbia had all but dumped his movie . . ."

This, of course, made Herbert Allen and Victor Kaufman sound as if they were carrying on a personal vendetta at the expense of Coca-Cola stockholders.

The other element of the *Vanity Fair* piece which troubled Hollywood was the scattering of testimonials.

Michael Nathanson, a Columbia production executive, was quoted as saying: "Puttnam has the best postproduction mind of anyone I've ever met." And Don Keough, in David's words, said: "David Puttnam . . . had the guts, sheer guts, to say, O.K., I'll do it. I'll do it my way."

In addition to the text, "Hollywood Knives" was accompanied by photographs. Not just any photographs, but *studies* by well-known photographer Annie Leibovitz. One shot even pictured David standing in front of a backdrop of the parting of the red sea from Cecil B. Demille's epic film *The Ten Commandments*.

The feeling in Hollywood changed drastically with the publication of the April issue of *Vanity Fair*. No longer was there a sense of annoyance or passive anger. Suddenly, there was a retaliatory mood brewing on the shores of the Pacific.

This time David Puttnam had gone *too* far.

I spoke to Don Safran after hearing about "Hollywood Knives."

"I think David Puttnam might have just created his own Altamont," Don stated, switching from his previous *Rashomon* analogy. (Altamont was the site of the ill-fated Rolling Stones concert which erupted into a riot in which a spectator was killed, documented in the film, *Gimme Shelter*.)

"I thought you said Ray Stark doesn't talk to the press," I remarked, noting Ray's quotes in the article.

"I can tell you that what I read in *Vanity Fair* doesn't in any way sound like Ray. For one thing, I know he never spoke to Tina Brown for the record. For another, I can't believe she would have used David Puttnam quoting Ray Stark. I know Ray was at a *Vanity Fair* party sitting with Tina Brown and Mike Ovitz, but I also know what Ray's rules are—even before sitting down with the media—and he always establishes that everything he says is off-the-record. He does that so he can relax and enjoy the evening."

As Don spoke, I realized the wall of silence in the David Puttnam affair was beginning to crack.

"Ray may want to speak to you after all," Don added, catching me by surprise. "So why don't you come to the *Biloxi Blues* premiere in New York on March twenty-third."

Biloxi Blues was Ray's newest film, a Neil Simon story produced for Universal Pictures.

"Ray will be there," Don concluded, "and perhaps we can have a drink together."

As the *Vanity Fair* article set off fireworks from Atlanta to Beverly Hills, I found myself growing curious about the writer of "Hollywood Knives." I wanted to meet the woman who single-handedly reignited the Puttnam-Hollywood war.

I called Tina and scheduled a meeting for 10:30 the morning of March 17.

On the Ides of March, another mortar shell, this one of nuclear proportions, detonated in New York. Instead of rhetoric, however, this blast—emanating from the office of CPE president/CEO Victor Kaufman—contained only figures. It was a press release which announced that Columbia Pictures Entertainment would declare a staggering $105,000,000 loss. Across the top of the page were the words: COLUMBIA PICTURES ENTERTAINMENT ANNOUNCES ITS THREE YEAR OPERATING PLAN AND LOSS FOR "STUB" PERIOD.

The release stated that Columbia Pictures Entertainment had completed the development of its three-year operating plan. According to CPE president Victor Kaufman, the company had "two objectives in mind . . . to concentrate on generating substantial cash flow from operations and to emphasize the importance of a strong balance sheet."

After outlining the future, Victor dealt with the present by offering the current balance sheet as "$3.5 billion in assets, $1.0 billion in net worth, $1.0 billion in outstanding debt, and in excess of $2.5 billion in available credit facilities, including outstanding indebtedness." Then the Columbia executive turned his attention to the past.

". . . the Company said that management reviewed its overall operations, including the large number of films produced or developed by the prior management. . . . As a result, the Company said that it anticipated recording an after tax loss of approximately $105 million for the two and one-half month 'stub' period ending February 29, 1988. . . . The loss, according to the Company, is primarily due to the write down of motion picture product produced by the Columbia Pictures studio prior to the combination, to the level of performance now anticipated for these films by current management and to a write-off of certain development costs. . . ."

A sum such as $105,000,000 commands attention all by itself. Announced in relation to David Puttnam's "legacy," it was riveting. Besides, reading between the lines, it was easy to see that $105,000,000 might be the tip of the proverbial iceberg.

Although the release did not specifically mention David Puttnam, the reference to the loss being declared after reviewing "the large number of films produced or developed by the prior management" and "primarily due to the write down of motion picture product produced by the Columbia Pictures studio prior to the combination" was enough of a clue. The effect of the statement was to reinforce the preexisting opinion of both Puttnamites *and* non-Puttnamites.

Puttnamites considered the write-down of unreleased pictures sufficient evidence that Columbia was sabotaging David's "legacy."

The Hollywood establishment, for their part, viewed the loss as justification for David's dismissal.

Ironically—even with a concrete figure like $105,000,000—the debate centered around intangibles. Since the pictures in question had not had a chance to prove themselves at the box office, the declared loss by Columbia really settled nothing on a definitive basis.

What Victor Kaufman was doing was applying a method dubbed "forward-based accounting," a common financial maneuver in the motion picture industry. Since studio executives were supposed to be able to predict which films would be box-office hits—their very job was based on that assumption—it followed that these same executives should be allowed the latitude to declare a loss as soon as it was evident that the loss was inevitable. Significantly, both the Internal Revenue Service and the Securities and Exchange Commission recognized forward-based accounting as acceptable.

The allure of forward-based accounting to current management is its allocation of loss within the period that films are approved rather than when they are released. The result is that the actual performance of each administration is synchronized with the time in which it is in power. By declaring the $105,000,000 loss now instead of later, Victor was assuring that the profits of any pictures he put into motion would not be diminished on the income statement by the losses of those approved by David Puttnam.

Notwithstanding the reality of the situation, Puttnamites continued to assert that Victor Kaufman was "burying" David Puttnam's "legacy."

To suggest that Victor Kaufman would purposely lose $105,000,000 just to strike back at his predecessor seemed to be a preposterous allegation. But it became a rallying cry for the pro-Puttnam faction of Hollywood nonetheless.

On March 17, at the appointed hour of 10:30 A.M., I walked into the tastefully decorated offices of *Vanity Fair* magazine to meet editor-in-chief Tina Brown.

Tina was tall, blond, and very elegant. She was also cordial, and explained in some detail the observations she had made when interviewing David Puttnam.

As I listened to Tina, David became multidimensional and began to emerge as a personality. It seemed obvious to me that Tina was fond of David and what he stood for—which may have accounted for her vivid dialogue—and it was equally obvious that she had spent a great deal of time and effort compiling "Holly-wood Knives." Both her fondness and diligence were evident in the article.

Just before leaving, I asked her how she was able to get Ray Stark to go on-the-record.

"I don't discuss my reporting methods," she replied.

Later that morning, I called David Puttnam's California office, located in his Coldwater Canyon home. David, I learned, was at his London office. I called London and left a message, describing at length the reason for the call. He phoned back within a half hour.

First of all, I was surprised by the rapid response and secondly, although I had never met or spoken with him previously, I was taken by his instant willingness to discuss the Columbia year. We achieved a spontaneous rapport and it was easy to see why so many journalists had become mesmerized by his accessibility and candid conversational style.

David was amenable to doing an extensive face-to-face inter-view, suggesting that the best time and place might be early April, in Toronto, Canada. He would be there from the tenth through the fifteenth teaching a seminar at the Canadian Centre for Ad-vanced Film Studies.

"I'm afraid I'm stuck here in England for a while," David said, "dealing with the government on this footpath I have on my country property. I want to move it but they won't let me."

David explained that there was a nine-hundred-year-old right-of-way crossing his country estate upon which the townspeople were free to walk anytime they chose. David said he was seeking to relocate that right-of-way some distance from his house. (I later found out that David's action caused quite a stir in England, be-coming nightly fodder on BBC and in the tabloids. Newscasters and journalists asked: "If David Puttnam was such a champion of the common man, then why couldn't the common man walk along the same path he had walked for nine hundred years?")

"How about five-thirty on the twelfth?" David asked. "I'll meet you at the Four Seasons Hotel."

The following morning, March 18, Liz Smith reported in her column in the *New York Daily News* that David Puttnam would appear in a special two-part interview on the *Today Show*. Under a bold-faced heading which said BEHIND THE FEAR & LOATHING IN LA-LA LAND, the columnist wrote:

" 'I felt that Hollywood was basically a fear-based community, that it ran on fear . . . that fear was an extremely bad element; not a combustible element that created good creative work. Creative people, in my experience, didn't respond to fear. They responded to encouragement and they responded to love,' says David Puttnam. His interview with reporter Nancy Collins will be seen on the 'Today' show Monday and Tuesday."

Liz Smith then outlined a bit of the background leading up to the interview before telling her legion of readers:

"So here's Puttnam talking to Collins and the first shocker is— 'I don't believe Ray Stark has any real power at all. If you believe he has power . . . but I don't believe it. That's exactly why [people in Hollywood] are rigid with fear and unable to do their jobs properly. That's exactly why I wasn't rigid with fear and didn't have that problem . . .' "

Next to the above paragraph was a picture of Ray in a tuxedo. It was the *only* photo in the column.

"This could be David Puttnam's Sarajevo," Don Safran observed of David's upcoming *Today Show* appearance. Don's analogies growing more ominous by the day. (Sarajevo was the site of the start of World War I.)

According to Don, Ray was startled. Having only met with David twice during the entire time he was at Columbia, Ray was at a loss as to why the ex-chairman/CEO was suddenly zeroing in on him.

"He's as annoyed as I've ever seen him," Don continued. "Not only is he being attacked publicly, no one is checking to see if there is any validity to these charges. Ray is not in national politics but he's being turned on like a rival candidate. It's a very strange reaction by the media giving anyone—in this case David Puttnam—that sort of forum."

Don paused.

"I can't promise anything," he finally said, "but I get the feeling Ray may just have had enough."

I hung up the phone feeling very fortunate that three such lovely women were helping me break through the impenetrable force field surrounding the Hollywood establishment.

First Tina Brown. Now Liz Smith. And, in three days, Nancy Collins.

At 8:38 A.M. on the morning of March 21, America awoke to hear *Today Show* host Bryant Gumbel say:

"The European influence in Hollywood has never been stronger. All of this year's Oscar-nominated films were directed by foreigners. Two of the strongest, *Hope and Glory* and *The Last Emperor*, were brought to American audiences by Britain's David Puttnam when he was head of Columbia Pictures. He had won an Oscar for *Chariots of Fire* but he had never run a studio before, and he didn't run Columbia very long. Contributing correspondent Nancy Collins is here with more of that story."

Collins noted David's outspoken criticism of Hollywood and called his selection as studio chief "surprising." Then she brought on the British producer with the words, "Today, in this exclusive interview, we hear David Puttnam's side of the story."

David opened with the "fear-based community" speech reported in Liz Smith's column and then it was back to Collins's commentary.

"He was . . . a filmmaker, not an agent nor a lawyer. Although the creative community was rooting for him, the business community, the power elite, felt threatened."

David then insisted he had been hired by Coca-Cola because ". . . they wanted to be very, very proud of their studio. They wanted the films that the studio made to reflect what they thought were the most positive aspects of Coca-Cola. That it was international. And celebrated the best things in life."

"But," Collins interjected, "they also wanted to make money, didn't they?"

"I assume so," David retorted. "But funnily enough it was one conversation we didn't really have. I mean, my films, that I've made, by and large have made money. In fact, the vast proportion of the films I've made have been profitable. So I assume that was implicit."

He went on to say that the movies coming out of Hollywood were of a "dreadful quality" essentially because of "a small golden group of people who regard themselves as having free passes."

Collins's voice-over next pointed out that David had "ruffled feathers" of people like Mike Ovitz and Bill Cosby.

"But most importantly," she concluded, "he offended producer Ray Stark . . . a major Coca-Cola shareholder [who] reportedly went to the parent company and demanded Puttnam be fired."

David's response: "Ray Stark has no power. . . . It's the Wizard of Oz. If you believe him, he exists."

The most astonishing aspect of the interview was that Collins didn't explore any of David's statements, many of which cried out for a deeper probe. For example, when David remarked that his films "by and large have made money," Collins accepted it as fact. What about *The Mission*, a $25,000,000 disaster at the box office? And what about the string of small films David produced prior to joining Columbia? How much money did they make? After all—despite what most people thought—all of David's past efforts did not perform as well as *Chariots of Fire*. And even the $30,600,000 in domestic rentals from that picture placed it far down *Variety*'s all-time film chart at number 128.

Granted, the *Today Show* is an electronic rather than a print medium and Nancy Collins was appealing to a consumer rather than a trade audience, so it was not necessarily *required* that she counter David Puttnam's comments. Yet her conversational rather than investigative treatment of the British producer was indicative of the media coverage surrounding the controversy: When David Puttnam spoke, it was gospel.

The next morning, it was Jane Pauley who informed viewers of Nancy Collins's second segment:

"*Hope and Glory, The Last Emperor, Housekeeping,* and *The Big Easy* are all films David Puttnam brought to Columbia during his tenure as chief operating officer. That tenure ended abruptly, and controversially, last October when Puttnam resigned after only eighteen months on the job. Although he won't be running a studio, Puttnam will be making movies. Contributing correspondent Nancy Collins talked to Puttnam about his film career in the second part of her exclusive interview."

"David Puttnam called his film company Enigma," Collins opened, "an apt name for a man who's often more famous than the stars of his movies."

David repeated his oft-stated doctrine of filmmaking before Collins once again returned to the subject of David's very high profile.

"David, because you came out of the advertising business, you obviously know how to sell things. And a lot of people think that you've sold David Puttnam better than you've sold any of your films and products."

David's answer: ". . . With *Chariots of Fire,* a very interesting thing happened. I became the story . . . And they said, 'Maybe David Puttnam is good copy.' And that's what happened. The journalists invented me . . ."

Of course, most in Hollywood believed it was the other way around, that David invented himself for the media. Regardless of who invented whom, however, it was clear that the invention was working. David had graduated from the pages of entertainment business trade papers with fifty thousand readers to network television, where millions would hear his message.

Not bad for an invention no one would claim credit for having invented.

CHAPTER
TWENTY-TWO

Just when Hollywood thought it was safe to continue business as usual, *Daily Variety*'s front-page banner headline screamed: PUTT-NAM AND H'WOOD: THE SEQUEL. While the message was shocking enough, the timing also added an element of surprise. The date was March 22, the morning of David Puttnam's second install-ment on the *Today Show*.

"Negotiations have not been finalized," *Daily Variety* noted of a new production deal the former studio chief was about to con-summate, "but the expectation is that the deal will be done and in place by May. If that timetable is met, the occasion may be celebrated with a burst of fanfare at the Cannes Film Festival."

This time several international companies would finance his foray back into filmmaking, including Japanese firm Fujisankei Communications International, Britain's Anglia TV, and Holly-wood's own Warner Bros. Pictures. Collectively, the amount David would be given to crank up the cameras was estimated at $50,000,000, a quarter of a million dollars less in production power than he had at his disposal when chairman/CEO of Columbia Pic-tures, but a substantial sum nonetheless.

Incredibly, David Puttnam was about to return to Hollywood *again*, after just seven months in the pastoral setting of the En-glish countryside.

Ray Stark and Don Safran had flown into New York a few days earlier for the *Biloxi Blues* premiere. The night before the film was to open—which was the evening of the second *Today Show* segment—Don called and asked me if I'd like to meet for coffee the next day.

"Why don't you come by the hotel about eight."

The next morning I met Don in the lobby of the Parker Meridien.

"We're going to have breakfast with Ray," Don said.

Ray Stark sat in his rambling East Side apartment sipping instant coffee from a mug. There were no maids, butlers, silver, or china. There wasn't even fresh-brewed coffee as Ray shed the indulgence of Hollywood for the expedience of Manhattan.

"Wizard of Oz?" Ray laughed, referring to David Puttnam's *Today Show* remarks.

It was a bizarre analogy, but one with a ring of truth. Perhaps David was referring to Ray's reclusive private life behind the curtain of major motion pictures he produced. In that case, Ray was sort of a movie biz Wizard.

Ray questioned other comments David had made the previous morning.

"Rigid with fear? I don't understand why he's saying these things. Especially after all this time."

It was obvious that Ray didn't like seeing his name bandied about in the media like loose change.

Perhaps the most unrealistic characterization of Ray Stark made by David Puttnam on the *Today Show* was that Ray had no power. If that was the case, then why did David bother to talk about him on national television? And, if Ray truly had no power, I wondered how he could have gotten David fired, a charge leveled often by David's supporters.

"Actually," Ray said, "Puttnam has a tendency toward self-destruction. It seemed he *wanted* to be fired."

During the next half hour, Ray made several observations about the sudden press interest in David Puttnam but he carefully avoided any direct refutations of what was being said.

"I'll see you tonight," Ray said as Don and I left. "At the *Biloxi Blues* party."

Although the subject of my doing an on-the-record interview never came up that morning, I couldn't help but feel I was getting closer every day. In fact, I reasoned that as long as David Puttnam kept talking, it was only a matter of time.

***

When I arrived at the Baronet Theater for the premiere of *Biloxi Blues*, the corner of 59th Street and Third Avenue was in the final throes of another murderous New York rush hour and looked more like a parking lot than an intersection. A flotilla of various vehicles jostled along, making imperceptible progress toward the outmoded Queensboro Bridge.

Commuters had come to expect, though never completely accept, the reality of fleeing a modern Manhattan island by crossing the East River via a structure designed to handle traffic of another era. Tonight, however, the delay was worse than usual and rivaled the massive exodus of a holiday weekend.

But the reason for the logjam was neither holiday nor weekend. Rather it was the flurry of activity in front of the Baronet Theater.

On Third Avenue, directly across the street from the Baronet, the beam from a giant spotlight crisscrossed a starless sky like an incandescent sword slicing its way through a black velvet curtain.

While the huge apparatus swung back and forth, limousines gathered at curbside, sending waves of anticipation through a burgeoning throng of onlookers. Each time a passenger disembarked, the curious crowd surged forward. And each time a "nobody" entered the theater, they fell back again with a disappointed sigh.

Barricades adorned with the admonition "POLICE LINE, DO NOT CROSS" separated the fans from the fanfare. The wooden obstacles strained and creaked against the group momentum, serving their purpose in psychological, not physical, terms.

A Universal Pictures release, *Biloxi Blues* was produced by Ray Stark, directed by Mike Nichols, written by Neil Simon, and starred Matthew Broderick and Christopher Walken. In other words, it had a pedigree of definitive Hollywood lineage.

Biloxi Blues was a "big" picture. The production cost $16,000,000, the advertising budget was set at $7,000,000 and—with a 1240-theater nationwide opening scheduled March 25—it would take another $2,000,000 just for prints.

I found Don Safran standing inside the lobby of the theater.

"How are you, Don?"

"Okay. It's just a little crazier than I thought. But then again, it always is."

I looked around. Don was right, it was crazy.

A young girl of about fifteen muttered as yet another unrecognizable face smiled his way into the theater. "Where is Matthew Broderick?"

Limousines had come and gone during the past half hour, but all had contained a collection of mere mortals.

"Where's Ray?" I asked.

"He'll be here. Right now I'm concerned about everybody else. We've got about half as many seats as we need."

The *Biloxi* invitation was slick, colorful, and expensive, with a set of dog tags tucked inside a glossy announcement. It was a unique publicity ploy which may have worked a bit too well considering the fact that Universal Pictures received 570 RSVPs for the Baronet's 360 seats. As a result, Universal was forced to rent two additional screening rooms and provide buses to those locations for the expected overflow. In theory, it sounded good. But in reality, busing someone from the hub of glamour to a remote site was akin to sending a comrade to Siberia. Who would be allowed in the Baronet? Who would be turned away?

Suddenly, a cheer went up outside and Don peered through the glass doors to see Matthew Broderick. On Broderick's heels was Walter Cronkite. Then Christopher Walken. Brooke Shields. Neil Simon. Heavyweight champ Mike Tyson. Actor Harrison Ford. Playwright Arthur Miller. Screenwriter/director Joseph Mankiewicz. Ray Stark. The stellar flood gates had finally opened, signaled by the staccato clicking of camera shutters and blinding flash of lights.

As Ray Stark made his way through a mass of humanity, it seemed to me that this premiere might be more meaningful to the veteran producer than any of the others that preceded it. *Biloxi Blues* had followed a two-part David Puttnam appearance on network television, so fate had placed Ray in a position of answering his detractor with actions rather than words.

"This is what I can do," would be his tacit message. "This is what the business of filmmaking is all about."

If *Biloxi Blues* was successful, Ray would have dramatically proved his point in grand fashion. If it wasn't . . .

The *Biloxi Blues* bash took place immediately following the screening, at the Horn and Hardardt Automat at 42nd Street and Third Avenue. With its coin-operated mechanisms, it was an unusual locale for such an event. Tonight, however, party goers noshed on free tidbits as the vending machines were rigged not to need quarters in order to dispense food. In some ways, the party could have been subtitled "Let them eat cake!"

Biloxi Blues grossed $11,000,000 its first week—more than *Hope and Glory* managed during its entire run—and ranked as the number-one film in America. Headlines from the pages of *Variety* told the story much like the script device in old black-and-white movies where newspapers spin, one by one, onto the screen:

'BILOXI BLUES' GREEN 985G, N.Y.

'BILOXI' BLASTS CHI, 200G

NO BLUES FOR 'BILOXI' IN L.A.

'BILOXI' BOOTSTRAPPING 409G IN D.C.

'BILOXI' 134G, SEATTLE

PITT. POWERED BY 'BILOXI,' 60G

'BILOXI' BIG 79G, ST. LOO

'BILOXI' BRAZEN 103G BY THE BAY

BALTO., 'BILOXI' BIG 56G

'BILOXI' 60G IN K.C.

Ray Stark had countered David Puttnam's remarks in a most convincing way. With numbers, and very big numbers at that.

Three weeks after David Puttnam's *Today Show* segments and Ray Stark's *Biloxi Blues* success, the Academy of Motion Picture Arts and Sciences hosted its annual Oscar extravaganza on April 11. *The Last Emperor* swept nine out of nine awards, giving Puttnamites the basis for a renewed rallying cry.

The following morning I boarded American Airlines flight number 932, which departed New York's La Guardia Airport at 11:22, banked left, and turned north toward Canada. It was a flawless spring morning with brilliant California-style sunshine.

As I settled in, I noticed actor Al Pacino in a seat across the aisle and actress Ellen Barkin directly in front of me. The impression created by the sunny skies and presence of two such familiar faces was more West than East Coast. Since I was on my way to see a man who was dominating movie business headlines, it seemed odd to be winging to Toronto instead of Hollywood.

Lately, though, Toronto had become a favored location for film production in the wake of ever-increasing salary demands by American trade unions.

U.S. movies shot in foreign sites like Toronto earned a special moniker—runaway production, as in "running away" from Hollywood. But producers didn't care since it saved a great deal of money.

I flipped open my briefcase and pulled out a yellow pad. As I rummaged around looking for a pen, an avalanche of business cards spilled into my lap. Each bore the distinctive *Variety* logo.

Next to me was a man who was ardently poring over a screenplay. Was everybody in the movie business?

He noted the lapful of cards: "You work for *Variety*?"

His accent was decidedly French.

I nodded.

"I'm a director," he offered.

He explained he was looking at U.S. locations for his next film and scheduled a stopover in Toronto on his return flight to Paris.

He loved Toronto: "It plays like any city I want it to be. New York. Los Angeles. Munich. Miami. Even Paris!"

Those in charge of luring filmmakers to Toronto regarded the chameleonlike nature of the northern hub as both an asset and a liability. Name a city, and Toronto had a section of town that could stand in for the real metropolis. Consequently, Toronto had appeared in hundreds of films, but rarely as Toronto. Usually as New York or Los Angeles or Munich or Miami or Paris.

The director spoke with passion about his craft, delivering a lecture on the purity of French cinema. By the time the plane touched down, I had been injected with a concentrated dose of European filmmaking concepts. It was a good precursor to meeting a British producer.

Admittedly, France and England share a continent and not necessarily a universal attitude on making movies. Furthermore, generalities usually do not hold up under scrutiny. Yet there does appear to be a certain altruistic thread running through the psyche of most European filmmakers, a collective notion that motion pictures were meant to be art, not commercial opportunities.

This postulation makes sense in a country where films are subsidized by the government. To Americans, where financing depends on convincing investors a project will make money, such an idea comes across as pompous and naive. The disparity in the two philosophies, of course, was at the heart of the battle between David Puttnam and Hollywood.

It was two o'clock when I checked into the Four Seasons Hotel, more than three hours before my scheduled meeting with David Puttnam. We had arranged to rendezvous at 5:30 and then travel to the Canadian Museum of Art for David's scheduled speech to the Canadian Academy of Motion Picture Arts and Sciences.

I checked in with *Variety* for messages, dialed my home answering machine, and went over my growing volume of notes. Having slid a chair next to a window, I was able to gaze out over the city as I worked. The Frenchman on the plane was right. It did look like New York. Los Angeles. Munich. Miami. Paris.

Finally, it was 5:30. I took a short elevator ride to the fifth floor and walked toward the door of David Puttnam's room.

Who would answer? An aide? A secretary?

David Puttnam greeted me himself. He was alone.

Although I knew what he looked like from photographs and television, it did not prepare me for his unassuming demeanor.

"Hello, Charles," he said, extending his hand. "I'm David Puttnam. It's nice to meet you."

He spoke softly, with a precise English accent.

Was this the man who had stirred up so much trouble in Hollywood? It didn't seem possible.

"There isn't time for a drink," he apologized, "the car is waiting downstairs."

When we reached the lobby, David turned to me and said, "By the way, no press are allowed at the affair. So—for tonight—you're not with *Variety*, okay?"

"No problem." Pretending to be somebody else promised to be an adventure.

I began concocting a cover, in case someone asked what I did. Screenwriter, maybe. Author. Fabulously wealthy American financier. It was great. A sort of real life *Mission: Impossible* episode or James Bond movie.

A Cadillac limo was parked in front of the hotel with a young woman from the Academy seated in the back. A round of introductions later and we were off.

Several people greeted us on the steps of the museum. We picked up another three or four stragglers in the main entrance hall. More from the administrative offices. By the time we reached the small theater which was to serve as the venue for the seminar, the entourage missing from David's suite had assembled in force.

David was asked to wait for a minute outside the door to the theater while a small mob milling around him was ushered in to take their seats. I stayed behind.

"Do you like doing these things?" I asked. "Giving speeches?"

David nodded.

In the past, David had addressed many audiences and his upcoming agenda listed still more speaking engagements. He was next scheduled for April 23 in Los Angeles at the 34th Annual Entertainment Law Institute cosponsored by the University of Southern California Law Center and the Beverly Hills Bar Association. An advertisement published in the trades described him as "Special Luncheon Speaker: David T. Puttnam. Producer, 'Chariots of Fire.'" According to the ad, David would explain "Hiring And Firing Practices In The Entertainment Business" to the gathering of attorneys.

I asked David why he invested so much time speaking to so many small groups of people.

He responded without hesitation: "If you believe in something, you have to keep saying it until you get the message across."

A woman approached. "Mr. Puttnam, whenever you're ready."

"See you afterwards," David said as he headed for the stage. I slipped in a side door and sat in the back row.

Applause grew into ovation. People stood. A woman three rows in front of me even wept.

David played the crowd like a veteran vaudevillian on a farewell tour. He slipped off his suit jacket. Loosened his tie. Rolled up the sleeves of his shirt. Then, slowly walking to the podium, he leaned forward on one elbow.

What an entrance!

David's delivery was eloquent. And—since most in attendance that evening were aspiring actors, actresses, producers, screenwriters, and directors who considered themselves victims of the very system David attacked—his words were hypnotic.

Immediately following the speech was a cocktail reception. As David sat on the arm of an overstuffed chair and held court, I walked around the room eavesdropping. What were they saying about David Puttnam?

"Incredible . . . he's wonderful . . ."

"Hollywood stabbed him in the back . . ."

"I brought a script with me . . . I'm going to give it to him on the way out . . ."

"David? There's no one like him . . ."

"I love his films . . ."

"I wish he were still at Columbia . . ."

About an hour later, I noticed David motioning to me.

"Ready?" he asked in a whisper.

"Whenever you are."

"Let's go."

As we worked our way toward the exit, a commotion arose by the door.

"What is it?" David wanted to know.

Since I'm six feet eight inches tall, I can see over most crowds.

"A TV crew," I replied.

An extremely appealing young woman was complaining bitterly to one of the organizers of the event. I couldn't make out what she was saying, but it was obvious that the face-off centered around the "no press" policy imposed for the evening. As David and I nudged closer, we heard:

"Please! I just want five minutes! Please! It's very important to me."

The voice belonged to a brunette beauty. She was from *City News*, which appeared on an independent Toronto television station. Behind her was a battery of equipment lugged by several surly crew members.

"Hi, I'm David Puttnam."

"Mr. Puttnam, if I could just have a moment, I would be . . ."

In the blink of an eye, high-intensity lights were illuminating David's face and an impromptu interview was under way.

That done, we began inching toward the door again. David was collecting business cards and shaking hands with every step.

"This is like being with a rock star," I laughed.

Back at the Four Seasons, we wandered into a small restaurant off the lobby.

"Is Patsy in Toronto?" I asked.

"No," David replied.

"It's a shame she wasn't with you last night to watch the performance of *The Last Emperor* at the Academy Awards."

David suddenly grew animated.

"It was great! Nine out of nine awards. And then the nominations for *Hope and Glory*. I was up *all night* with calls about the Oscars."

The conversation shifted gears as David probed my background and then asked me what I expected to accomplish with my planned *Variety* article.

"I want to get *both* sides of the story. Besides talking with you, I want to get the Hollywood version too."

"You mean Ray Stark?" David howled. "He'll *never* talk to you. At least not for the record. He never talks to the press, you know."

"That's what I've heard. But I intend to try anyway."

"It won't do you any good. You won't get any farther than Don Safran."

As dinner progressed, David dove into a general overview of his filmmaking philosophy. I'd heard it before. Read it dozens of times. But listening to the infused passion of the former chairman/CEO gave it all new meaning.

David appeared very tired as he spoke—which was understandable in that he was awake most of the night before—so we both agreed it would be better to continue the next day. We designated a time, noon, and a place, Norman Jewison's office, where a press conference regarding the Canadian Centre for Advanced Film Studies was to be held. Norman was cochairman of the Centre.

Actually, it was the Centre which had drawn David to Toronto in the first place. He had agreed to teach a filmmaking seminar for a small class of twelve students.

Arrangements for David to become a Canadian professor for a week had been made long before he declined to renew Norman's production deal at Columbia Pictures. It would be interesting to see if the two men were functioning smoothly on an academic basis after such a professional chasm regarding the philosophy of filmmaking.

It was 11:15 when I walked into my room and snapped on the television. Checking the TV listings, I found *City News* and switched to that channel. A few minutes later, the news anchor announced:

"The producer of Oscar-winning *The Last Emperor* was in town tonight and we have an *exclusive* interview."

The shot switched to the pretty brunette who had shown up at the reception.

After her two-minute question-and-answer with David, she stared straight into the camera and cooed:

"They say he's controversial. I found him fascinating!"

Her appraisal was typical of the reverent tone most in the media adopted when covering David Puttnam. The lead-in, too, typified media coverage of David Puttnam. "The producer of *The Last Emperor* was in town," the segment had begun. Indeed, he was not. Jeremy Thomas, of course, was the producer of the film. And he was in California, not Toronto.

Considering Jeremy's reaction after the Oscar ceremony, it's a good thing the "producer of *The Last Emperor*" wasn't in town that night.

And it's a good thing he wasn't tuned to *City News*.

CHAPTER
TWENTY-THREE

After a short taxi ride through the amorphous streets of Toronto, past the section that substituted for a Brooklyn neighborhood in *Moonstruck*, I arrived at Norman Jewison's office for the scheduled noon press conference.

Norman's presence, and that of Garth Drabinsky, president of Cineplex-Odeon Corporation, was to be expected. As cochairmen of the Canadian Centre for Advanced Film Studies, they would announce the formation of the Second Monday Reel Club.

The club would solicit memberships via one-thousand-dollar minimum contributions and would be strictly limited to seven hundred members. Participants would enjoy private screenings on the second Monday of each month for their tax-deductible contribution.

Norman and Garth were performing a duty as cochairmen, but what was David doing there?

David had always been a supporter of the Canadian Film School and—since he was temporarily a film professor at the Centre—presumably attended the press conference as a member of the faculty. Yet none of the press materials indicated that David would be there and, in fact, there was no mention at all of the British producer. Despite his unofficial status, however, he appeared to be *hosting* the event, enthusiastically greeting media representatives as they trickled in the door.

I studied the scene, paying particularly close attention to the interaction between David and Norman Jewison. They spoke to arriving journalists but not to each other, although there wasn't any clearly visible evidence of tension between them.

Norman was open and friendly to his guests. The bearded director seemed to know everyone by name, making several reporters feel important as he recalled some anecdote from the last time they had met.

But Garth Drabinsky, a hefty man of forty, seemed put out by the intrusion into his busy day. He may have had a warmer side, but he treated the group gathering in Norman's office with apathy.

Pleasantries aside, Garth Drabinsky was obviously an effective businessman. Since the formation of Cineplex-Odeon in 1979 with the opening of one multiscreen complex in Toronto, the company had grown to be one of the largest exhibitors in the world, claiming ownership to over fifteen hundred screens in more than five hundred theaters. One of its divisions, Cineplex-Odeon Films, quickly became Canada's largest independent film distributor, leading to a joint venture with Robert Redford's production entity, Wildwood Enterprises, as well as other Hollywood filmmakers.

Garth's efforts culminated in the 1986 purchase by MCA of 49 percent of Cineplex-Odeon Corporation for $219,000,000.

It was an unlikely trio. Norman Jewison, Garth Drabinsky, and David Puttnam standing shoulder-to-shoulder. The relationships and events that tied them together were convoluted and intersecting.

First of all, there was the *Moonstruck* incident. Did David turn down the project or didn't he? Following the termination of Norman Jewison's deal at Columbia Pictures, the director resurfaced at MGM with the major motion picture starring Cher and Nicholas Cage. Immediately after *Moonstruck* soared to the top of the box-office charts, Hollywood speculated that the film was one which David Puttnam could have had as part of his "legacy." David, however, had maintained that the project was never submitted to him. Perhaps this was one mystery I could easily solve.

Garth Drabinsky's connection to David Puttnam centered around the theatrical release of *The Last Emperor*. The film was all set to open in a few hundred Cineplex-Odeon theaters in late 1987, but Columbia pulled it at the last minute. Instead of a broad release, the studio had decided to do a slower "roll-out" in 1988 with the

Oscar-nominated motion picture in what the studio described as an attempt to capitalize on the Academy Awards.

David's supporters, of course, didn't see it that way. They cited the sudden reduction in the number of theaters as an example of Columbia's apathy toward the British producer's motion picture product. Another debate erupted and rumor had it that Garth Drabinsky and Columbia Pictures Entertainment president Victor Kaufman were no longer on speaking terms because of the eleventh-hour change in the release pattern of *The Last Emperor.*

The press conference finally commenced. Norman sat on the left, Garth on the right, and David, as usual, in the middle. Norman and Garth outlined the Second Monday Reel Club and then opened the floor for questions.

Although David had not uttered a word at that point, the first query was directed at him.

"Mr. Puttnam, how do you feel about not receiving a single thank-you from the makers of *The Last Emperor* at the Academy Awards?"

There was an instantaneous feeling of tension created by the question. The press had been invited to learn about the Second Monday Reel Club. Not to interview David Puttnam.

Sensing the suppressed anger emanating from his two associates, David issued a very brief reply which said, in effect, those who produced the picture deserved all the credit.

But then the dam burst. Reporters began firing more questions, all at once, all aimed at David Puttnam. Camera shutters rat-a-tat-tatted away. And flash units bathed David in bursts of illumination.

"Mr. Puttnam, what did you think of Columbia's write-down? Is it fair?"

"Mr. Puttnam, do you feel you were betrayed in Hollywood?"

"Mr. Puttnam, could you tell us about your new production deal with Warners?"

"Mr. Puttnam, I've heard that . . ."

Norman smiled politely. Garth fumed, visibly angry.

"Mr. Puttnam, I wonder if you could address . . ."

"Wait a minute!" Garth bellowed. "We didn't invite you here to talk about David Puttnam!"

There was a stunned silence followed by obligatory interest in the Second Monday Reel Club.

The media had shown its allegiance once again. Even though

an endless stream of pro-Puttnam print had been evidence of the love affair, the intensity of the passion had to be seen to be believed. David was given the press attention of a visiting head of state rather than a deposed studio chief.

Questions about the club waned, so Garth, who seemed anxious to return to his duties at the rapidly expanding Cineplex-Odeon Corporation, rose and launched into a wrap-up statement. Before he could finish, however, he was interrupted by David.

"Garth, I'd like to be the very first member of the Second Monday Reel Club."

It was a perfectly timed offer.

As applause rattled the room, Garth looked on in horror as David slipped out a thousand-dollar check and stole the show.

Once again, cameras clicked away, this time capturing the official charter member of the Second Monday Reel Club, David Puttnam, smiling as he handed the cofounder of the Club, Garth Drabinsky, the requisite dues.

"Thank you, David," Garth managed. "This certainly is a surprise."

The event officially over, Norman and Garth stood in the front of the room and talked informally with two reporters. But the real action was taking place a few feet away. David had broken off from the trio and had taken dozens of the media with him.

An hour later, David was on camera doing his twentieth interview, tireless in seeing to it that his "message" was understood.

Finally, at 3:00, there were no reporters left. David and I walked down the street to Pane Vino, a small Italian cafe. It was completely empty.

"You're amazing," I told him as we sat down. "Don't you ever get sick of all the attention?"

David laughed. "Not really."

I pulled out a cassette recorder and placed it on the table.

"What happened?" I asked.

The two words might have formed an inadequate question in any other situation, but not here and now. David knew exactly what I meant.

He stared away for a moment, as if rewinding a mental tape, sighed, then fixed his gaze on the small cassette deck. He spoke slowly and deliberately.

"Let's go back through it precisely. . . ."

***

David began his recollection of events by describing the circumstances surrounding his quest for the top spot at Columbia Pictures in spring 1986.

"Without doubt, Warren Beatty, maybe Dustin as well, but certainly Warren, went to Fay Vincent when the rumors started about my going to the company, and said, 'This is a catastrophic thing to do, you mustn't do this, it's bad for the company and could be disastrous for *Ishtar*.' They lobbied actively against my going there.

"Fay, I gather, listened to them, heard them out and said, 'We're going to make our own decision. . . .' This was at a time when nothing had been settled anyway '. . . If David decides he's prepared to join us, we'll make that decision.' I think he was gentlemanly with them."

"The reason Warren Beatty was against your appointment," I interjected, "wasn't that because he was upset when you started talking about *Reds* the way you did? In 1981."

David pushed his plate aside and leaned over the table.

"That's an interesting word, 'upset.' Upset is a loaded word. 'Upset' is supposed to mean that he's not distraught, he's merely upset. It's a *regal* word. He's not angry, he's 'upset.' He wouldn't want to debate with me. He's 'upset.' And it's always, 'a spokesman for Warren Beatty said.' I don't understand it. If he's got a problem, why not say so?"

David grew suddenly tense.

"I had a lot of problems with *Reds*. Not with the film itself, but with the affluent manner in which it was made.

"Anyway, I went to this dinner at a friend's and they told me much worse stories about Warren than I had ever heard before. And I said, 'Why doesn't this ever get in the press?' Everything I ever seem to do wrong is in print the very next day. And someone said, 'Don't be silly, no one is going to say anything negative about Warren. He's part of Hollywood's royalty.' That was the word, 'royalty.' I loathe privilege. I loathe all forms of privilege. And the idea that someone—anyone—could be above criticism really pissed me off."

It surprised me that a British subject would rail against royalty, an integral part of English history. Maybe, since modern-day England recognized Kings and Queens only as figureheads, he wasn't aware that in Hollywood the caste system was not a distant memory of centuries past. It was a way of life.

David went on.

"And it just so happened, a few days later, I was doing an interview about *Chariots of Fire*, and I was asked about *Reds* and I said, 'It upset me immensely to be forced to spend a year getting a director I was working with to conform to a set of rigid disciplines to avoid going over budget while someone else was being given carte blanche to exceed his budget.' And that's when all this thing with Warren started. And they blamed me for losing *Reds* the Academy Award, saying I put the boot in. When will these people grow up?"

For the first time since we met the day before, I saw a flicker of fury from someone who seemed completely able to control himself until now. Obviously *he* was "upset."

David did have a point, however, about the "spokesman" aspect of Hollywood. It was true that Warren had not given an interview in years, decades maybe.

Neither of us spoke for a moment, as David recovered from his fitful recounting of the events of 1981 as they pertained to Warren Beatty.

"I think I've been utterly consistent in my views," David asserted. "I formulated a set of views fifteen years ago and I've deviated remarkably little from them."

I prodded David back into the story.

"So, Warren and Dustin were not in favor of seeing you become chief executive of Columbia Pictures. What else was going on while you were negotiating? Who else played a part during your talks with Fay Vincent and Coca-Cola?"

David stared away for a moment, thinking, remembering. Suddenly his face paled and he took a deep breath.

"Then you get to the Ray Stark thing."

The "Ray Stark thing," as David dubbed it, was not a simple matter.

"I think at one point," David recalled, "Ray climbed on the bandwagon to the extent that he felt: 'Puttnam is coming here, so I might as well make the best of it and maybe even help.' But the decision was already basically made."

That was not the way I had heard it. I pressed: "Didn't Ray make a phone call? At your request?"

David relented.

"There was one particular issue over Pat Williamson, who was head of the international division. I had made it clear that I wasn't prepared to join so long as the international division didn't report to me. It was not a negotiable issue. I gather that Ray called Keough and told Keough: 'That's a stupid thing to hang a deal up over, and, in any event, it was quickly sold.' "

David continued, describing his own eleventh-hour talks with Donald Keough regarding the Columbia job.

"What is important for you to know," David elaborated, "and this is absolutely categoric, is that on at least three occasions, once by me and twice by Patsy, maybe even twice by me, the issue of Ray was raised together with the problems that could be caused in-house. And on all of those occasions, specifically Don Keough stated that he has no currency here. He's our problem, not your problem. You just get on with the job. They were utterly emphatic.

"It wasn't a case of 'try and mollify him,' it wasn't 'do us a favor, keep him off our back.' There could have been a dozen answers. Any one of which I could have accommodated. But the message clearly was, 'Forget it, don't worry about it. Get on with the job.' "

David looked drained from the recollection.

What David was so concerned about was the possibility that Ray would be able to force a picture on Columbia because of his influence in the highest echelons of Coca-Cola and his friendship with Herbert Allen. Or, more to the point, David did not want to be placed in a position of rubber-stamping whatever film Ray wanted to produce at the studio.

David's paranoia may have been more perception than reality. Just as David had cultivated a certain image of himself, so had Ray Stark, and that was one of an *independent* producer. Despite the perception that he was somehow "connected" to Columbia Pictures, Ray had produced pictures at many different studios during his career and, in fact, his last two pictures—*Biloxi Blues* and *The Secret of My Success*—had both been at Universal. In any case, David made Ray Stark an issue.

It occurred to me that a little more common sense may have been called for when David arrived at Columbia. I said as much.

David replied: "The idea—and this is me being a bit moralistic—of me giving someone a deal to make an expensive film—

we're talking about twenty million dollars—because he's a friend of Herbert Allen is something I could never see myself doing. Doing that would have indicated my being assimilated into the system. I couldn't do it. I'm just the wrong person."

"But Ray Stark has had a long—and presumably profitable—relationship with Columbia," I noted. "Why didn't you do a film with Ray? Say, one movie a year or something like that?"

Pondering for a minute, David offered the following scenario: "If Herbert Allen had said to me when I arrived there, 'Do us a favor and give Ray a picture a year,' I would have answered, 'Well, hang on, if I do that, that's going to be the beginning of an endless series of conversations.'—'No, I'm going to make sure that doesn't happen. Give him a picture a year.' I would have said, 'O.K., but I take them off my budget. Instead of me having a production budget of a hundred and twenty million a year, I'll take a hundred million a year plus this one for Ray. It must have nothing to do with my accounting. If Ray goes over budget, that's your problem.' I would have dealt with that."

Incredibly, David was offering both sides of a conversation that had *never* taken place. In fact, Herbert Allen had not at any time discussed the subject of Ray Stark with David Puttnam, something David readily acknowledged. However, David still seemed to be grappling with his perceived dilemma pertaining to Ray, even to the point of concocting an imaginary meeting with Herbert Allen. David seemed fixated on Ray Stark. It was peculiar.

In any event, it was clear that under certain circumstances, David Puttnam *would have* greenlighted a Ray Stark project. Quite a turnaround in less than a minute!

Staying on the subject of Ray Stark, I asked David what he thought of *Biloxi Blues*.

"It wouldn't have been a film with any interest for me because I don't think it will work overseas. It's high-priced domestic cinema. It may end up turning a small profit. But it isn't something that would interest me. There's nothing new about it."

David certainly was brave in his assessment of what was at the time the nation's number-one motion picture. I wondered how different the story might have been if *Biloxi Blues* had somehow landed at Columbia during David's tenure. A number-one movie, and Ray's blessing, would have done a lot to keep the American wolves from the Briton's door.

I pointed out that David's tastes in movies were quite different from Hollywood's and that he had voiced his opinion about that very subject quite often.

"In essence, you said Hollywood was a 'despicable place' and you could never work there. Yet, you accepted the job at Columbia."

"Deep down, I wasn't comfortable about having done this. A terrible thing happened to me in a way, I mean I was put in the most terrible situation.

"When I shook hands with Fay and Dick Gallop in New York—and the only other person there was my lawyer Tom Lewyn—something in my heart of hearts told me I should not be shaking hands with them. Really, what I would have liked to have done is got out of that room without having made a final commitment.

"But, in a way circumstances conspired, every little thing I had asked for including the Pat Williamson problem had been agreed to. And I had no cause to procrastinate . . . if there had been one unresolved issue, I could have said, 'I want to think about that.' There was nothing. Every single thing I had brought to the table had basically been agreed. And they said we've got a deal. And my lawyer quite rightly said, 'David, you can't muck about, we've got it sorted out.' So, I did it, I shook hands, and I liked Fay and I trusted him—he's a man of his word—so as I shook hands I knew I had made a deal.

"And I really felt on the horns of a horrible dilemma. I guess what I'm trying to say to you is, all things being equal, if I hadn't shaken hands at that moment, I would have picked up the phone and called Fay and said, 'Look, I'm making a mistake and I suspect you're making a mistake.' But we had shaken hands. And I felt I was obligated to him. I've always known Fay to be an utterly, utterly, utterly honest man. An honorable man. A man of his word. That's a part of it."

This was unexpected. The most controversial chairman/CEO in Hollywood history almost didn't take the job. All of this craziness came within a handshake of never happening. Yet, I wondered why a handshake held such heavy commitment when his three-year contract obviously didn't. After all, he had said he resigned.

"What about your three-year time cap?" I asked. "Why was that so important to you?"

"O.K., so then I had to deal with this sense of selling out. I had always said to Fay, three years . . . I talked to the kids and I talked to Patsy about leaving England . . . We have a house in the country, actually I was leaving a lot. We all agreed on three years—we were going to go to Boston anyway for a year—to turn one year into three years didn't seem like such a terrible thing."

David grimaced.

"I'd said a lot of stuff in my life about not wanting to go back to Hollywood, and for the sake of my own dignity, I had to time-cap it. There was a fifty-fifty chance I'd never even complete the three years anyway. In effect I was saying, 'You can't fire me, I'm already leaving.'

"It was very, very important to my sense of dignity that I hung on to this three-year notion. I was very conscious of what I had said and I felt I was defusing that argument by saying I was only coming back for three years."

Demonstrating that it was truly "important" to him that the time-cap be made public, David had sought out the *Los Angeles Times* soon after becoming chairman/CEO of Columbia Pictures and said: "I will walk out of here on March 31, 1990."

David leaned back in his chair and smiled faintly.

"Fay will tell you, he always thought I would do it but he never thought I would talk about it. He was appalled I started telling people it was three years only."

I made an observation regarding the frequency and intensity of his attacks on Hollywood.

"Yes, David, but you kept saying over and over that you hated Hollywood."

"I can't really say I don't like it. I just don't feel comfortable in Los Angeles, it's not my home. The problem is, people personalize things. If I were to tell you, I really don't feel comfortable in New York, you might take it personally because you live in New York. I get quite upset when people say, 'I don't like London,' I really do. So I know very well that's a personal issue. It's a dumb thing to hang on about."

David offered an explanation for his initial anti-Hollywood diatribe following his term as president of Casablanca Filmworks.

"At the time I had made those earlier statements, I was very angry, very upset, and believe me, the fall of 1979 was not the time to go back to England. I was not going back to anything attractive.

"I also believe I was a bit more specific. I seem to remember talking about the fact I didn't think I could achieve culturally or artistically—I hate both words—what I wanted to achieve in the United States. It's fair to say that if I had a legitimate cultural voice, that it had to be a British voice. That's what I think I was trying to say. I think that's what I was saying. I don't ever remember saying, 'I don't like America.' I did say I didn't feel comfortable there."

I was fascinated. David evidently was able to find peace within himself by limiting his term to three years and at the same time justify his verbal assaults on Hollywood. He must have felt he was not entering into a marriage with Hollywood, just a temporary live-in arrangement. It wasn't a *real* commitment. He was just passing through.

I laughed. "A lot of people were stunned by your public revelations. What about the production deals? There was quite a furor when you allowed many of those deals to expire."

"To an extent, we all live on both sides of the street. When on the outside, I wanted the studios to push money out. But when I went inside, I also knew that wasn't the most economical way of development. I wanted to bring money back in."

Admittedly, David Puttnam sat atop a unique vantage point when he took over Columbia Pictures. As a producer, he knew all the ploys that independent producers use to extract money from a studio chief and as a studio chief he felt he had to police the Hollywood establishment for doing exactly what he had always done as an independent producer.

"What about Norman Jewison's deal?" I asked. "What about *Moonstruck*?"

"In reality, his deal was up. I'm now told that the studio read *Moonstruck*. I don't know if the studio did, I certainly didn't. I mean it certainly wasn't submitted to David Puttnam."

At this point, I felt I was seeing the David Puttnam/Hollywood battle clearly for the first time. I was witnessing just how convincing David could be. How obsessed he could be in making his point unmistakably understood. I saw firsthand just how charismatic David Puttnam really was, and, at the same time, just how clever.

Once again, without warning, the subject turned abruptly to Ray Stark. There seemed to be no way David could resist steering the conversation in that direction. After listening to David blast Ray Stark for a full five minutes, I finally interrupted.

"You know, David—and I hate to harp on this—but it strikes me that you could have perhaps been more diplomatic than you were . . ."

"You mean in the case of Ray?" David interrupted.

"Yes, and other people, too."

"There wasn't anybody else," David reacted.

CHAPTER
TWENTY-FOUR

David launched into another speech about the problems he had with Ray Stark, only this time he provided a list of questions which he wanted Ray to answer.

"You should put this to Ray . . ."

"I'd like you to ask Ray . . ."

"I'd like to know why Ray . . ."

David finally paused, so I attempted to get him back on track regarding the events during his term at Columbia.

"You inherited quite a few properties. *Ishtar*, and . . ."

"*Ishtar* was a nonevent for me. I stayed right out of it."

"What about *Leonard Part 6* and Bill Cosby? When you took over, you said Bill Cosby was happy with the film."

"Yes, very happy. Now we all agree that *Leonard Part 6* was a disaster, but, at the time, no one had seen *Leonard Part 6* including Cosby. *Leonard Part 6* might have been *Ghostbusters* for all anyone knew."

I couldn't believe the reference to *Ghostbusters*. Considering all the controversy surrounding *Ghostbusters II*, it was an odd measurement of success for David to use.

"You have to remember," David continued, "that at this time—late August—Cosby was phoning Fay Vincent saying *Leonard Part 6* was fantastic, phoning Keough saying not only was it fantastic, it was going to do hundreds of millions of dollars."

The giddy feeling about *Leonard Part 6* had dissolved when David brought in Briton Paul Weiland to direct it, and another Briton, Alan Parker, to produce it.

"One of the criticisms," I pointed out, "is that you brought over a lot of English filmmakers."

David bristled.

"Let's deal with that. First of all, when I first took the job, we were desperate for product. We had no product. First thing you do, the first thing anyone would do, is you draw on your own resources.

"If you are about to start a film you say: Who do you know who has a film? Who do you know that you could hook in? It just so happens that the films that I knew of that were getable, one was *Housekeeping,* I read the script and I loved it. John Boorman was walking around with *Hope and Glory* and I loved it and I admired John and I wanted to get it. Ridley Scott sent me a copy of *Someone to Watch Over Me,* which had been put in turnaround, I read it and I liked it. And Gregory Nava had *Destiny.*

"So I picked up within three weeks of starting and closed deals on these four pictures. Three of which happened to be by British directors."

David then fell into a discussion about the philosophy of film-making. After a few minutes, I once again pushed for specifics. Despite David's declaration that he preferred to bring "small" films to Columbia, there had been one glaring exception: *The Adventures of Baron Munchausen.*

"What about *Munchausen?*" I asked.

David looked at me as if I had said some ancient ritualistic word, some forbidden invocation which embodied all the evils of the world.

"*Munchausen,*" he sighed, "was a margin call. We *needed* a broad-appeal Christmas film. When you're filling out your schedule, you're looking for certain categories of film. So *Munchausen* was a convenient pick-up for us.

"My big concern wasn't that it wouldn't be a quality movie, it was what it would cost. So I froze our investment at approximately twelve million dollars. Eighteen million five hundred thousand, less six million five hundred thousand which was put up by RCA/Columbia Home Video.

"Everyone who's seen the footage thinks it's sensational. If we got it right, Columbia will have acquired an approximately forty-million-dollar picture for twelve million."

I wondered about the rest of the money. We were talking about over ten million dollars. More, actually. Who would fill in the gap?

"David, what about the overage? Where's the rest of the money coming from? The completion guarantor, Film Finances?"

"Yes. Absolutely. The total amount committed was eighteen million five hundred thousand from us, about two million from Germany. They did a very good deal in Italy; indeed, I think it was another two million five hundred thousand. They probably collected one way or another about twenty-four million dollars."

David mulled the amount over for a moment before adding:

"I gather that Richard Soames reinsured through Lloyds."

Completion bond companies go into a deal based on the premise that the budget will stay within the original parameters. On *Munchausen*, the costs had almost doubled.

"I bet Richard Soames was upset," I said, stating the obvious.

"I'm afraid I had a row with him," David recalled. "I went into the press when they talked about firing Terry Gilliam. It was deliberate, I had to protect our investment. We couldn't stop them from firing him, so I made it clear that the notion of a Terry Gilliam film without being directed by Terry Gilliam was laughable. My intention was to make them feel insecure about whether we'd accept delivery."

With that observation, David illustrated the intimidation a studio can employ when a film is a "negative pick-up." Film Finances, already into the picture for a whopping $16,000,000, certainly didn't want to do anything which would allow Columbia to legally reject the finished film, and thus be forced to underwrite another $20,000,000 or more.

"You know, the interesting thing, not only was the studio rock solid about the project, all of our initial worries about the budget, our being absolutely emphatic that we would *not* do it without a completion bond, all the holdups were caused by the production, not us. We were always there.

"We had, in fact, one guy, our very best lawyer, work nonstop to clear up their rights problem. Nonstop for two months. I would say the studio operated above and beyond the call of duty. They were magnificent, everyone at the studio."

David leaned back in his chair.

"But it may well be an incredible film. This time next year

we'll be sitting here saying, 'What an incredible film.' But the truth of the matter is, it isn't David Puttnam, it was David Picker's incredible tenacity. I probably would have walked away when all these rights problems came up, but David Picker and Fred Bernstein were really loyal to the project."

It struck me that even the *explanation* of the origin and development of *The Adventures of Baron Munchausen* sounded like a story worthy of the baron himself.

David then slipped into philosophy again.

"It all comes down to responsibility. It comes down to responsibility for what you do, responsibility for the films you make and responsibility for the manner in which you make them. If you can't step up and say, 'This is what I believe in, these are the ideas I live by,' I was brought up to believe that to fail in this made you less of a man.

"I'm beginning to regret that my father gave me a set of values which may be irrelevant for the 1990s. That's the way I was brought up. Make your mistakes, admit them, enjoy your triumphs, and be a man. Don't worry about what other people think; if you're doing a good job you'll come out ahead."

After his brief statement of purpose, David returned to the facts. For another hour I listened as he pinpointed the beginning of the end . . .

"April was the high point. From that point on, little things started to slip . . ."

And the middle of the end . . .

"There was a meeting in June where Herbert Allen and I got into an argument about the relationships with Ovitz . . . from then on it wasn't ever as positive as April . . ."

And the approach of the end . . .

"When I went down to Atlanta in August, I had a long discussion with Fay. I said, 'Fay, you've got to tell me, if you or Don have a problem, you've *got* to tell me.' And I accused him of being elliptical or Jesuitical. I said, 'Don't hint. If there's something wrong, say so.' And we had a very good conversation for several hours. I said, 'You've got to put things on the line. You've got to let me know where I am. Otherwise, I'm going to start boxing with shadows. If you've got a problem, tell me. If I can solve it, I'll solve it. If I can't solve it, I'll let you know."

And then the end itself . . .

"The other important thing to touch on is the nature of the breakfast with Keough and Goizueta after the announcements of the Tuesday. I met them on a Thursday.

"When I had breakfast with them, they stressed repeatedly that this was just a financial rationalization and an amalgamation of the two companies, it was being done to make the thing work better for Coca-Cola, they would like very much for me to sort the situation out with Victor. It didn't mean massive staff changes. None of the people in the studio should be worried.

"I thought that Don should go there and reassure them personally because there were a lot of concerns. 'No, no, no,' he said, 'everything's fine.' So I can take that back as a message? 'Absolutely.' "

By now, David looked completely drained. He appeared to be not just recalling the events of his tenure at Columbia, but *reliving* it. Yet he continued, this time not in a chronological order, rather he randomly pulled issues out of the past.

On his outspoken behavior:

"The greatest irony is when journalists write, 'It's a pity he was so ready to talk to the press.' A journalist saying it's a pity that someone talks to the press! That's pretty bizarre. Are they advocating that people don't talk to the press? I don't understand. Even if you thought it, it's an odd thing to write."

On his preference of an Audi over a Rolls-Royce:

"To the extent that it's any issue at all, I think it reflects badly on Hollywood, not on me. I drove an Audi because I like four-wheel-drive cars and that's a different style of driving and they have the best four-wheel drive. It's as simple as that.

"What you have here is a conflict of British and American—or at least West Coast—attitudes. The West Coast ethos is that if you've got a enough money to buy a Rolls-Royce, buy the damn thing. Flaunt it. The British ethos is, if you've really got a lot of money, you drive a little Austin. Preferably a very old one. This doesn't make the British right or the Americans wrong. It makes them totally different. I was brought up to believe that it was more elegant to be discreet about what you have."

There were, of course, many jabs at Hollywood:

"Hollywood has a caste system but no merit system. Therefore, the people can acquire rank without bothering with merit. Whenever that happens, what you're looking at is the beginning of a collapse. I mean historically, whenever and wherever there has ceased to be an equation between rank and merit, you're always on the verge of collapse. You might be able to sustain things for a year, or even ten years, but sooner or later the system rots away from inside.

"One of the things I want you to ask Mike Ovitz: 'If you have as much power as we read you have and if you have this terrific ability to maneuver and manipulate for your clients, why aren't the resulting movies better?' What has actually happened is that the power has switched from the studios to the agents, or at least the artists *through* their agents. So, how come we're not looking at a wonderful renaissance of quality films? And we aren't."

Sometimes David would appear to be concluding the interview, as he did when he commented on Fay Vincent:

"At the end of the day, maybe the only naive person in all of this was Fay Vincent. And, in a way, maybe the person who has been hurt worst by the whole thing is Fay Vincent. He's a good man. I don't think you'd find a better man. He's a much finer man than me. I've got many, many flaws. Fay doesn't happen to share them."

But then David would grapple with another aspect of his term. Finally, however, he did finish.

"You know, the other interesting thing that you should try and pin is when people say, 'Bloody Puttnam, he shouldn't have done this.' Well, *who* shouldn't he have done this to? Himself? Has he hurt you? Has he hurt this business? What you're going to hear is that a lot of the things he wanted to do were helpful and it's a pity they weren't done. At the end of the day, that's the answer you're going to get. What always gets quoted is, 'Well, he shouldn't have done this.' There's no follow-up question like 'Why?' "

David covered his face with his hands and sighed, not in sorrow, but in sheer exhaustion. As David had promised when we sat down, we had gone "back through it precisely."

And, now, as dusk melted into darkness, there wasn't much left for David Puttnam to say.

David and I walked back to the hotel, taking our time. The fresh air seemed to revitalize both of us. For my part, I felt as if I had been infused with more information than could be assimilated at one sitting. For David, it had been a catharsis, a lightening of excess mental odds and ends.

"I never do interviews of more than ten minutes each," he noted with a laugh. "This one about did me in."

Once at the Four Seasons, we talked for a few minutes in the lobby as David waited for a friend to arrive.

"If you need anything else," David offered, "give me a call."

"Now if I can just get everybody else to be as precise as you were."

"Everybody else? Like Ray? Herbert?"

"Yes. And Dick Gallop. Marty Ransohoff."

David laughed. "They'll never talk to you. Ray *never* talks to the press. Neither do the rest of them. They're always shadowy figures. They *never* come forward. Haven't so far. And never will."

The first thing I did when I walked in the room was dial American Airlines. I was scheduled out of Toronto early the next morning but thought I might as well head back to New York that night.

My next call was to Don Safran. I informed Don that I had just spent two days with David Puttnam. Don was amused.

"I bet you never got to ask a *second* question."

"Seriously, it was quite revealing."

"I'm sure it was. But there is another side to the story."

"That may be. But so far David is the only person willing to give me his version. It doesn't look like Ray is going to talk to me, so it's the only account I've got. But it's going to make a hell of a story, that I can tell you."

"How long are you going to be there?"

"Another two hours. I'm packing now."

"Look, Ray has a picture to deal with, so it's a case of first things first. I'm not promising anything, but I'll get back to you."

My suitcase was only half packed when the phone rang.

"Pack the lightweight clothes on top," Don began, "that is if you can come to L.A. next week. Ray has agreed to talk to you."

"Before I make the trip, do you mean on-the-record?"

"Yes. But there are ground rules. Come out and we'll discuss it."

When I walked into *Variety* the following morning, I found Roger Watkins, *Variety's* editor, sitting in his office, typing away at a computer keyboard. Roger knew I was going to Toronto to interview David Puttnam, but his reaction had been rather apathetic.

After all, Roger had covered the outspoken British producer extensively when he was *Variety*'s London bureau chief during the 1980s.

After describing my meeting with David, I said: "Next week, I'm flying to L.A. to interview Ray Stark."

One of the many goals Roger had set for *Variety* under his stewardship was to bring the Hollywood establishment, long absent from the paper's pages, back to the fold.

"Ray Stark? Really?"

"Yes. And I'll be contacting other people involved in David's year at Columbia. I think after they find out Ray is willing to talk to me, they might give me their version of events too."

Suddenly, the article I was planning to do took on a whole new meaning to Roger. He grabbed a pen and began jotting down notes.

"I want to use pictures. Can you get pictures?"

At that point, *Variety* did not use photographs. Using them here would be a major departure from the past.

"We'll do a big spread," Roger continued. "Like nothing *Variety* has done before. When can I have copy?"

He grabbed his calendar and looked up at me waiting for an answer.

"It could be a very long piece," I told him. "It could very easily be two parts. Or more."

"How about May eleven and eighteen," Roger shot back. "Those two issues, eleven and eighteen, go to the Cannes Film Festival. Perfect!"

And that was that. In the space of five minutes, Roger formulated a rough layout and penciled in two publication dates.

"Good luck, mate," Roger said.

I walked out of Roger's office and began a series of phone calls to the key players in the David Puttnam/Hollywood drama. Until now, Hollywood's side of the David Puttnam affair had been like a silent film. It was about to become a talking picture.

CHAPTER
TWENTY-FIVE

Don Safran picked me up at the Beverly Hilton and we wended our way toward the Georgian home where Ray Stark has lived for the past thirty years with his wife, Fran. It is located in Holmby Hills, less known to non-Californians than Beverly Hills or Bel Air, but far more exclusive a neighborhood than either.

The house was impressive. Huge rooms. Intricate woodwork. Classic architecture. And a priceless collection of original art.

A moment after we arrived, Ray jogged down the steps and we moved to a table overlooking a garden. As Don had said would be the case, first came the ground rules.

"I will be responsible for anything I say," Ray began, "but I don't want my remarks to be paraphrased, moved around for dramatic purposes, or taken out of context. I want my quotes verbatim."

A fair enough demand, I thought, for what could be the start of a most unusual and exclusive story.

"I'm talking to you because *Variety* is a newspaper of record," Ray continued. "You can have your tape recorder and I'll have mine. I say this because I think it's a little dangerous sometimes to treat the press too casually. I have always liked and respected Tina Brown, the editor of *Vanity Fair*, and our conversations about the movie business have always been confidential and off-the-record. But, as a reporter, in doing a piece on Puttnam, she referred to a conversation that she and I might have had. Unfortunately, the quotes she attributed to me were inaccurate and she never called to verify any of the conversations Puttnam had attributed to me. Perhaps you can credit that to Puttnam's way with the media, and, perhaps, unconsciously, her loyalty to a countryman. In any case, it is not typical of either the editor Tina Brown or *Vanity Fair*, since she does preside over one of the few popular magazines of any literary quality. As a matter of fact, I want you to check with Tina Brown to confirm my recollection of the facts concerning my conversation. I insist you extend her this courtesy."

"Can you give me an example," I asked, "of how Tina misquoted you?"

"Attributed to me were phrases I would have never used," Ray replied, "like 'Rule Britannia' and 'compatriot.' "

The *Vanity Fair* article had quoted Ray as saying: "Well darling, it's a bad day for Rule Britannia. Your compatriot turned out to be a real asshole, didn't he?"

Ray smiled.

"I've never used the words 'Britannia' or 'compatriot.' But she got 'asshole' right. That's more international. Anyway, what I said was, 'It's a bad day for British Columbia,' in reference to Columbia Pictures, which I thought was funny.

"In any case, with this article, I'll want to read my quotes before they go to print."

That, too, was reasonable enough, since I had made the same deal with David Puttnam.

"I have no problem with that," I told Ray.

"Good," he laughed. "Maybe we'll have some fun."

I pulled a tape recorder from my briefcase but Ray shook his head no.

"No, not today. I'll block out a few hours tomorrow."

The next day Ray, Don, Ray's assistant Janet Garrison, and I convened around a large round table in Ray's Beverly Hills office.

"Let's start when David was seeking the Columbia job," I suggested. "Didn't he come to you for help?"

"Yes. I thought he was a bright young entrepreneur producing interesting movies like *Local Hero*. Years earlier, a friend had asked me to help David when David was pursuing an executive position with Columbia in London. As it happened, things didn't work out.

"So, in 1986, when David called me and said it was important that he see me, we made a date for four o'clock that same afternoon. It was June twenty-second, 1986."

Ray looked at Janet for confirmation and she nodded.

"It was a beautiful day and we sat out in the garden," Ray continued. "He gave me a big bear hug. Can you imagine, a big bear hug! As I recall, David said, 'Ray, you have to help me. I don't know what to do. I've been offered this fabulous deal. It's more money than I ever heard of or expected, and it's a wonderful opportunity for me. Ray, you are like a father to me.'

"Actually—although I rather liked him—I couldn't see myself adopting him.

"David then explained his predicament. I can't remember his exact words, but he said something like 'The problem is, Fay won't let me have any control over international, and I don't want to take the job unless I feel I can do my best, and my best is international. I don't know very much about domestic, but with international, I really think I could help.' "

Ray offered an aside—"By the way, you should check with David and get him to tickle his schizophrenic memory"—and then turned his attention back to the story.

"It seemed to me, if they were going to take an Englishman, they really should utilize his knowledge of English distribution. So I told David I would try to help him communicate his point to Atlanta, certain that David would incorporate the input of Pat Williamson, the bright and experienced head of Columbia's worldwide distribution.

"My recollection is that David said, 'One thing, though, Ray. I have to know that if there's something you want to do at Columbia which I don't like, I have to know that you're not going to push it on me.'

"David surprised me. I said, 'Bullshit, David. If you didn't care for one of my projects, I'd be out of your office quicker than you could blink an eye.'

"He gave me another big hug and said something like, 'You're terrific. You've really made this a wonderful afternoon for me.'

"Now a lot has been made about this idea of me supposedly trying to force David to do my pictures. It's absolutely absurd. David Puttnam's references to me about wanting to work at Columbia are hallucinatory. I never pushed anyone into making a film and—even as a large stockholder of Columbia—when they didn't like my projects, I took them elsewhere.

"For example, when David Begelman and Stanley Jaffe were at Columbia, I went to the studio with the idea of doing *Smokey and the Bandit* with Burt Reynolds for three million dollars. Stanley was adamant that he didn't want to be associated with this kind of picture. I never went to David Begelman—who was my friend, and over Stanley—to ask him to intervene. Instead, I submitted the picture to Universal, where Ned Tanen was smart enough to immediately take the project. It cost three million dollars and grossed over a hundred and twenty million, which was great for Burt Reynolds, who probably made twelve million dollars for eighteen days' work. Only God and Lew Wasserman know how much Universal made with *Smokey* and the two sequels and a rip-off TV show.

"I submitted *The Goodbye Girl* to David Begelman at Columbia and Ted Ashley at Warner Brothers. They couldn't see the potential of *The Goodbye Girl*. So I went to Metro, where Danny Melnick was head of production at the time, and he made it.

"I've been associated with a great many successful pictures away from Columbia. I've even helped Columbia to the extent that when one executive at Columbia didn't want to do *California Suite*, I brought it to Paramount. But when that Columbia executive was replaced by a new executive who wanted the picture, I went back to Paramount and received an okay to bring the picture back to Columbia.

"So the worst thing I did was make five successful pictures away from Columbia. I think *The Secret of My Success* will earn more money than all of Puttnam's projects at Columbia."

Next we moved chronologically to David Puttnam's appointment.

"In your view, Ray, how did David wind up in Hollywood after all the things he said? What exactly happened?"

"At the time, Columbia was being run by Fay Vincent. He was brought in because of the unpleasant problems Columbia had had during the Hirschfield-Begelman-Kerkorian period. Fay was an SEC lawyer who had the dignity and proper background that should have gone well with a conservative company like Coca-Cola.

"On the other hand, Fay did not have the vaguest idea what the entertainment business was all about, and in the learning process, he made a lot of mistakes. The first one was letting Frank Price go. Frank had been on a run and was a tremendous piece of manpower at the studio.

"Then there was the possibility of getting Michael Eisner. Instead, Eisner wound up as chairman of the Walt Disney company and is credited with the amazing comeback of that studio.

"I remember meeting with Victor Kaufman and others who strongly recommended Michael Eisner, as I did. But Fay felt he didn't want to give him that mantle of power that he eventually bestowed on David Puttnam.

"I think Puttnam's lawyer approached Fay about the job and Fay—just grasping for any straw that came along—probably thought, 'Gee, here's a gentleman. Here's a man who wants to change an industry that I don't particularly like myself. He wants to change the whole image of the film industry and this could be wonderful for the image of Coca-Cola from the aesthetic and intellectual point of view.' Fay then persuaded Coca-Cola that hiring David was the right thing to do. So that's really how David wound up at Columbia. He just walked into the job because there was no one else around who met Fay's criteria of being the antithesis of a Hollywood personality. Victor—who was *really* the best bet—was still running Tri-Star. And there just wasn't anyone else available."

"David arrived in Burbank," I noted, "and everyone, it seems, was in favor of his appointment. Even you."

"That's correct. As I said, I liked Puttnam when he was starting out. However, as Puttnam grew older and perhaps not wiser, he decided it was a rather good idea to have money, instead of just the masturbatory fun of sitting on the set for ten weeks. His attitudes changed a lot.

"But even before his attitudes became evident, the pictures he made were an indication that what he said wasn't what he did. He said he was against big-budget movies, for example. Yet the last film he did before coming to Columbia was *The Mission* for Warner Brothers. The picture cost twenty-five million dollars or more, apart from marketing. Then, later, he approved *The Adventures of Baron Munchausen* for about twenty-five million dollars. And I think you'll find that *Munchausen* will be a big loser.

"Then he talked about social relevance in cinema. After doing *Midnight Express* for Peter Guber over at Casablanca, he said he had to seek the absolution of a Jesuit priest. He should have visited his guru instead. It's funny, but David was involved with a hit in that movie and he didn't even know it.

"David expresses guilt over *Midnight Express*, yet his first film at Columbia was *Someone to Watch Over Me*, which was peppered with sex and violence. I wonder if he had to go back to a Jesuit priest after that film.

"If you look at my record as a producer, you won't see any films with violence or promiscuity or overt sex. The discreet love scenes in *The Way We Were* were the most explicit of any Rastar film. I will put up *Reflections in a Golden Eye* or *Fat City* or *The Night of the Iguana*—all three of which I did with John Huston— against anything David has made on the basis of social content. However, whether it was *Smokey and the Bandit* or any of the other films, there was never a drop of blood or a broken bone.

"My objective has always been to make films that entertain and/or explore relationships, certainly not to preach. I feel that when people pay money for tickets they should receive what they paid for, which is entertainment. Otherwise they would go to a tabernacle.

"After more than one hundred films, I'm doing a film this year that will be a first for me in its emphasis on sex and violence, a movie called *Revenge* starring Kevin Costner and Anthony Quinn, with Tony Scott directing. I became involved because of John Huston, who showed me the Jim Harrison novella, upon which the film is based. John and I loved the story and he wrote a screenplay for me. I really wanted to work with John again, but that was not to be. Sadly, he was too ill. However, I still felt it could be made tastefully. But then, I've hedged on this new direction by also putting into production a strongly contrasting film, *Steel Magnolias*, a very charming and humanistic story, based on an Off-Broadway play by Robert Harling.

"On the other hand, Puttnam does pretend to elevate society with his films, which leaves him very vulnerable when you consider some of his projects. When you take a film with very graphic violence like *The Beast* or a vulgar little film about a talking penis like *Me and Him*, one can hardly say that David was bringing on the new dawn of elegant, intelligent, socially relevant filmmaking.

"I was a lucky man, indoctrinated by the best. Sam Goldwyn. Charlie Feldman. Darryl Zanuck. David Selznick. Men who had humanity and whose films had themes that stretched out to the audience. They didn't make cult movies that are eccentric for the sake of being eccentric. They didn't pretend that the movies they made had some greater meaning."

As Ray talked, he was insistent and very precise. There was no particular anger in his voice, just a tone of exasperation on occasion, especially when I asked the main reason he didn't like David Puttnam.

"I don't dislike David," Ray countered. "I just don't respect him. I don't understand the basic truth of David. I think that if David had kept an open mind and a closed mouth, he might have been successful. There's nothing to dislike. I didn't know him that well. We never had any more than passing conversations, which David has distorted or fantasized.

"Yes, I became very open in my criticism of David Puttnam. But that was nothing personal. I criticized him when I saw that he was dropping top, top filmmakers with whom I would have loved to been involved. Norman Jewison, Taylor Hackford, Danny Melnick, Larry Kasdan, Ivan Reitman. Within moments they were connected with other studios which had been trying to get them for years. David was not only blowing off these talented and proven filmmakers but insulting them as well.

"And what was he bringing in? There were no David Leans, more like a migration of well-meaning, unproven young English people who really had little filmmaking experience in America."

I pointed out that David, because of his perception that Ray was an adversary, had often expressed the feeling that Ray had "gotten" him and caused him to be fired.

"People say that because of my relationship with Columbia and, perhaps, Herbert Allen, but Herbert is above studio intrigue. He is a very straight, highly intelligent, conservative, and witty man and a dedicated investment banker. It may be difficult for some people to understand that talking business is just one of the ancillary pleasures of a twenty-five-year relationship.

"I did talk to Fay a number of times and told him that I thought David was on the wrong track in getting rid of these talented people and antagonizing a bright, knowledgeable, very creative and constructive agent like Mike Ovitz who does enjoy the trust and admiration of many very special clients who believe in him. He does have the ability to take his clients anywhere that's best for them.

"There are maybe one hundred bright people in Mike's company, all with one objective: finding good stories and linking them to the right talent. It would seem very helpful to a studio, for example, if someone were to call and offer a package with Bill Murray and *Ghostbusters*. David should have embraced Mike Ovitz and CAA, Jeff Berg and ICM, and Sue Mengers and the William Morris Agency too. If you don't have their support, you're not in the movie business.

"It was naive of Puttnam to lecture CAA and Mike Ovitz, who knows more about getting movies made than Puttnam ever will know.

"Sure, agencies are tough. That's what the business is, as is every art form, every sport. A studio chief should be tough enough to negotiate with these agencies and stand up to them. Puttnam never understood that he had to earn his way, not talk his way. His responsibility was not that of an evangelist, but to make movies that audiences want to see.

"I couldn't understand why David seemed intent on alienating these people. Why antagonize your peers when it would be easier and more fun to enjoy doing business with them?

"David constantly spoke out against 'packages.' I wish people would come to me with star-name packages. Someone calling to tell me that they have Tom Cruise and Dustin Hoffman for a movie or Debra Winger and Warren Beatty for a movie. I would love to be offered a tasteful, entertaining project that stood a chance of making a profit. I see nothing naughty in the words 'making a profit.' "

Ray shook his head, as if in disbelief.

"The most important thing David lost—or never had—was his perspective and sense of responsibility. When you are in control of a couple of hundred million dollars a year, you have to say, 'I just can't waste it on bringing a chum over from England. Or I can't waste it on a quaint little project.' You have to say, 'How can this money be spent so (a) I don't lose anything for the company, and (b) try to make money for the company, and (c) make films that will embrace my ideals yet will still entertain and be of some social relevance.'

"Even that's a difficult point. What exactly constitutes social relevance? I remember a film with Gregory Peck about anti-Semitism called *Gentleman's Agreement*. I remember saying to Darryl Zanuck—whom I consider to be one of the *great* filmmakers—'It's strange, Darryl. You can take the picture two ways: one, as having been an important treatment regarding the dangers and the trauma of anti-Semitism, and, at the same time, it could also be viewed as a *blueprint* for anti-Semitism.'

"David didn't have to make action/adventure pictures. He could have made classy pictures as long as they had the potential for success.

"You know, making a picture is like making a chocolate soufflé. You put in the right ingredients and hope it rises. David was making chocolate soufflés that turned into brownies.

"So David lost his perspective. His ego was and is so intense that he just lost sight of his goal. If David truly was interested in young filmmakers, he should have been a professor and sacrificed the million dollars a year he was receiving to run a studio. David received a mandate that is very rarely given to a studio chief, that of complete control. And instead of holding that up as something sacred, he exploited it. He used it for self-indulgent cronyism, paying off old debts.

"It's a shame. But David just lost track of what he said he was going to do. They say absolute power corrupts absolutely. In this case, it was true.

"The logical thing for David to have done when he took over at Columbia is what Dawn Steel is doing today. She's making movies and not lecturing. The day Dawn took over the studio she was responsible for generating a massive cash flow of hundreds of millions of dollars by merely confirming plans for the *Ghostbusters* and *Karate Kid* sequels."

Ray stood up, walked around the table, and then sat back down.

"We should discuss specifics. The press has been terribly careless with the facts. And I want to straighten a few things out once and for all."

"So does David," I informed Ray.

"What do you mean?"

"Well, when I was in Toronto David presented me with a list of questions that he wanted me to pose to you. He'd say, 'Why don't you put this to Ray,' and then give me a question about some incident during his time at Columbia."

"Oh, he did?" Ray said with a grin. "Then let's get to it."

CHAPTER
TWENTY-SIX

I scanned the notes from my interview with David Puttnam. David had suggested that "an interesting question to Ray" might be "Why don't you run a studio?" According to David, Ray had told him: "I never saw a way of making a buck."

Ray took a deep breath, obviously annoyed at the implication inherent in the statement.

"I have never run a studio. But I can say with humility—my short suit—that I have been offered many opportunities.

"For a brief period I was one of the major stockholders and head of production at Seven Arts. And I realized that you have to report to a board of directors and to stockholders. And that's why I've never gone public with any of my companies. They've always been private. I've never had a board of directors I've had to answer to.

"So when David says I've never run a studio, it isn't because of lack of opportunity. Most people in the industry know that I'm not interested in being an administrator. I am an entrepreneur. I am a producer. I am a man who really loves the fun of being involved in the making of movies."

I read another one of David's challenges: "Ray Stark would kill for an Oscar. He'd do anything. If you told him he could buy one for ten million dollars, he'd be there with a check so fast, you wouldn't believe it! Why don't you ask him?"

This time Ray smiled.

"Well, I did receive the Irving Thalberg Award, and then there are my films which have received dozens and dozens of Oscar nominations and many Academy Awards in so many different categories."

Again Ray stared at me, waiting for a question, and again I obliged with a passage from David's interview which he had directed at Ray.

"Ray's deal is basically constructed—in case anyone ever told you differently—in such a way so that if he makes a reasonable film, reasonable, not a successful film, he makes two million dollars. That's the way his deal is structured. That's a very, very, rich deal. That's my opinion. Other people may think it's a reasonably rich deal. He has offices on the lot and probably gets seven hundred fifty thousand to a million dollars a year, all his overhead paid."

"I know it sounds crass," Ray responded, "but I use it here only as a point of fact and for illustration. As David implies, I *have* made a great deal of money for myself, but I have also made a lot of money for those studios involved. I made money with successful motion pictures, not with up-front deals. I am not paid unless a picture is produced. I'm not like David Puttnam, who is paid a million dollars a year to try to make movies. If my film is successful, I am, too. I profit from success, which is as it should be. Puttnam profited from gross failures. How proud can he be of that?"

Ray placed his elbow on the table. "Any more questions from the little professor?"

"Yes. David said, 'Try and find out why Ray Stark dislikes David Picker so much.' "

"First of all," Ray answered, "I don't dislike David Picker. As I remember, during our conversation at my house that afternoon, Puttnam asked my opinion of Picker. And I told him that David Picker is a very nice man, yes, and he did do well when he worked for Arnold Picker, who ran United Artists. But then I pointed out that Picker has since run three production entities and they have all let him go. I also mentioned that Picker's last film, which he produced and his wife, Nessa, directed—it was called *Leader of the Band* and was a three-million-dollar effort for Vista—had a brief regional release, lasted three weeks in Texas, and was considered a disaster.

"But Puttnam told me: 'It doesn't matter to me; what's important is, I know I can trust him. David Picker helped me get my start and I owe it to him.' Puttnam even talked about this during his self-promoting eulogy at the 'Reel Truth' seminar. He told the story about Picker financing his first big picture.

"This is from a man who has been making speeches on cronyism and has been lecturing on the immorality of returning favors. Not very consistent, is he?"

As Ray spoke, I recalled something David had told me in Toronto: "Hollywood may work on the basis of favors done and favors given, but I don't."

"The next time the subject of David Picker came up," Ray continued, "was when I met with Puttnam right after he arrived. By the way, that was the meeting where Puttnam said I walked into his office without an appointment."

Janet Garrison, who was following the chronology of events with a calendar, pointed to an open diary.

"The meeting was at Columbia in Burbank," Janet noted, "and Ray is not usually there, but in his Beverly Hills office. Ray drove over specifically for the appointment and sat in his office at Columbia Plaza West and waited for Mr. Puttnam to finish another meeting. Then they called us and said Mr. Puttnam was ready. Ray walked across the parking lot to see him. It was a scheduled appointment."

"That's specific," Ray asserted. "And the wonderful thing about this meeting was that I went to see Puttnam because I had a project which Columbia and I owned called *Earthly Possessions*, based on a book by Anne Tyler. We were talking to Sean Penn and Jessica Lange, and I thought I should discuss it with Puttnam to see if he was interested.

"I said to him, 'I have this good little movie,' and Puttnam said, 'Okay, talk to David Picker about it.'

"Well, there was a personal problem. A few years back I hired David Picker's wife to write a screenplay of the book for Marsha Mason and it turned out very badly. I filed it away. So I said, 'David, there's no use in talking to David Picker about it.' And David said, 'You're right. He'd resent it.'

For the next hour, Ray and I talked about dates and times and places and people. Ray requested that these observations be off the record because he wasn't sure about them.

"You must check these things out for yourself."

Then I asked Ray about his thoughts on power.

"People think I have all this power," Ray laughed. "They think I can just pick up the phone and get any project that I want into production. The reason for this misconception, I think, is because I basically don't talk to the press. So they don't have any idea of how hard I work to develop a project and get it made.

"I'm successful because I am tireless in trying to make what I believe in come to pass. I'm a very good salesman. And I probably have as good a record with successful films as anyone around. So naturally the studio will listen to me a little more carefully. But ultimately it's their decision whether or not to make the film.

"There are many films that I would have liked to have made that I haven't been able to, and a lot of pictures have taken me ten years to start. I'm *still* working on *Sweet Libby*, which Puttnam said publicly that he didn't like. He's quoted as saying it was not his kind of movie. That's his privilege, but I wish I knew what kind of movie was his kind of movie, looking at the mishmash he's put together at Columbia.

"Anyway, *Funny Girl* took nine years before cameras rolled. *The Way We Were* took five years. I spent four years working on *Revenge* before taking it to Puttnam, who turned it down. Now it's being done at Columbia with Kevin Costner and director Tony Scott. I wouldn't say that would be indicative of a man who can just pick up the phone and make a motion picture deal at a whim.

"Puttnam plays around with the word 'power' and we all have our own definition of it. But power, as I see it, is the ability to use salesmanship and be persuasive in convincing someone of something in which you believe. And, of course, the purest power is tenacity and the truth.

"The other reason I have been successful in the motion picture business is that I like most of the people in the industry and I believe most of the people in the industry enjoy working with me. Some don't, but I am at least on friendly terms with almost everyone. If someone is not my friend, I don't go out of my way to make him an enemy.

"Finally, if I *say* I'm going to do something, chances are that I probably will deliver a film that is reasonably successful. If I have any power at all, it's a positive power of suggestion and a positive power of a track record. At the risk of sounding redundant, I did far less to hasten David Puttnam's departure from Columbia Pictures than he did himself.

"If only he had devoted his time to making pictures that people wanted to see, he would still be in Hollywood with hundreds of millions of dollars in production resources and total autonomy at a major studio, one of the most powerful men in town."

Despite his protests, Ray Stark is among the most influential producers in the movie business. And few would disagree that Ray knows a great deal about making movies. So Ray's appraisal of what could have been in the case of David Puttnam had all the credibility of Ray's credentials and experience to back it up.

David Puttnam could have had it all. Most people had been saying it all along. Now none other than Ray Stark concurred.

I thanked Ray for his time.

"Call me whenever you like," Ray offered.

It was an invitation I would accept.

"And good luck with your story," Ray added. "This will be the first one with *both* sides represented."

During the next few days, I met and spoke with several other key players in the Puttnam/Hollywood controversy. Certainly, having talked with Ray Stark helped in gaining on-the-record interviews with the typically silent motion-picture majority. And most related a story that was radically different from David's recollection of events. By the time I left L.A. on a midnight flight, I had a briefcase full of cassette tapes and dozens of pages of notes. It had been a most interesting trip.

After landing at Kennedy Airport, I had just enough time to stop by my apartment and head to a scheduled meeting with Herbert Allen at 711 Fifth Avenue.

Fifth Avenue, to me at least, is a spectacular sight any time of the day. But I had rarely seen it at 8:00 A.M. and I couldn't ever remember seeing it so early on such a beautiful spring morning. Cartier's windows sparkled like the diamonds inside the famous jewelry store and the soft leather cases on display at Mark Cross seemed to be melting in the sun.

The outer office of Allen & Company looked like a scene from the movie *Wall Street*. Dozens of brokers and investment bankers sat hunched in front of computers, staring intently at rows and columns of numbers as they raced up, down, and across the monitor screen.

Herbert Allen seemed to be the epitome of reason. His words were measured, though in no way guarded, and he usually spoke plainly, getting his message across in no uncertain terms. For example, the first thing I said to Herbert was that I would honor the confidentiality of any off-the-record statements he made. It was the first thing I had said to everyone, including David Puttnam.

"*Everything* I say," Herbert replied, "is on-the-record."

Our discussion of David Puttnam's term began with Herbert's reaffirmation of the fact that the Hollywood establishment was initially very supportive of the British producer.

"I was very positive toward David Puttnam. Puttnam appeared to be a competent producer and I'm sorry for him and for Columbia that his reign was not successful. We were all rooting for him."

But, as Herbert pointed out, things started to deteriorate almost immediately and David soon found himself locked in mortal combat with Hollywood. Herbert expressed puzzlement at David's account of many key elements in the controversy, including David's assertion that Coca-Cola had sought him out for the job.

"David Puttnam had his lawyer call Fay Vincent and essentially apply for the job. I think the misconception arose when Fay and Dick Gallop flew to London for the first meeting. They did it to accommodate David's schedule—he was finishing *The Mission*—and because Fay was anxious to fill the position. Fay wanted to get a reading on David as soon as possible since there were other candidates under consideration."

Herbert, bewildered by David's willingness to alienate major Hollywood filmmakers, told me that "David's job was to make pictures, not enemies," and then described a meeting in Atlanta which represented the only confrontation between him and David.

"It [David's freewheeling speech and treatment of Hollywood filmmakers] involved a policy of the board of directors," Herbert added.

"He let a lot of people get away," Herbert elaborated. "Martin Ransohoff after *Jagged Edge*. Dan Melnick after *Roxanne*. Norman Jewison, which cost us *Moonstruck*. Taylor Hackford."

Then there was the apparent double standard David practiced while at Columbia.

"His criticism of cronyism was inconsistent with his hiring practices," Herbert observed, in reference to the preponderance of Britons brought to the studio.

And of David's verbal jabs at highly paid actors, Herbert remarked:

"I never fully understood Puttnam's criticism of the star system in view of his own contract demands. There seemed to be an inconsistency."

Herbert, considering his position on the Columbia board, was restricted to some degree in what he could say. He did confirm several factual points and made a few suggestions as to who I should consult for further confirmation.

"It is in the best interest of the studio," Herbert concluded, "and the filmmakers involved, that the final chapter not be written in newspapers by David Puttnam."

On April 23, David Puttnam was back at a podium again, adding to his version of the "final chapter." This time at the California Law Symposium. Although I happened to be in New York, David made sure I received a copy of his forty-nine-page speech.

I spoke to several people who had attended the symposium and they reported that David was at his best, his delivery at once crisp and passionate, his words eloquent.

Incredibly, he compared his year at Columbia Pictures to the trial of Socrates! Noting that several thousand years ago Socrates was put on trial for "challenges against contemporary authority," David said: "He was found guilty of heresy and nonconformity; but the memory of his trial should be sufficient to remind us all of the necessity to hold fast to our beliefs; lest they too slip away, and find us fleeing towards an uncertain future."

David quoted George Bernard Shaw: "George Bernard Shaw advised us to 'be true to the dreams of our youth.'" He chided the American creative community by citing a passage from the book *In Search of Melancholy Baby* by exiled Russian writer Vassily Aksyonov: "I see with mounting astonishment that for all its scope, the American literary, theatrical, and cinematic establishment has certain traits in common with a general store: preference for the hot item, fear of risk, sheer panic at the thought of innovation." And he used two movies—*Broadcast News* and *Inherit the Wind*—to make his point.

From *Broadcast News*, David invoked a speech by Aaron Altman, a character in the film: "What do you think the devil is going to look like if he comes around? He will be attractive and he will be nice and helpful . . . he will just bit by bit lower standards where they are important. Just coax along flash over substance. Just a tiny bit at a time."

The fictionalized Clarence Darrow from *Inherit the Wind* provided David with the following challenge: "Why *did* God plague us with the power to think? Why do you deny the one faculty which lifts man above all other creatures on earth: the power of his brain to reason?"

Then David offered yet another opinion about the ills of America: "As I see it, the United States is in genuine danger of becoming the lost land, at least of my youthful dreams, and in some cases, almost certainly yours. There is disillusionment wafting though the heady winds of the American dream."

There was the familiar reference to socially relevant cinema—"I also sincerely believe that artists, and those who work with them, have a considerable moral responsibility to carefully select projects which attune themselves to the *needs* of their audience, projects which *at the very least* offer them a sense of values . . ."—and, as usual, the call for a new era in filmmaking, this time using the words of French director François Truffaut: "Young filmmakers must make up their minds not to tread in the footprints of the 'old' cinema."

The balance of the speech was full of self-analysis:

"The nature of my character is to fight for my right, and that of other filmmakers, to make those films in which we passionately believe, and which genuinely reflect an individual humanist vision. A form of arrogance, I suppose, because it requires an inordinate amount of belief in oneself to risk the failure that lurks behind every creative choice. . . .

"It is a necessary thing for me to continue to maintain my belief in the power of the individual mind to think and make a difference. I will continue to believe in the possibility of work which celebrates the dignity of man, which strengthens the hope of an uncertain future. . . .

"So criticize please, but know too that it is my right, indeed I have no other choice, than to be who I am. Just a man, wiser perhaps by virtue of his experience, but a man still enthused about the future, and passionately in love with life and the movies. A man still unable to compromise in matters that remain close to him and which form part of his upbringing."

Like a politician, David garnered more and more votes from a mesmerized audience with each poetic phrase. He cited passages from the statement he gave to Don Keough and Roberto Goizueta in July 1986. And then ended with his trademark flourish:

"In closing, like Cyrano, I, and many like me, ask simply, 'What would you have us do? Seek for the patronage of some great man, and like a creeping vine on a tall tree, crawl upward, where I cannot stand alone? No thank you! . . . But, to sing, to laugh, to dream, to walk in my own way. . . . To travel any road under the sun, under the stars. . . . Never to make a line I have not heard in my own heart; yet, with all modesty, to say: "My soul, be satisfied with flowers, with fruit, with weeds even; but gather them in the one garden you may truly call your own." ' "

By the next morning, David Puttnam once again dominated the pages of *Variety, The Hollywood Reporter*, and the *Los Angeles Times*. Again a hero, again a visionary. Only this time, no longer chairman/CEO of Columbia Pictures, he was perceived by the media as a martyr too.

And a martyr, as history has clearly shown, can be so much more effective than a leader.

So can an exile, which was what David was about to become, at least temporarily. Unable to enter England for tax reasons, David would fly to Japan to complete negotiations on the $50,000,000 production fund which would place him back in Hollywood and then, when he could do so without fear of taxation on his multi-million-dollar settlement, continue on to London.

Awaiting the return of the idealist from Britain would be a legion of ardent American disciples who, ironically, became even more impassioned when David Puttnam publicly mourned the failure of the American dream.

The American dream, of course, was alive and well among the Hollywood establishment. And they didn't appreciate a Briton telling them it was dead.

CHAPTER
TWENTY-SEVEN

As I continued my investigation into the David Puttnam/Hollywood controversy, I felt like I was in the middle of a movie that might be entitled *Citizen Puttnam*. Just as the search for the meaning of the word "Rosebud" took many surprising twists in the classic film *Citizen Kane*, the quest to gain an understanding of the enigmatic David Puttnam was propelled by astonishing revelations.

One of the more shocking statements came from Warren Beatty:

"I have never met or spoken to Mr. David Puttnam," the actor/producer/director said, "nor have I ever had the slightest communication with him of any sort. I have never made any public comment about him because I have never wanted to aid what appears to me to be his quest for publicity, which he generates by publicly attacking coworkers who are well known."

Incredibly, David had been engaged in a public feud for *seven* years with a man he had *never* met!

Mysteries were commonplace in the wake of David Puttnam's departure and one of the most hotly debated issues involved the box-office hit, *Moonstruck*, which was released by MGM. Could *Moonstruck* have been a Columbia picture? David had always insisted he never saw the script and reiterated this to me during our interview in Toronto. Hollywood insiders insisted he had read the screenplay and turned it down. So I called the director of the film, Norman Jewison, to find out.

"I was under contract to Columbia at the time as far as first refusal was concerned," Norman related. "I submitted the script to Columbia to David Puttnam's attention."

"Do you know if he read it?" I asked.

"Well, my agent, Larry Auerbach, received a letter from David, turning it down. I would think so."

A letter?

I called David.

"David, I just got off the phone with Norman Jewison and he said that . . ."

"I've got one thing to clear up," David interrupted, "because I did some checking on my own. While I was at Columbia we did turn down a script called *Moonglow*, which did eventually become *Moonstruck*. The letter I sent out to Larry Auerbach was the sixth of September, which means it was at the end of the first week I was there.

"As we got four thousand scripts in, and as I'd done nothing but read scripts in the previous two months—I *only* read scripts— it could have been one of the ones I read. I have no idea.

"In the letter I sent, it sounds as though I did. I said 'I'm pretty sure in my own mind that this is the one decision I'm going to regret and at least half of me hopes I will regret it.'

"It's an unusual letter—the only one like that I wrote—it sounds to me as though I must have been right on the edge."

I checked back with Norman to confirm the *Moonglow* title.

"It was called a lot of things," Norman related. "Originally it was called *The Bride and the Wolf*, and at one time it was called *Moonglow*."

Another mystery which was still unsolved when I started my pursuit of the controversy was the Bill Murray slur. Did he make a disparaging comment about the star of *Ghostbusters* or didn't he? David firmly asserted he did not.

Compiling a list of people who had attended the luncheon where David was rumored to have made the statement, I logged repeated confirmations that it was indeed uttered by the then-studio chief. No one, however, would say so for attribution. Ultimately, I met with Los Angeles attorney Tom Hansen, who did come forward and relate the events of that day for the record.

At every turn, David Puttnam's account was at odds with other participants in the drama, as it was regarding the monetary expectations of his year at Columbia Pictures. David had often said the subject of making money was never an issue during the contract talks.

"You should ask Dick Gallop," David suggested in Toronto when queried about the fiscal responsibility of his job. "He sat quietly through *all* of this. He, in effect, made the deal with me. He was certainly the point man on the deal with my lawyer."

Taking David's advice, I met with Dick Gallop, who, until then, had never spoken to the media about the negotiations.

"It was made clear to him," Dick told me, "and he accepted the fact that Columbia was a profit-making venture. That was made clear from day one. There was no question, through direct conversations at that meeting, that making popular pictures and making the studio money was the essence of the assignment."

After hearing Dick Gallop's appraisal, I called David in London.

"You talked to Dick Gallop?" David asked. He seemed very surprised.

"Yes. And he said there was no question about the commercial aspect of filmmaking. He said that it was made *very clear*."

"I suppose it was implicit," David allowed.

I called Dick Gallop for a reaction.

"It was *explicit*," Dick shot back.

Why would David indicate Coca-Cola was not interested in making a profit at Columbia Pictures? Why would David deny making the Bill Murray remark? Why would David assert that he had never seen *Moonstruck*? Why would David carry a long-term grudge against Warren Beatty, someone he had never met?

All these questions rendered *Citizen Puttnam* a most complex individual. Rather than a portrait of a visionary filmmaker, there were snapshots of contradictions. Even clear-cut events suddenly splintered into contradictory recollections, as evidenced by conversations I had with producer Peter Guber and British film financier Jarvis Astaire.

I had called Peter Guber merely to gain some background information regarding David's stint as president of Casablanca Filmworks. Instead, Peter offered a fascinating revelation regarding David's true role in *Midnight Express*, a role the media had played to the hilt.

"I conceived *Midnight Express*, not David Puttnam," Peter said. "I saw a newspaper article about Billy Hayes and acquired the rights to the story on my own. I arranged for a book to be written, hired Oliver Stone to write a screenplay, set Alan Parker as director, and brought in Alan Marshall as producer. I then signed Giorgio Moroder to do the music and began financing the film with my own money.

"The picture was a go long before David came to Casablanca. Immediately upon joining Casablanca, David asked to coproduce *Midnight Express* with Alan Marshall."

With a coproducer, Alan Marshall, and a fully developed script, David Puttnam's involvement, although significant, was not as total and unassisted as the media liked to imply.

"To be fair," Peter Guber concluded, "David acted as line producer on *Midnight Express*."

After completing *Midnight Express*, David had been scheduled to produce *Agatha*, a film starring Dustin Hoffman. Since he never made it to the set, I endeavored to find out why. I located Jarvis Astaire, who stepped in as producer of *Agatha*, in London.

"He couldn't produce the picture," Jarvis recalled, still sounding angry about the 1977 incident, "because he could only come into England twenty days the rest of the year. He was getting a tax breather."

After speaking with Jarvis, I contacted David, who had previously blamed a "malevolent" Dustin Hoffman for his withdrawal as producer. David stuck to his version.

"I didn't produce *Agatha*," David bristled, "because it became a movie out of control. I saw in that film how *not* to make a movie. How any star can't be allowed to decide what's right for a movie."

"What about the tax breather?" I asked. "Are you saying that's not true?"

David didn't answer immediately.

"I don't recall anything like that," David said finally. "Nothing like that at all."

A few days later I obtained a copy of a letter David had written to Jarvis Astaire citing tax reasons for his absence from the set.

"I'm afraid," David had written, "that my tax accountants advise me I can only come into England twenty days the rest of the year. . . ."

Sometimes my investigation would beget a previously unknown example of David's less-than-straightforward dialogue with

Hollywood. A case in point was David's termination of the production deal Columbia had with former studio president Dan Melnick.

"I had a contractual commitment that was running out," Dan remembered, "and David indicated a strong desire to continue the relationship. It was a unique relationship. I funded my own development and then made a distribution deal with Columbia which was advantageous. David said he wanted to change that and take over the development costs. We struck a deal. He committed verbally on the phone."

Dan related how he was readying himself to implement the deal when David called him back.

"David said, 'This is embarrassing but Fay doesn't want to make any rich production deals.' "

After speaking with Dan Melnick, I called David.

"Dan said that the reason you gave for terminating his deal was that Fay Vincent didn't want to renew it."

"Well," David replied, "I wouldn't want it to be implied it was Fay's decision. I may have told Fay, but it was my decision. It was not personal. I admire Dan Melnick. I just felt that the terms of the deal were too rich to live with."

David Puttnam's severing of Dan Melnick's relationship with Columbia was particularly surprising since it followed the Melnick-produced box-office hit *Roxanne*, starring Steve Martin and Daryl Hannah.

"The picture was committed by Guy McElwaine," Dan said of *Roxanne*, a film the media had often referred to as one of David's approvals. "It was all in place with a start date by the time David arrived at the studio. David's involvement was limited to authorizing an additional sum of money so we could close our deal with Daryl Hannah.

"At the time, David was out of the country. I called him and said: 'If you agree with the additional sum please transmit the information to your staff.' "

Dan Melnick's agreement was just one of the many production deals consummated by Guy McElwaine and later dispensed with by David Puttnam. I called Guy to get a reaction regarding the transition between him and his successor. Guy recalled his first meeting with David:

"David said: 'I don't know what I'm doing here, Columbia is set up pretty well.' I had set producer deals: Jewison, Kasdan,

Hackford, Melnick. And there were the 'franchises,' *Ghostbusters* and *Karate Kid*. And *Jagged Edge II*."

Although it was usually the Hollywood-grown movies David Puttnam *did not* approve which fueled much of the controversy during his term, one that he did greenlight even before arriving in Burbank, *Leonard Part 6*, created quite a stir because it ran completely contrary to David's filmmaking credo. It boasted a big budget *and* a major star. Later, David explained that he had no choice other than doing the picture, considering Cosby's close ties with Coca-Cola.

"But he did have a choice," Tri-Star president David Matalon countered. "I would have been happy to have made *Leonard Part 6*. And I'd like to believe it would have been quite a different movie with an American point of view."

Certainly, *Leonard Part 6* would have been a "different" movie under Matalon's supervision. David Puttnam had brought in two Britons, director Paul Weiland and producer Alan Marshall, to work on the Cosby project, a move which was akin to assigning a young American filmmaker to oversee the *very* British *Benny Hill Show*.

However, the prospect of Tri-Star, Coca-Cola's other motion picture subsidiary, having a major box-office hit with Coca-Cola's highest paid spokesman must have seemed to David to be too terrifying a risk to take. A switch from Columbia to Tri-Star, of course, could have been easily accomplished without in any way alienating Cosby. One Coke subsidiary or another would certainly not have mattered to anyone involved.

While I had David Matalon on the phone, I asked him about the now infamous *Rambo* statement David had made during his first trip to Coke headquarters. It had been an unfortunate example to use, since *Rambo: First Blood Part II* was the highest-grossing film ever for Tri-Star Pictures.

"I'm very proud to have distributed *Rambo*," Matalon countered. "In fact, I was surprised when I heard what David said about the film. I have to believe David never screened *Rambo*. He must have been reacting to *Rambo* the phenomenon and not *Rambo* the film."

Although Matalon tried to remain gracious, he finally stated tersely: "*Rambo II* made more money than Puttnam's total production lineup."

Beyond the specifics, there was the philosophy. David Puttnam

and Hollywood could not have been further apart in this respect.
As my interviews explored the ideology of filmmaking, the responses grew more impassioned.

Producer Marty Ransohoff, whose *Jagged Edge II* was nixed by
David because the studio chief was philosophically opposed to
sequels, offered a rebuttal to David's rhetoric regarding social
responsibility in cinema and to his preoccupation with low budgets.

"Social responsibility?" Marty laughed. "When you're running
a public company, you have a corporate responsibility as well as
a responsibility to hundreds of employees. The studio is like a
train that steams along. If you want to talk about social consequences, what are the social consequences if the train stops? It's
very easy to make heavies out of a few guys on the inside who
have the responsibility of turning a buck. What about the jobs
they are responsible for? What about the banks? Stockholders?
People who invested their life savings in good faith? This in itself
indicates social responsibility."

Turning his attention to the cost of a film, Marty offered the
conventional Hollywood view.

"What *should* a picture cost? The average medium-budget film
might cost six million and change below the line. The important
point here is that the below-the-line figure should not go up more
than one to one point five million regardless of what the above-
the-line appetite ultimately is. So the below-the-line figure should
not drastically alter the final budget.

"From that point on, the above-the-line could be three million
or ten million or more, depending on cast—primarily stars—and
the choice of director. So the difference between a ten-to-eleven-
million-dollar picture and a seventeen-to-eighteen-million-dollar
picture is really the stars and the director. These are the huge
variables. This is the judgment call.

"It has to do with the three A's of filmmaking: Attitude, Approach, and Appetite. The three A's themselves will dictate what
range the picture is in.

"If you elect to go out and make a seven-to-eight-million-dollar
movie, which in all likelihood means no major stars or major director, you could be looking at drastically reduced cable and cassette income. And that income could be as much as forty percent
of the total. You're looking at quantifiers—cast, director—which
went into the machine. It goes right back to the three A's.

"*The* consideration in evaluating what a picture should cost is the potential audience."

Marty also challenged David's aversion to big-name, "high-priced" directors as well.

"The first thing I attempt to do when developing a picture is tie up a top director. I use two criteria. One: Is he a good direc-tor? Two: Is he capable of attracting talent? As far as what that director is worth, there are basically established prices. The prices being paid top directors are justified because of the talent they can attract, as well as the artistic talents they bring to the movie. Generally, the first question a star asks is "Who's the director?" The *second* question is "How much am I being paid?""

Another concept which placed David and Hollywood at opposite ends of the spectrum was the idea that movies should make money, something David dubbed "the tyranny of the box office."

Bertram Fields, Los Angeles movie business attorney who represents Warren Beatty and Dustin Hoffman, had this to say:

"Mr. Puttnam is fond of saying that we should not be subject to the 'tyranny of the box office,' which means, as I understand it, that studio executives shouldn't base their decision to make a picture on the picture's chances of commercial success.

"That melodramatic statement may be appropriate coming from someone who makes pictures with his own money (something I don't think Mr. Puttnam has done). But someone holding that view could never, in good faith, accept a position as head of a major studio responsible (directly or indirectly) to public shareholders. Those people have invested their savings in the company in order to make a return on investment. It's the legal and moral duty of the studio head to maximize that return. A studio head who ignores the probable appeal of a picture to the consuming public, whether in the interests of art or ego, is betraying his duty of trust to those investors.

"The test of the free marketplace is fundamental to our economic and political system. If Mr. Puttnam wants to escape its 'tyranny,' he should make pictures with his own money, not that of trusting and innocent investors.

"Actually, I suspect that Mr. Puttnam's raging at the 'tyranny of the box office' may stem from a realization that the pictures he developed for Columbia to produce will fare badly in the marketplace. His statement is somewhat like that of the slumping baseball player who wails that we must free ourselves from the 'tyranny of recorded batting averages.' "

Besides being socially relevant, low budget, and free from the tyranny of the box office, David advanced the notion that films should have foreign appeal. Former Columbia president Frank Price was quick to qualify that postulation.

"There was nothing new in being involved in foreign-based pictures of quality," Frank noted. "I founded Triumph Films to deal with low-budget films and foreign films. But we discovered that it wasn't profitable. At least not for a studio the size of Columbia Pictures.

"Even before Triumph, Columbia was always known as an international studio. We made films that had a worldwide appeal. Certainly *Gandhi* and *Ghostbusters* did well in foreign territories and, in fact, American-produced pictures have typically done well overseas.

"On that basis, *The Last Emperor*, for instance, was a dumb deal. In order to profit from American success, to take advantage of nine Academy Awards, you need foreign, video, all the ancillaries. So David didn't really understand the foreign aspect of American movies. He may have known foreign films within a foreign environment, but he obviously didn't understand the foreign market in relation to the export of American movies."

Frank paused and then continued with an assessment of David's year at the studio.

"Being a British producer is different from running an American studio. It doesn't even remotely resemble it. He was in a totally unfamiliar community in a job he didn't understand. It was like taking someone who had only flown Cessnas and putting him in the cockpit of a 747."

Frank shook his head.

"What David Puttnam did to Columbia really offended me."

I pressed: "Can you give me examples?"

"It's immoral not to utilize an asset like *Ghostbusters*. There is an obligation to do a sequel. If you're head of a studio, there are certain things you are *obligated* to do. *Ishtar* is another example. David kept saying he never saw the picture. As the head of a studio, you really can't go back and say you had nothing to do with it."

Notwithstanding David Puttnam's actions, more than anything

else it was his words, his dalliance with the media, that seemed to generate the most ire in Hollywood.

"Puttnam is a man who likes to play with words," Ray Stark observed when I asked him about David's apparent fascination with newsprint. "He's anti-semantic. What suits him at the moment becomes the basis of a speech. In some cases he says I have no power, I'm like the Wizard of Oz, the power is only there if you believe in it. In other instances, he tells stories of what he considers to be my power, how I make phone calls to help his cause or to hurt his cause. These are nice turns of phrase, but that's his primary interest—not me, not power, not threats, not even films—but to use all of these in trying to woo the media for his own personal gain."

Indeed, this was a most puzzling aspect of David Puttnam's personality. Why did he seemingly go out of his way to alienate the very people he might need to call upon during his term at Columbia Pictures?

Frank Price offered one possible explanation:

"To an outsider like David Puttnam, the Hollywood establishment may have appeared bigger and more fearsome than they actually are."

Certainly, *Citizen Puttnam* was an elusive figure. Much had been written about *what* he did and said but very little illustrating *why*. Where was the underlying impetus for his behavior?

Just as "Rosebud" turned out to be nothing more meaningful than the name of a sled, Hollywood felt David Puttnam was motivated by nothing so lofty as a noble cause. Instead, the old guard speculated that the British producer was driven by a thirst for personal glory and a nagging insecurity which manifested itself in a very vocal hostility.

Perhaps they were right. Nothing else seemed to make any sense.

CHAPTER
TWENTY-EIGHT

Word spread from *Weekly Variety* in New York to *Daily Variety* in Los Angeles that the Hollywood establishment, including the reclusive Ray Stark, was headed for the pages of *Variety*. The reaction within the paper ran the gamut from the elation of *Weekly Variety* editor Roger Watkins to the consternation of *Daily Variety* editor Tom Pryor. Reporters lined up on one side or the other, most firmly behind Tom Pryor.

I was somewhat puzzled by Tom's reluctance to run a piece that contained dozens of exclusives. More puzzling was the fact that he had made this determination *before* even seeing it. Naturally, I wondered why the veteran editor was so adamant about not running the article.

I didn't have to wonder long, however.

On April 27, Hollywood was stunned by an editorial carried in *Daily Variety*. Entitled "Puttnam's Legacy," it was written by Tom Pryor.

"Never mind all the baloney that has appeared in print," Tom Pryor wrote, "about the short-lived head of Columbia Pictures speaking his mind too freely. To list his transgressions: criticizing power-broker agents, some domineering stars and certain individuals with Columbia-Coca-Cola ties.

"The irony is that the name David Puttnam is likely to be more prominent in the history of Columbia, already splintered via Tri-Star, than its founder Harry Cohn, a curmudgeon measured against the most autocratic of the founding fathers of the 'picture business.' "

To Hollywood, it was inconceivable that Tom Pryor would compare Harry Cohn, a movie business legend who had *built* an entire studio, to David Puttnam, a man who had spent just one year at Columbia Pictures. Cohn had fostered hundreds of filmmakers during his career, among them David Puttnam's own hero, Frank Capra.

The editorial was filled with praise for the departing studio chief:

"And what cardinal sin did David Puttnam commit? He went to the heart of what plagues the film business. . . .

"Puttnam's instinct was right. . . .

"It has not been proven that Puttnam was a creative failure. He was a victim of political skullduggery, which Coca-Cola may regret down the road."

That morning—the morning Tom Pryor told the world how he felt about David Puttnam—my phone never stopped ringing.

Marty Ransohoff: "I just don't understand what made Tom write that editorial."

Ray Stark: "Tom's a nice guy, but he must be bucking for early retirement."

In fact, Ray had been used as a point of reference in the piece. ". . . as Ray Stark can remember well . . ." Pryor noted, preceding a section on the golden days of Hollywood.

Call after call expressed bewilderment.

"Obviously," Don Safran conjectured, "*Variety* is being held hostage by the editors of *Mad Magazine*."

While Tom Pryor had alluded to "political skullduggery" as the reason for the professional demise of David Puttnam—seen as a victim of an organized effort—I soon found that the sword cut both ways. Within days, there were rampant rumors about my upcoming *Variety* two-parter.

I was told by several callers that my article was being viewed by David Puttnam's supporters as part of a Hollywood conspiracy to discredit him.

David Puttnam also called.

"Charles, I felt we had a good conversation in Toronto. I felt you understood the facts. But now I think you've been seduced by Hollywood."

I was exasperated.

"David, I have not been seduced by anyone. I told you when we first spoke that I wanted to get *both* sides of the controversy. Isn't it fair for Ray Stark and Herbert Allen to have an opinion?"

"I'm not saying that, I'm just saying . . ."

For a moment—David was calling from England—I thought the line went dead.

"David? Hello? David? . . ."

"You spoke to Herbert Allen? Not on-the-record?"

"Yes."

David was inconsolable.

"You see, that proves Ray Stark is behind this. Herbert would have never talked to you if Ray hadn't asked him to talk to you. Can't you see what they're doing?"

"David, it would be naive to think that Ray and Herbert don't talk to each other. Obviously, they all talk to each other all the time. And it's equally obvious that they must have discussed who was talking to me and why. If everybody was off-the-record, your point would be valid. But they are not 'shadowy figures,' as you described them, anymore. As I promised you many times, I will not print one single unattributed word. You will know who is saying what. This is not a conspiracy, David. This is an article, that's all. Everybody else is just doing what you have done all along."

"No they aren't. I've been telling the truth. They're lying."

"Even if they are, this time it's on-the-record."

"They're lying on-the-record, then."

Again there was silence.

"Like I told you before," David concluded, "what is frightening is that they'll say *anything*. This is what troubles me about the whole situation."

During his most recent speech, David had said ". . . scholars and educators are warning us to hold firm to the first amendment rights of free speech and open discussion . . ." and advanced the "value of a single individual, and his right to think and express himself . . ."

Why, I wondered, was it okay for David to speak his mind but no one else was supposed to return the favor?

If Hollywood had a united political mechanism which ground David's career into dust, then this nefarious group had nothing on the army of Puttnamites who seemed to be working overtime in an attempt to undermine an article that had not yet even been written. A day didn't go by in which I didn't hear about another disparaging remark regarding my alleged unholy alliance with the Hollywood establishment.

Once again the trail led to 711 Fifth Avenue, this time to Victor Kaufman, president and chief executive officer of Columbia Pictures Entertainment.

"I don't want to be drawn into the media controversy regarding David Puttnam," Victor said, explaining that his status as head of a public company precluded taking a public stance on an ex-employee. "But I will say this. It would seem that the facts speak for themselves in this case."

I asked Victor about the weekend meeting between him and David when it was decided that David should leave Columbia.

"Was he fired, Victor?"

"I can't talk about it. That's part of the settlement agreement. Neither of us can comment about what transpired in that meeting."

"It hasn't stopped David from talking about it," I pointed out. "Is he violating that agreement?"

Victor didn't respond, but his silence, of course, said as much as words might have.

By May 1, the media had heard about the planned *Variety* piece. Now, in addition to almost daily calls from David Puttnam as well the key Hollywood players, I began receiving an endless stream of inquiries from the press.

New York magazine. *Los Angeles Times*. London *Times*. *Washington Post*. *New York Post*.

My life became a circus. So much so, I realized that there was no way I could possibly deliver the article in time for a May 11 publication date. I met with Roger Watkins and he reluctantly rescheduled the two-parter for May 18 and May 25.

Even something as simple as a week's delay created a controversy with phone calls speculating that *Variety* didn't want to print the article at all because of the vicious nature of the attack on David Puttnam. Of course, the article was, as yet, still unwritten.

***

Over the next few days, I flew back and forth between Los Angeles and New York more often than a member of most flight crews.

On one trip, I met with Dawn Steel. Full of energy, she spoke more about the future than the past, demurring on questions regarding David Puttnam by noting, "I wasn't there."

Her only comment for attribution was as follows:

"Columbia Pictures and David Puttnam have one thing in common. A need, desire, and obligation for the pictures made during his administration to succeed."

As the article's publication date approached, David Puttnam sent me a copy of a letter from Thomas Schuly, the producer of *The Adventures of Baron Munchausen*. Schuly had made several negative remarks in the press about David during the past few weeks and had written to say:

"With regard to some press articles I very much regret certain statements given by me and Terry [Gilliam] and we thus have to ask for your 'generous and benevolent understanding' . . . but sometimes the difficulties we had to face nearly brought us to desperation and losing our minds . . . Sorry for that!"

David was letting me know that at least one of his critics was contrite after blasting him in the press. It was a subtle attempt, I felt, to provide impetus for me to reconsider chronicling Hollywood's reaction to his year at Columbia.

Although I had a lengthy interview with David as well as access to him for further comment, I wanted to speak to some of David's supporters as well. Few returned my calls. Those who did, like ICM head Jeff Berg, refused comment.

Upon learning this, David urged me to keep trying, and even gave me home phone numbers of some of his former executives. In addition, David would often call me with an update on someone's whereabouts.

"You can reach him at the Beverly Hills Hotel," David might say.

Greg Coote. David Picker. Fred Bernstein. They all ignored my queries.

"I suppose I can't blame them," David told me as it became evident that his friends would not step forward. "They have a career to think about and I'm not the most popular person in Hollywood at the moment."

It was a gracious comment to make under the circumstances.

As the clock ticked toward May 18, I sequestered myself in my apartment and hammered away at the keys of a computer. Late one afternoon, I received a call from Peg Tyre, writer of the "Intelligencer" column in *New York* magazine.

She asked general questions about the article, which I was happy to answer, and then she wanted to know what Ray Stark and Herbert Allen had said. Since it didn't make much journalistic sense to "scoop" my own newspaper by giving quotes from the Hollywood establishment, I declined to elaborate on the comments from Ray and Herbert. Finally, after much urging and assurances, I did speak to Peg Tyre *off*-the-record.

A few days later, I picked up a copy of the new issue of *New York Magazine*. In the "Intelligencer" section, a headline announced: COLUMBIA PUTS PUTTNAM IN HIS PLACE.

"The powers of Columbia Pictures," Tyre had written, "have finally decided to speak out about David Puttnam's departure . . . Herb Allen and Ray Stark . . . gave interviews to *Variety* reporter Charles Kipps to refute Puttnam's claims . . . In the interviews, Allen claims there was no concerted effort to oust Puttnam. He complains Puttnam was contemptuous of the star system while acting like a star himself—dallying with the press and demanding a lucrative, ironclad contract. Stark charges that Puttnam moved too slowly on small projects and came to Hollywood with his mouth open and his ears shut."

Almost immediately, I received a call from Ray Stark.

"Why are you offering my quotes out of context to another publication?" Ray demanded, obviously upset to read a paraphrase of his words in *New York* magazine.

The next call was from Herbert Allen.

"I just saw *New York* magazine," he said.

I braced myself.

"It's no big deal," Herbert remarked.

I was relieved. I must have sounded harried, however, because Herbert noted that I shouldn't take the whole thing "so seriously.

"This is not a *real* war," Herbert observed. "No one is going to get maimed or killed. At this point, no one is even going to lose their job. Besides, all the players here are big boys. And they're all worth a lot of money. So this is not going to affect their lives in any consequential way. Just remember that only words are flying back and forth. That's all. So why not go out and have a little fun with it."

When the London *Times* contacted me at home on the evening of May 9, I was still feeling reverberations from the experience with *New York* magazine.

"I really can't talk about it," I told John Cassidy, London *Times* New York bureau chief.

"I understand," Cassidy replied, and hung up.

But the next day Cassidy called *Variety*. Editor Roger Watkins and publisher Syd Silverman were both at the Cannes Film Festival, so Cassidy spoke with Syd's son, Mark Silverman, who is the associate publisher of the paper. Mark obviously had been more cooperative than I had been.

On Sunday, May 15, the London *Times* ran the headline: HOLLYWOOD BIGWIGS' REVENGE ON PUTTNAM.

"Hollywood is taking its revenge on David Puttnam," Cassidy reported. "The British film director . . . will this week be described as an abrasive and close-minded foreigner by the Tinseltown powerbrokers who saw him off.

"In an article to be published in *Variety* magazine, the bible of the American film industry, Columbia film executives and producers accuse Puttnam of being contemptuous of the star system while acting like one himself. They say he gave jobs to British cronies but needlessly created Hollywood enemies, a trait that threatened Columbia's commercial future.

". . . But Mark Silverman, the acting publisher of *Variety*, denied that his magazine's article was a hatchet job on the British producer."

What followed was a four-column piece which alluded to many of the quotes in the upcoming part one of the two-parter.

Needless to say, it was a major transgression. After getting a fax of the article from London, I called Mark at home. He had already heard from his father, whom he described as "very annoyed."

I wasn't particularly happy either, but after my revelations to *New York* magazine, I had no room to talk.

"Do you think the Hollywood guys will be upset?" Mark asked.

Mark need not have worried about a reaction to his interview with the London *Times*. The London tabloids had much more explosive fare emblazoned across their pages the following day.

David Puttnam had been caught frequenting what the tabloids claimed was a London brothel. And he had been accused of making love to the musical accompaniment of Mozart melodies, with a pair of headphones firmly clamped on his head.

CHAPTER
TWENTY-NINE

Early Monday morning, May 16, the fax machine in my den began humming away and a copy of the London tabloid *News of the World* inched into view. The headline was bizarre:

TOP STARS IN ROYAL VICE GIRL SCANDAL

DAVID PUTTNAM 'PAID FOR THRILLS'

TYCOON DID IT TO MUSIC

MOZART TURNED HIM ON!

According to the *News of the World*, this is what happened:

"TV charmer Nigel Havers and film mogul David Puttnam were revealed last night as clients of the VIP vice girl used by Fergie's dad. . . . Vice girl Barbara revealed how she and millionaire film producer David Puttnam made love to a Mozart tape at the Wigmore Club. She said the bearded Hollywood tycoon arrived equipped with a personal cassette player and two sets of headphones. At first we'd have sex to the music of Dire Straits. We got so worked up, the headphones would sometimes fall off. Then I surprised him with a Mozart tape. . . ."

It was an outrageous turn of events. Already embroiled in a major controversy in Hollywood, David Puttnam was now suddenly mired in a sex scandal in London. Whether or not there was any truth to the accusations, just being *accused* was embarrassing enough.

Word of Wigmore wafted across the Atlantic and then across the North American continent, finally drifting into Hollywood like laughing gas. While worth its share of chuckles, the affair seemed destined to dissipate overnight, proving to be just a bit of much-needed comic relief in the overly serious debate between David Puttnam and his former colleagues. After all, many doubted the veracity of the British rags anyway.

Ironically, the Wigmore scandal would probably have been brief had it not been for one man: David Puttnam. Over the next two days, David himself nourished the anemic tale by granting interviews to the very publications that charged him with sexual misconduct.

Headlines in the *Sun* and *Daily Express* like MY VICE DEN SESSIONS, BY FILM BOSS: I ONLY WENT FOR A MASSAGE, HE SAID; MY WIFE KNOWS ABOUT MY MASSAGE SESSIONS, SAYS PRODUCER; and PUTTNAM: I SAW NO VICE served to *enhance*, not diminish, the credibility of the story. Pictures, too, added to the circus. In one photo, a smiling David and Patsy Puttnam, sitting side-by-side, arm-in-arm, were seen talking to reporters on the lawn of their nine-hundred-year-old country estate.

Just as he had done in Hollywood, David Puttnam kept talking. And talking. And talking. Never before had the tabloids had such a cooperative subject.

The next morning, after being up all night making last-minute changes, I worked with Mark Silverman on the layout of the article, to be entitled THE RISE AND FALL OF THE COCA-COLA KID. By noon, four pages were ready for the camera.

Then came the first of several calls from *Daily Variety*. Tom Pryor was resisting running the piece.

For the next three hours, Mark spent a great deal of time on the phone with Tom Pryor in California and Roger Watkins, who was attending the Cannes Film Festival. Ultimately, it was resolved that *Daily Variety* would publish the "Puttnam piece," despite the vigorous protestations of its editor, Thomas Pryor.

On May 18, every newsstand in New York sold out of *Weekly Variety* by 9:00 A.M. And by 8:00 A.M. California time, there wasn't a copy of *Daily Variety* anywhere.

Although Tom Pryor had indeed run the article, he placed it on

CHARLES KIPPS

page 15. Hollywood hummed. It did not escape regular *Variety* readers that David Puttnam had always been featured on the *front page* and that Pryor's "Puttnam's Legacy" had run on page two, but when Frank Price and Ray Stark and Warren Beatty and a full complement of Hollywood big-leaguers decided to speak out, the best Tom Pryor could manage was page fifteen!

No one, however, had any trouble finding it.

There was one difference between the *Daily* and *Weekly* versions of the article, in that Tom Pryor had cut two sentences from the story. The missing section read:

"Until now, Puttnam has been performing a soliloquy for the press. A lone figure monopolizing the media with an eloquent delivery of controversial barbs aimed at his former employers and colleagues."

It was an odd thing to edit out of a four-page article.

Once again, I was deluged with calls from the media, insistent on knowing what Ray Stark and Herbert Allen had to say in part two. I wasn't prepared to go into that aspect of the next segment, so I declined comment in most cases. However, I did speak to reporter Pat Broeske on Wednesday night and she filed a story the next day which led the Calendar section of the *Los Angeles Times:*

PUTTNAM VS. COLUMBIA . . .

THE SEQUEL

STUDIO TELLS ITS

SIDE IN *VARIETY*

"David Puttnam has been giving *his* side of his dispute with Columbia Pictures for months—in newspapers, magazines such as *Vanity Fair,* on the 'Today' show, and in speeches in Los Angeles and elsewhere.

"On Wednesday, Columbia started talking too. For the record and, notably, in the show-business bible, *Variety.*"

Broeske, after describing the banner headline in *Weekly Variety,* noted that "Wednesday's *Daily Variety* was more subdued . . ." and went on to point out the two missing sentences in the *Daily* version.

What Broeske may not have realized—as it turned out no one

in the media realized it—was that she was knocking on the door of a major "inside" story: the friction within the hallowed halls of *Variety*.

Later that afternoon, another article appeared in Los Angeles, this one in the *Daily News*.

Reporter Frank Swertlow seemed miffed at the unkind words the Hollywood establishment had reserved for David Puttnam and said as much. But the most startling passage of the piece was the following account of an interview with Tom Pryor:

"Tom Pryor, editor of *Daily Variety*, said the decision to publish the story was the New York office's and that he would not have published it. 'It was too little, too late,' he said . . . He also said this was the first time that *Daily Variety* has ever published such a lengthy profile."

The following Friday, May 20, the *New York Post* devoted the entire lead page of the "City Weekend" section to the *Variety* article. The words H'WOOD SQUARES OFF stretched the width of the page under which was a large-type deck: CONTROVERSY OVER FOR- MER COLUMBIA PICTURES EXEC DAVID PUTTNAM IS BREWING ALL OVER AGAIN.

"If Hollywood is looking for a mystery script to film," *Post* reporter Martin Burden pointed out, "it has one right in its back- yard, one that could run to as many fascinating sequels as 'Friday The 13th,' which recently premiered its seventh episode.

"And this one would have the best of ingredients—names (ac- tors Warren Beatty and Bill Murray, movie mogul Ray Stark, among others) and money (how about $432 million for starters?). Plus a lot of controversial comments."

Over the weekend, I spoke to David Puttnam.

"I haven't read it," David said of the *Variety* piece. "If I read these things I'd go crazy."

That was all David had a chance to say. Patsy grabbed the phone.

"They're lying," Patsy declared. "I was in Atlanta and I can tell you that the subject of making money *never* was an issue. Never! You don't know how devious these people are. They'll stop at nothing to get what they want. I can't believe you gave them space in *Variety*."

Patsy and I spoke for some time as she refuted every word of the article. Finally, David returned to the phone. He sounded weary and, although the subject never came up, I felt that the Wigmore scandal was at the root of his lethargic tone. Certainly, the *Variety* article was like the second half of a one-two punch, but having Hollywood call you a liar seemed to me to be far less a personal affront than having a London tabloid call you a john.

On Monday morning, May 23, *Daily Variety* carried a piece by Will Tusher which was headlined: DAVID PUTTNAM ON HIS 'SILENT' DETRACTORS: LUDICROUS CLAIM.

"Former Columbia Pictures chairman David Puttnam," Tusher began, "has challenged as 'ludicrous' that until now his detractors have been silent while he had had the media stage to himself. . . .

". . . 'The whole thing is rather ludicrous,' Puttnam said. 'The notion that Columbia or whatever they call themselves are reluctantly being forced to react to me when, in fact, all of this only relates to me reacting to stuff in the media, is really a joke.

" 'I think it's fair to say I was on the receiving end of an inaccurate leak in the *Wall Street Journal* and a viciously inaccurate piece in *Manhattan* magazine. . . .' "

I couldn't believe it. My *own* paper offering a refutation of my article!

Jake Eberts, who had funded the crown jewel of David's filmography, *Chariots of Fire*, called me after reading part one of the *Variety* series. We spoke at length, Jake openly offering his observations regarding the brouhaha surrounding his longtime friend, David Puttnam. Since Jake had been given *three* projects while a host of Hollywood filmmakers were absent from David's slate, he seemed a perfect candidate to address the issue of "cronyism."

"If that's the word you want to use," Jake Eberts said, "then I believe in it. This is a classic business for people who operate on the basis of relationships, on the basis of close personal understanding of each other's strengths and weaknesses. And there's nothing wrong with that kind of relationship. David uses it when it pleases him and doesn't when it doesn't. But there's nothing wrong with using your old relationships, because you trust them."

On Wednesday May 25, part two of the Puttnam saga was published. As with part one, there was a flurry of media activity. Most noteworthy was an analysis of the *Variety* piece in *The Washington Post*, written by Kim Masters.

"Over the last several weeks, an extraordinary and quite lengthy series . . . appeared in the daily and weekly editions of *Variety*, the industry publication of record . . .

"Instead of settling the controversies sparked by Puttnam, the series created friction . . . [Tom] Pryor—editor of *Daily Variety*—admitted that he opposed publication of the articles. 'I'm embarrassed up to my bloody ears,' he said."

On June 21, following a series of talks with *Variety* management, Thomas M. Pryor, the distinguished editor of *Daily Variety* for nearly thirty years, retired. Considering Pryor's contribution to the paper, it was a sad footnote to a brilliant career that it ended in the wake of the Puttnam/Hollywood controversy.

As summer turned into fall, everyone in Hollywood was waiting for the other shoe to drop. Most expected David Puttnam to launch a renewed verbal flurry following the *Variety* article, but the British producer who had once electrified the media with impassioned sermons was now as silent as a Trappist monk.

Besides the filmmakers and executives I had spoken to before, many more called and expressed a willingness to talk—*on-the-record*—about their experiences with David Puttnam.

Screenwriter Howard Franklin, for example, provided a glimpse of how David dealt with the outside world as he related his exasperation over the fate of *Someone to Watch Over Me*.

"As a writer," Howard remarked, "I was not well served by David Puttnam."

Bob Robinson, business affairs executive vice president during the first half of David's term, offered a rare look at what it was like inside Columbia Pictures itself.

"I first had questions about David Puttnam's prospects for success in running the studio in a profitable manner during the summer of 1986 when Warner Brothers relinquished and Columbia acquired two projects which David had developed at Warners and wanted to pursue at Columbia, *The Cory Aquino Story* and *The Boys of Beirut*. These projects appeared to be the kind of stories that find their best audience acceptance in today's marketplace as network television movies or miniseries or as original programming for HBO, and not projects that would interest American moviegoing audiences.

"At the same time, Warner Brothers would not sell to rival Columbia certain projects which David had earlier developed at Warners and wanted to move to Columbia, like *Fat Man and Little Boy*, to be directed by Roland Joffe. These projects were retained by Warners."

One evening, I was surprised by a call from Don Simpson, who, with Jerry Bruckheimer, had produced *Flashdance, Beverly Hills Cop, Beverly Hills Cop II,* and *Top Gun*. Don told me about his meeting with David at a Thai restaurant and then offered this appraisal.

"David Puttnam tried to make the job something it could never be. The job is picking projects which are accessible. Yet David's movies were movies that the audience could not gain access to. It is my feeling that he thinks movies of value are those that appeal to a very select group of people rather than to the general audience."

Don Simpson also noted that "the media latched onto David Puttnam because they thought, 'here is a man with a valid point of view.' My observation, however, is that the point of view was unworkable. He had a bush-league, cynical point of view."

And, of the Hollywood reaction to the British invader, which the media had characterized as "anger and rage," Simpson asserted there was no violent response at all: "Hollywood started out *be*mused and went to *a*mused."

Notwithstanding the public debate, however, Don Simpson pointed out that there was just one aspect of David Puttnam's term that really mattered:

"Except for people in the motion picture industry, no one gets the arcane nature of this business. The fundamental factor in Hollywood is: How good are you at the job. David Puttnam failed to perform. He didn't fail because of what he said or did, he failed because of what he didn't do. It wasn't the animosity he created that was his downfall. In the end, it was his performance."

Indeed, the time had finally come for David Puttnam's "legacy" to speak for itself. In fact, it was *already* speaking.

By Summer 1988, sixteen movies from the David Puttnam "legacy" had been released by Columbia Pictures. The aggregate cost of the films was $155,806,000 and the domestic box-office take tallied $122,743,000. Since less than half of this amount flows to the studio as income—in this case $50,551,000—the preliminary tally represented a loss of $105,255,000. But, before calculating profitability, other factors had to be considered. The cost of prints and advertising, for one.

Columbia had spent $81,500,000 in distributing copies of the films to theaters and in marketing campaigns. Thus, the loss on theatrical exhibition totaled $186,755,000 at that point.

An additional $19,180,000 in income had been derived from foreign and ancillary sales (video, television, etc.), but the amount was inconsequential due to the fact that *The Last Emperor*, the biggest grosser on the slate with $40,000,000 in box office, was a negative pickup which precluded Columbia's participation in these valuable after-markets. Besides the limits placed upon the studio by contract, there were the limitations of salability for pictures like *Pulse*, *Stars and Bars*, and *Zelly and Me*. With U.S. box office of $44,000, $125,000, and $74,000 respectively, not much interest had been generated overseas or in the electronic media.

As the negative figure rapidly mounted, it became clear that the "legacy" was not headed down a road to financial success. But the *reason* the slate had failed became the basis of a *new* debate, especially after David's charge in the May 18 *Variety* article that Columbia was "strangling my smaller pictures at birth."

Impetus for David's statement stemmed from the budgets for prints and advertising which were *expected* for the individual films versus what was *actually* spent. For example, Columbia might have opened a film like *Stars and Bars* with a $4,500,000 marketing effort. Instead, the studio spent just $600,000. Likewise, $3,800,000 had been tentatively earmarked for *Pulse*, but the reality turned out to be $500,000. And *Zelly and Me* received a $300,000 treatment rather than a considerably higher amount which had been originally discussed.

There was, however, an explanation for the drastic reduction in prints and advertising. Before laying out millions of dollars in marketing, all studios "test" a film via "sneak previews." If the audience reaction is less than favorable, the movie is issued cautiously to selected regions and then, only if the box office warrants it, is it spread into wide national release. David Puttnam's slate had so far performed poorly both in sneaks and in regional theaters. On that basis, Columbia had moved to cut its losses.

Despite the cool reception at theaters, another rallying cry for

David and his supporters was: "*All* of the films in the 'legacy' have not yet been released!" And that was true. Among the films waiting in the vaults was one done entirely in authentic Gypsy language and another in Serbo-Croation. Then there was a Japanese film with no dialogue at all. And a movie about a man and his talking penis. And a picture about the adventures of a three-hundred-year-old German baron.

The first half of David Puttnam's "legacy" had cost Coca-Cola over $150,000,000. With eighteen more films to go, it looked as if it was going to be a *very* expensive bequest.

CHAPTER

THIRTY

On September 12, David Puttnam broke a four-month media hiatus with an appearance on *World of Ideas*, a new **PBS** series hosted by Bill Moyers. But his dialogue with Moyers was devoid of any specifics—not once did viewers hear the name Ray Stark or Warren Beatty or Mike Ovitz—and was merely a generic recycling of his time-worn speech on social responsibility.

Even the normally cool Moyers bristled at one point during David's diatribe.

"But I go to the movies to be entertained," Moyers sighed, "not to be lectured. Do I really want David Puttnam sitting there saying, 'What kind of moral instruction can I give Bill Moyers when he pays me seven dollars?' "

Two days after seeking the legitimacy of public television, David Puttnam officially announced the financing arrangement that had been rumored for months. A multinational alliance consisting of Warner Bros., the Japanese firm Fujisankei Communications International, British Satellite Broadcasting, and the venture capital arm of National Westminster Bank would make $50,000,000 available for the production of six films over a four-year period.

In a September 15 *New York Times* article, David indicated that the financial partners would have a say in which projects were greenlighted under the deal.

"One of the lessons I learned at Columbia," the former chairman/CEO told the *Times*, "is that there is absolutely no point whatsoever in jamming some movie down the throat of a distributor who doesn't want it."

On October 7, *The Beast* stalked across American screens. With no big-name Hollywood actors, a story line involving the Russian/ Afghanistan conflict as seen through the eyes of a Russian soldier, and a good portion of the dialogue in Pushtu dialect, the film grossed a beastly box-office total of just $96,000. After sharing that amount with exhibitors, Columbia Pictures netted $22,000, not even enough to buy an Audi.

Besides its poor performance at theaters, *The Beast* awakened the ire of long-suffering critics. *Los Angeles Herald-Examiner* reviewer David Ehrenstein wrote: "When the full story of David Puttnam's period at Columbia Pictures is finally written (and here's hoping that it will be sometime soon), a special chapter should be set aside just to discuss 'The Beast.' For, more than any other hapless programmers green-lighted by the pompous headline-hungry British 'filmmaker,' this attempt at mixing melodrama and humanistic 'think' piece is most characteristic of the rank incompetence he successfully sold to an ever-gullible Eastern press as artistic integrity."

The outlook for David Puttnam's slate was so bleak, Columbia Pictures began a serious program of damage control regarding the remaining films.

The first picture to be affected by the crisis management strategy was *The Adventures of Baron Munchausen*. Scheduled as *the* Christmas picture (every studio has *at least* one movie geared toward the year-end rush to the box office), *Munchausen* was yanked from release at the last moment. The film did open in Germany, the only territory in which it was issued, and performed worse than any major holiday movie the country had seen in decades. At Columbia Plaza East, the gloom was permeating. If the saga of a German folk hero failed to attract an audience in *Germany*, it didn't take much of an extrapolation to figure out how it might play in Peoria.

Besides *Munchausen*, there was one other picture in the unreleased portion of the "legacy" with a sizable production cost, and that was the $30,000,000 *Old Gringo*, starring Jane Fonda. Also scheduled for Christmas 1988 release, *Old Gringo*, too, was postponed, leaving Columbia Pictures without the flagship holiday extravaganza so necessary to the bottom line of any studio.

With *Munchausen* and *Old Gringo* tucked away for the moment, Columbia tried to lessen the rate of monetary descent by reducing the weight of the load. *The Big Picture*, a movie that pokes fun at the film business, was placed on the sales block, as was *Me and Him*, the "penis movie." There were no interested parties. Some of David's other "smaller pictures" apparently held more appeal. For example, *Bloodhounds of Broadway*, a musical comedy with rock star Madonna in the lead, and *Earth Girls Are Easy*, an extraterrestrial comedy, were sold to other distributors.

As the "legacy" offered up one disappointment after another, the blind adoration once bestowed on David Puttnam by the media turned into wide-eyed realization. The following appraisal by the revered British publication *The Economist* illustrates this dramatic reversal in attitude.

"He failed in Hollywood because his tastes were middlebrow, without the vulgarity that brings in crowds or the intellect that wins critical acclaim. Nor, when the spotlight was on him, did he have the genius of an Irving Thalberg or a Darryl Zanuck—the ability to stamp one's will on the product of a studio."

Under attack in the media—an unusual situation for David Puttnam—the former studio chief ventured back onto the pages of *Variety* via an interview with London bureau staff member Don Groves. Groves summarized his talk with David by observing: "The producer lamented the overall standard of British scriptwriting and said he was looking increasingly to Eastern Europe where he believes more challenging and stimulating films are flourishing despite lack of resources."

Having once denounced Hollywood as not equal to the British film industry, David Puttnam now chided the British film industry as not equal to Eastern Europe.

Of course, Eastern Europe is not big on freedom of speech, something David might do well to consider before basing his operations there.

On March 6, 1989, Tri-Star Pictures was combined with Columbia Pictures into a new entity called the Motion Picture Group. Although the merger in September 1987 had brought Columbia and Tri-Star together under the umbrella of parent corporation Columbia Pictures Entertainment, the companies had operated as two separate divisions since that time. Now there would be just one corporate structure.

The union of Columbia and Tri-Star provided a hint of what might have been for David Puttnam, as his successor, Dawn Steel, was given the responsibility of running *both* studios. Tri-Star president David Matalon became executive vice president of Columbia Pictures Entertainment, while Jeff Sagansky, president of production for Tri-Star, would report to Dawn Steel after assuming Matalon's vacant post.

By the time of the combination, Columbia Pictures had chalked up another $72,289,000 in losses resulting from the David Puttnam slate of films, placing the deficit from Puttnam era product at $239,864,000. But the box-office bloodbath was far from over. In fact, the first two films released by the Motion Picture group, *The Adventures of Baron Munchausen* and *Hanussen*, were both cinematic reminders of an earlier regime.

With little advance warning, Columbia announced the March 10 release of *The Adventure of Baron Munchausen*. Exhibiting an uncharacteristic sense of humor, the Columbia publicity department tagged the press screening invitation by pointing out: "Gilliam believes in the Baron and after THE ADVENTURES OF BARON MUNCHAUSEN, you will too. After all, we have the film to prove it!"

Munchausen exploded on American screens. Literally. The opening scene was an extreme closeup of a cannon loudly belching forth fire and smoke. From that moment on, there was no respite for the timid moviegoer. A brassy and deafening music track rumbled under a relentless succession of battles, beheadings, and special effects. This was not a movie for the faint of heart.

Ironically, *The Adventures of Baron Munchausen* is set in a city that is under siege by hostile forces. In the midst of this raging war, an acting troupe is carrying on with a play about the baron, depicting him as "the greatest liar of all time." Suddenly, the *real* baron arrives on the scene to save the city and salvage his reputation. But would *Baron Munchausen* ride to the rescue of the embattled David Puttnam?

After the movie's third week of release, *Variety* reported that

Munchausen had logged $3,198,063 in ninety-two theaters, hardly a number of consequence for a $44,000,000 picture.

Despite its abysmal performance in Germany the previous Christmas, *Munchausen* fared considerably better in other territories. Box-office success in Europe, however, is a relative concept. For example, *Munchausen* managed to climb to the number one position in France after two weeks of release with just $1,478,858 in receipts, and became one of the hottest movies in Belgium and Switzerland with two-week tallies of $165,704 and $78,162, respectively. Meanwhile, first-week attendance in England ($115,983), Spain ($309,310), and Greece ($102,412) provided a small measure of additional consolation.

Ultimately, *Munchausen* was crushed by the weight of its own gargantuan budget. When the cannon smoke cleared, Columbia Pictures had lost nearly $25,000,000.

Also released on March 10 was *Hanussen*, a film directed by Istvan Szabo, the man David Puttnam considered to be the "best pound-for-pound director in the world." No one expected *Hanussen* to be a blockbuster box-office hit. It wasn't. Everyone expected *Hanussen* to be nominated for a Best Foreign Language Film Oscar. It was. (The movie had been released for a brief period a few months earlier in order to qualify for the Academy Awards.) Unfortunately, Istvan Szabo never got a chance to thank David Puttnam for his efforts, since Danish film *Pelle the Conqueror* won the Foreign Language category.

David was mentioned at the 1989 Academy Awards ceremony, however. Sean Connery and Michael Caine were standing at the podium about to present an Oscar when Roger Moore, sporting a full beard, walked onto the stage.

"He looks like David Puttnam," Michael Caine exclaimed to Sean Connery. Then, turning toward Roger Moore, Caine remarked: "I thought they sent you back to England."

The day after the Oscars, *Daily Variety* carried an editorial that had everyone in Hollywood feeling a vague sensation of déjà vu. Headlined PUTTNAM WORDS WORTH REMEMBERING, it was written by former *Daily Variety* editor Tom Pryor.

"Remember David Puttnam?" Pryor began. "He was, of course, at one time chairman of Columbia Pictures, and the most dynamic personality in Hollywood."

The David Puttnam Slate of Films*

	Release Date	Cost (Dollars)	Prints and Ads (Dollars)	No. of Screens	Box Office (Dollars)	Rentals (Dollars)	Foreign/ Ancilliary (Dollars)	Profit (Dollars)
Released								
The Big Easy	08/21/87	6,000	6,900,000	1,189	17,000,000	7,400,000	60,000	554,000
Someone to Watch Over Me	10/09/87	16,800,000	10,000,000	855	9,700,000	3,900,000	3,900,000	-19,000,000
Hope and Glory	10/16/87	11,000,000	5,000,000	316	9,600,000	3,800,000	1,870,000	-10,330,000
Housekeeping	11/06/87	6,500,000	900,000	25	1,500,000	513,000	275,000	-6,612,000
Leonard Part 6	12/18/87	27,400,000	9,300,000	1,127	5,000,000	2,300,000	1,050,000	-33,350,000
The Last Emperor	12/25/87	6,000,000	16,000,000	829	40,000,000	16,500,000	2,650,000	-2,850,000
School Daze	02/12/88	7,000,000	4,000,000	232	14,600,000	6,000,000	135,000	-4,865,000
Pulse	03/11/88	9,000,000	500,000	120	44,000	18,000	600,000	-8,882,000
Vice Versa	03/11/88	13,200,000	10,000,000	1,176	13,500,000	5,300,000	2,150,000	-15,750,000
Stars and Bars	03/18/88	8,000,000	600,000	25	125,000	41,000	1,000,000	-7,559,000
Little Nikita	03/18/88	15,000,000	3,000,000	383	2,000,000	800,000	1,750,000	-15,450,000
White Mischief	04/01/88	1,500,000	2,000,000	94	2,800,000	1,100,000	820,000	-1,580,000
A Time of Destiny	04/08/88	9,500,000	2,000,000	214	1,100,000	500,000	0	-11,000,000
Zelly and Me	04/15/88	2,300,000	300,000	28	74,000	16,000	20,000	-2,564,000
Vibes	07/22/88	18,000,000	7,000,000	957	1,800,000	763,000	2,150,000	-22,087,000
The New Adventures of Pippi Longstocking	07/29/88	4,600,000	4,000,000	850	3,900,000	1,600,000	750,000	-6,250,000
Rocket Gilbralter	08/26/88	7,000,000	1,000,000	30	214,000	79,000	60,000	-7,861,000

Film	Date							
Punchline	09/30/88	19,000,000	14,000,000	917	19,300,000	8,600,000	1,950,000	−22,450,000
The Beast	10/07/88	10,000,000	1,000,000	25	96,000	22,000	1,800,000	−9,178,000
Things Change	10/21/88	8,000,000	4,000,000	101	3,500,000	1,300,000	1,050,000	−9,650,000
Physical Evidence	01/27/89	10,900,000	4,600,000	695	3,500,000	1,500,000	6,500,000	−7,500,000
True Believer	02/17/89	12,000,000	9,000,000	895	8,300,000	3,400,000	1,950,000	−15,650,000
Hanussen	03/10/89	500,000	115,000	2	83,000	14,000	0	−601,000
The Adventures of Baron Munchausen	03/10/87	23,000,000	10,000,000	117	5,500,000	2,600,000	6,500,000	−23,900,000
Total		246,206,000	125,215,000	—	163,236,000	68,066,000	38,990,000	−264,365,000
Unreleased								
Eat a Bowl of Tea	07/21/89	2,000,000	500,000	—	—	—	—	—
Me & Him	08/04/89	5,900,000	55,000	—	—	—	—	—
Milo & Otis	08/25/89	0	175,000	—	—	—	—	—
The Big Picture	09/15/89	6,000,000	500,000	—	—	—	—	—
Old Gringo	10/06/89	30,000,000	12,000,000	—	—	—	—	—
To Kill a Priest	10/13/89	7,500,000	1,000,000	—	—	—	—	—
Time of the Gypsies	10/20/89	1,400,000	500,000	—	—	—	—	—
Blind Fury	01/12/90	9,000	3,000,000	—	—	—	—	—
Total		52,809,000	17,730,000	—	—	—	—	—

* This chart reflects total estimated costs borne by Columbia Pictures for the motion pictures listed above. The text, however, addresses costs in terms of initial budget projections and/or contractual amounts. Because of the propensity for film costs to escalate, some figures in this chart may be slightly higher than those given in the text. Figures here are as of July 1989.

Pryor reported that David had sent him the text of a speech he'd delivered in England. In that speech, David had said that the "true role" of television was "to serve the needs of society."

"If necessary," David had stated, "society even needs protection."

Later in the piece, Tom Pryor quoted one of David's oft-repeated doctrines ". . . as Puttnam knowingly says of the motion picture: 'Good or bad, they tinker around inside your brain, they steal up on you in the darkness of the cinema to form or conform social attitudes.' "

The first time these words had surfaced was in the letter David had handed to Roberto Goizueta and Don Keough in Atlanta in 1986. Then, the phrases had sounded eloquent and enlightened. Now the words seemed maudlin and meaningless, no longer a bold proclamation for the future, but a naive notion from the past.

Nevertheless, Tom Pryor and many other diehard devotees still regarded David Puttnam's utterances as sacrosanct.

"To all of this," Pryor wrote of David Puttnam's remarks, "there's only one response: Amen!"

From the moment David Puttnam got off the plane in Los Angeles in 1986, he began blasting the methodology of American filmmaking. In the summer of 1987 he journeyed to the Cannes Film Festival where, as a featured speaker on "British Day," he sharply criticized the British film industry. And in September 1987, he talked about the inadequacies of Canadian filmmakers during a keynote address at Canada's Festival of Festivals in Toronto. Everywhere David went, it seemed, he found fault.

Given his penchant for attacking on home soil, it might forever remain a mystery why the Australian Film, Radio, and Television School risked inviting David Puttnam to preside over a series of seminars on production. Immediately upon arriving in Sydney on April 3, David held a press conference in which he charged that the Australian film industry has been turning out "self-consciously domestic productions."

Over the next few months, seven remaining "smaller pictures" would be released without fanfare or sold to a distributor with a scaled-down distribution machine. Megabudget *Old Gringo* would be further delayed and held for release in fall 1989. Regardless of how well *Old Gringo* performed, however, it was a safe assumption that the film would not generate the $700,000,000 in box office ($300,000,000 in rentals) required to redeem the David Puttnam "legacy."

The final verdict was in. The slate of pictures David Puttnam held out as celluloid witnesses in his defense would *not* vindicate the filmmaking philosophy he had espoused while chairman/CEO of Columbia Pictures. Instead, it would indict him.

The shouting now over, the "legacy" now played out as a monumental failure, a sense of order returned to the filmmaking universe. David Puttnam was once again an independent producer, Ray Stark was back producing for Columbia Pictures, and names like Michael Douglas and Cher began popping up on Columbia's projected slate of new films. Another indication of normalcy was the start of principal photography on two of the three sequels David Puttnam had refused to make: *Ghostbusters II* and *Karate Kid III*. *Jagged Edge II*, although not yet before the cameras, was back on the development track. Except for the $300,000,000-plus tab, which had taken a bite out of the income statement, all was well at Columbia Plaza East.

On June 16, 1989, *Ghostbusters II* was unleashed into 2,410 theaters across America. By the end of the evening, the supernatural comedy had broken the all-time box-office record for a Friday night with $10,252,829. The frantic pace continued on Saturday with $10,890,325, also a record, followed by $8,329,740 for the biggest nonholiday Sunday night in the history of the movie business. This all added up to the most money *ever* earned on a three-day weekend opening, an incredible $29,472,894.

The spirit of the David Puttnam era at Columbia Pictures had haunted Hollywood since David's resignation two years earlier. Finally, that stubborn spirit had been brutally exorcized. Yet questions remained.

Why did David Puttnam come to Hollywood?

The most likely answer is simple enough: money. Even David himself admitted that the salary was one of the things that had attracted him to Columbia Pictures. And when he entered negotiations, it was not David Puttnam, the champion of cinematic purity, sitting at the bargaining table; it was David Puttnam the individual, out to make the best deal he could for himself. Admittedly, he did well. The contract, which was not tied to his performance in any way, specified that he would be paid $1,000,000 a year and, in the event of a termination, would receive a settlement of $5,000,000 *after taxes*. As it turned out, the gross amount required to net him the indicated $5,000,000 was $7,000,000.

Incredibly, David Puttnam became chairman/CEO of Columbia Pictures with an agreement that was *more valuable* if he was *fired* than it was if he fulfilled the contract. Had he stayed the entire term, he would have been paid $3,000,000 before taxes for three years. Instead, his pretax compensation was $8,000,000 ($1,000,000 in salary and $7,000,000 in severance pay) for *one* year's work.

"I am allowed to fail," David had told the *Los Angeles Times* in 1986. Perhaps he should have said: "It would *behoove* me to fail."

Why did David Puttnam act the way he did? Why did he criticize Hollywood? Why did he choose inaccessible subject matter as the basis for his films?

It is possible that David Puttnam did not want to succeed. It seems unlikely, however, that the strong ego driving David Puttnam would condescend to willful surrender. His refusal to assimilate in the Hollywood mainstream was probably more owing to the fear of failure rather than to some preordained program of systematic incompetence. It was far safer to take an unconventional approach to filmmaking and blame the poor performance on the Hollywood system than it was to work within existing Hollywood parameters and, in the event of box-office disaster, have no one to blame but himself.

One thing was certain about David Puttnam: He was full of contradictions. He decried "cronyism" but made production deals with dozens of his former associates. He called the rate of spending in Hollywood "insane," yet his last film as an independent producer before joining Columbia was the $25,000,000 *The Mission*, and, while at the studio, he approved the big-budget pictures *The Adventures of Baron Munchausen* and *Old Gringo*. He said stars were paid too much but ensured that he would be paid more than most stars. He chided the creative community for having no sense of social responsibility, then lived at various times as a tax exile in order to avoid paying British taxes.

Again, it comes down to the same thing. Money. In fact, the David Puttnam–versus–Hollywood encounter was analogous to a much broader battle: art versus commerce.

David Puttnam purported to represent "art" and portrayed

Hollywood as the "commerce" side of the equation. Of course, this was not exactly the case, since the art David championed was *his* conception of art, and the commerce Hollywood achieved was not without artistic effort.

Other than religion and politics, there may be no more volatile source of argument than art versus commerce. Ardent supporters of public television do not usually mix well with viewers addicted to situation comedies. Those who hold subscriptions to the opera generally do not find soul mates at a rock concert. And people who would stand in line for hours to buy a ticket to a Broadway musical may not be overly excited with a free pass to an action-adventure film.

David Puttnam attempted to blur these comfortable categories. He tried to inject his brand of elitism into a Hollywood system designed for the masses, failing to understand that there is more than one form of entertainment.

The media, boasting a high percentage of "intellectuals," quickly latched on to David Puttnam as the messiah of meaningful motion pictures. But meaningful to whom? Was *Chariots of Fire* more meaningful by virtue of its appeal to a relatively small but sophisticated audience than was *E.T.* with its nearly half-billion dollars in box office?

Obviously the media thought it was, as evidenced by the constant references to "Oscar-winning producer" David Puttnam. Each year there is an "Oscar-winning producer," which means there are dozens of filmmakers deserving of that title. Yet David Puttnam was the only one who was so designated by the press. (That description has since changed to "former studio chief" David Puttnam, the most negative ramification, as far as David is concerned, to stem from his year in Hollywood.)

Is there a lesson to be learned from David Puttnam's sojourn in Hollywood? What was the point of all the sound and fury? Who won and who lost?

The last question is easiest to answer. When measured financially, certainly Coca-Cola lost and David Puttnam won. Other than that, there were no clear winners or losers. Most participants in the drama merely experienced a brief delay in a game that had been in play long before anyone ever heard of David Puttnam.

As to the point of all this, perhaps there really wasn't one. After all, nothing changed as a result of David Puttnam's short term at Columbia Pictures. No major shifts in philosophy occurred, no drastic modifications in the way films are made.

But there was definitely a lesson to be learned, one that Hollywood will not soon forget:

Never hire a studio chief who needs a visa to work in California.

INDEX